Flourish at Forty: Rewriting the Midlife Success Script

By:Mustafa Nejem

Table of Contents

Introduction to the Book

First and foremost, I'd like to thank you from the bottom of my heart for picking up this book. Here's the deal: it's about some really intense stuff. The things we'll be diving into, they're just as profound as they are universal aspects of life that we all experience. They run deep into our minds, how we feel in relationships, and why we have to live on Earth. While each and every one of us goes through it differently, we can't deny that there are parts of these experiences that are faced by everyone at some point in time.

After doing tons of research and talking with people from different walks of life, I've come to realize something. Pointing out these thoughts is priceless for readers who want more answers or even just a little bit of entertainment. My biggest hope is that this book helps make your life better in any way possible. If it helps you see your personal experiences under a new light or if it just gives you an intriguing chapter to read, then I'm happy.

While I do understand that there's no way a single piece of work will ever cover everything related to what we'll discuss today fully, I still tried my best to merge all the unique perspectives and experiences contained within these pages.

When it comes down to it though? It was impossible not to let my own thoughts slip in here from time-to-time. So with that being said… Let's dive into topics like emotional intelligence and spirituality from many angles! Some chapters here go deep into proven theories made by professionals while others talk about stories passed down across generations that have taught us valuable lessons about life.

Other times, we'll discuss real-world examples so you can get a better grip on what exactly I'm talking about when explaining things. All throughout this journey though? The goal always remains the same: show people how much they all have in common by showing them the many faces of their shared humanity.

Just understand that what you're about to read isn't meant to be taken as answers. Instead, think of it as a "push in the right direction". You've got your own mind for a reason, and I just want to help you get the most use out of it as possible. Even though perfecting yourself is something that never stops… It doesn't hurt to have some inspiration along the way.

With all of this being said though… I do invite you to come with me and celebrate life and its many opportunities for everyone trying their best at being human (and growing while doing so).

Chapter 1

The Midlife Milestone

Welcome to a new chapter of life - turning forty! This significant milestone marks the beginning of a transformative journey into midlife. As we bid farewell to our thirties and enter this new phase, it's natural to reflect on the experiences and lessons that have shaped us thus far. In this section, we will explore the significance of turning forty and embrace the opportunities it brings for personal growth and self-discovery. Let's embark on this journey together and navigate the challenges and joys that lie ahead.

Embracing the Milestone

Turning forty is a significant milestone in one's life, and rather than fearing it, it is crucial to embrace this new chapter with open arms. Embracing turning forty opens doors to personal growth and self-discovery, empowering individuals to embark on a transformative journey of inner exploration.

Entering your forties comes with a newfound sense of confidence and wisdom. It is a time when you can reflect on past experiences and use them as stepping stones for personal growth. This is an opportune moment to reassess your priorities and pursue the things that truly bring you fulfillment.

In this chapter, you have the chance to discover who you are and what you truly want out of life. It's a chance to shed societal pressures and expectations and become more authentic and true to yourself. Embracing turning forty allows you to break free from the constraints of the past and embrace the possibilities of the future.

40's, as you embrace this milestone, you may find that personal growth becomes a natural outcome. Exploring new hobbies, learning new skills, and pursuing passions that have been put on hold become more attainable and enjoyable. It's an opportunity to nurture your mind, body, and soul as you delve into self-discovery and expand your horizons.

This chapter of your life offers immense potential for growth and a chance to align your values with your actions. Embrace turning forty as an invitation to cultivate self-acceptance, to let go of self-doubt, and to pursue personal fulfillment without reservation. Seize the opportunities for growth and embark on this journey of embracing the milestone of turning forty with confidence and enthusiasm.

Reflecting on the Past

As we enter our forties, it is natural to start reflecting on the experiences and lessons of our past. Turning forty marks a significant milestone in our journey, a time when we can pause and gain valuable insights from our life experiences.

Reflecting on turning forty allows us to appreciate how far we have come and how much we have achieved. It gives us an opportunity to celebrate our accomplishments, learn from our mistakes, and make adjustments for a brighter future.

Life experiences are powerful teachers. They shape our perspectives, values, and priorities. By reflecting on our past, we can better understand ourselves and gain clarity on what truly matters to us. We can identify patterns, recognize areas of growth, and make conscious choices that align with our authentic selves.

Looking back on our history can equip us with the tools to handle future hurdles bravely and firmly. It supplies us with the necessary insights to deal with novel complications and choose wisely. In difficult times, our past guides us, boosting our self-assurance and drive.

So, as we take the big leap into our forties, let's ponder over our history and acknowledge its teachings. This way, we can build a future that's rewarding and significant.

Altering Viewpoints

In one's forties, entering a fresh life chapter usually prompts a deep change in viewpoints. This key moment enables a mindset shift, boosting personal and professional enhancement.

While managing the forties' trials and triumphs, we start to reconsider what's truly vital. The lessons learned previously supply a firm base for this fresh stage, enabling us to adapt a more optimistic and receptive mindset.

Altering viewpoints at forty means shedding restrictive views and welcoming broader world perceptions. It's about questioning old ideas and welcoming new potentials. With this fresh perspective, we build the nerve to chase our interests and discover fresh growth paths.

A mindset shift influences our entire life, from personal connections to career goals. It motivates us to convey our thoughts better, look for new adventures, and take measured risks. By accepting change and adopting a progress-focused viewpoint, we welcome new success and fulfillment possibilities.

Let's look at how to handle relationships in your 40s and balance work-life healthily. Our goal is to provide valuable advice to help you do well during this life change.

Handling Relationships

Relationships get intricate and vital as we hit our forties. Family and friends become central in our lives, molding our identity and offering support.

Our forties bring a mix of emotions to family life. We balance the needs of older parents and our growing children. It's a complicated dance with generations, where patience, understanding, and open talks help maintain good relationships.

Friends also change during our forties. Our friends may change as priorities shift and jobs demand more. Some friendships grow, others fade. Giving time to build significant bonds with like-minded people can help create a better support system and shared moments.

Authenticity Matters

Being authentic becomes crucial at this life stage. Sincere expressions of our needs and limits build trust and deepen ties. They enable us to form relationships built on mutual respect and understanding.

In our forties, everyone deals with unique troubles and chances to grow. It's key to show understanding and care to keep connections strong. This helps us help each other through the good times and bad.

We'll look at ways to balance life in the next part. Balancing our many relationships becomes more vital in our forties. Things like taking care of ourselves and finding work-life balance are key to feeling good in all parts of life.

Chasing Life Balance

Finding balance in life is extra important in our forties. We tend to juggle lots, like work, family, and personal stuff. So self-care and harmonious work-life balance should be high on our list.

Taking care of ourselves is key to feeling good during this stage of life. By making time for stuff we like and helps us relax, we look after our body and mind. This could be working out, a hobby, quiet time, or catching up with family and friends.

Also, getting a good work-life balance is a must for happiness and feeling satisfied. In our forties, we often have a lot of experience and skills from our jobs. But it's just as vital to make time for stuff away from work. By keeping our hopes realistic and sharing tasks, we can dodge burnout. This helps keep a healthy, doable work-life balance.

Remember, life balance in your forties is not about achieving perfection in every aspect of life. It's about finding a rhythm that allows you to thrive while maintaining a sense of harmony. Prioritizing self-care and work-life balance will not only benefit you, but also positively impact your relationships, productivity, and overall well-being.

Health and Wellness

As we enter our forties, prioritizing our health and well-being becomes increasingly important. Taking care of our physical well-being is essential for maintaining a vibrant and fulfilling life. Here are some tips to help you maintain a healthy lifestyle in your forties:

Eat a Balanced Diet

Adopting a balanced diet is crucial for fueling your body with the nutrients it needs. Include a variety of fruits, vegetables, whole grains, lean proteins, and healthy fats in your daily meals.

Stay Active

Engaging in regular physical activity is vital for maintaining good health in your forties. Find activities that you enjoy, whether it's going for a brisk walk, practicing yoga, or playing a sport. Aim for at least 150 minutes of moderate-intensity exercise each week.

Get Enough Sleep

Quality sleep is essential for overall well-being. Aim for seven to eight hours of sleep each night to allow your body and mind to rest and rejuvenate.

Manage Stress

Stress management is crucial for maintaining a healthy mind and body. Explore stress-reducing techniques such as meditation, deep breathing exercises, and engaging in hobbies or activities that bring you joy.

Doctor Visits

Do you remember to go for your regular doctor visits and screenings? These vital checks help to flag up any possible health issues early. They keep you healthy and well.

Look after yourself. Follow these tips, keep good health and live a joyful life as you step into your forties.

New Starts

Do you view turning forty as a crucial milestone? It's when we often start new life-chapters. You may be thinking about a different job or a fresh start in your working life.

Being in your forties is a special time, full of fresh opportunities and challenges. You get to think deeply about your skills, loves, and life's aims. You can then do what truly makes you happy.

Think of your work-change of choice as your own personal gift when you hit forty. Remember, you bring your rich past work experience and wisdom. This base is priceless as you look at new work areas or roles, or even begin your own venture.

Though starting a fresh work journey is thrilling, it does need careful thought and planning. Identify your skills that are transferable. See if there are any gaps that may need learning or training.

Get help from mentors or career coaches. They can tackle obstacles and boost opportunities along your changeover.

Diving into Fresh Careers

Making a career move in your forties says you're courageous. You're ready to dig into fresh careers, keep your mind open. The job world is changing fast! There are tons of jobs for all kinds of interests.

You should take time to pick out what new paths excite you. Learn their requirements. Industry insiders can help you with advice and links for your change.

Power of Your Old Skills

Switching careers isn't forgetting old skills. Leadership, talking effectively, and solving problems are useful everywhere. Think about skills you've built over time. How can they be cool in another career? This helps you show your worth to possible bosses or customers.

Passing Hurdles

Changing careers in your forties is exciting but may have difficulties. Fitting into a new job, starting a network in a new field, potential roadblocks - all can be tricky. Still, with grit, drive, and a keen spirit, these hurdles can be passed.

Ask for help from your network of friends, family, or mentors when changing careers. Know that stumbling blocks can lead to growth. Every step towards this fresh start gets you closer to a satisfying career in your forties.

Building Purpose and Meaning

Nearing our forties, we start seeking purpose and meaning. This life-altering journey lets us match our actions to our values and passions. This leads to personal satisfaction and fulfilment.

To seek purpose in your forties involves introspection. Set aside time to identify your skills and interests. What sparks joy and engagement in you? What causes are important to you? This self-knowledge can guide you to areas where you can make a significant impact and achieve personal fulfilment.

A way to seek purpose is to align your job with your values and passions. Ask yourself, does your current job satisfy you? Does it mirror your core beliefs? If not, look for opportunities that let you do work meaningful to you. This could mean changing careers or modifying your current role to something more rewarding.

Treading New Paths

Discovering new hobbies can also help you find purpose and meaning in your forties. Take part in things that pique your interest and make you happy. Join a group, volunteer for a cause you love, or acquire a new skill. Such experiences can widen your perspective, connect you with similar people, and give you a sense of purpose beyond work and family.

While pursuing personal happiness is important, finding purpose also involves making a positive impact on others. Consider how you can contribute to your community or society at large. Whether through acts of kindness, supporting charitable organizations, or using your skills to help others, making a difference can bring a deep sense of purpose and fulfillment.

Embracing the Journey

As you embark on the journey of finding purpose and meaning in your forties, remember that it is a process rather than a destination. Be open to new experiences, take risks, and embrace challenges along the way. Understand that finding personal fulfillment requires ongoing reflection, adaptation, and growth.

By cultivating purpose and meaning in your forties, you can transform this significant stage of life into a period of self-discovery and personal growth. Embrace the opportunity to align your actions with your values, pursue work that brings you fulfillment, and make a positive impact on the world around you. This journey will not only enrich your life but also serve as an inspiration to others.

Redefining Success

In our forties, success takes on a new meaning as we redefine our goals and aspirations. It's a time of reflection and self-discovery, where we have the opportunity to align our achievements with our true values and desires.

Instead of measuring success solely based on societal norms or others' expectations, we can now focus on setting new goals that align with our own personal growth and fulfilment. This allows us to create a more meaningful and authentic definition of success.

As we step into this chapter of our lives, we have gained valuable experience and wisdom that can guide us in redefining our path. We can reflect on our past accomplishments and learn from our failures, using these insights to shape new goals that align with our passions and purpose.

Setting Meaningful Goals

Setting meaningful goals in our forties involves a deliberate and intentional approach. We can ask ourselves probing questions, such as:

What truly brings me joy and fulfilment? What impact do I want to make in the world? How do I want to grow and evolve personally and professionally?

By contemplating these questions, we can uncover our deepest desires and aspirations. This allows us to set goals that are aligned with our values, bringing a sense of purpose and fulfillment to our lives.

Measuring Personal Achievements

Gone are the days of comparing our success to others or chasing external validation. In our forties, we have the wisdom to recognize that personal achievements should be measured based on our own unique journey.

Instead of solely focusing on external markers of success, such as wealth or status, we can now prioritize internal growth and personal satisfaction. We can celebrate the milestones that truly matter to us, whether it's overcoming a personal challenge, nurturing meaningful relationships, or making a positive impact in our community.

Embracing our individuality and defining success on our own terms allows us to cultivate a sense of fulfillment and contentment in our forties.

Embracing Aging with Confidence

Turning forty marks a significant milestone in life, where embracing the natural process of aging with confidence becomes crucial. In our forties, we have the opportunity to develop self-acceptance and embrace the changes that come with growing older.

Self-acceptance is a powerful tool that allows us to appreciate and love ourselves for who we are at this stage of life. It is about recognizing our strengths, accepting our imperfections, and embracing the wisdom that comes with age. By cultivating self-acceptance, we can approach the aging process with grace and confidence.

One strategy for developing self-acceptance is to focus on the positive aspects of aging. Instead of fixating on physical changes, we can shift our perspective to appreciate the wisdom, experience, and resilience that we have gained over the years. Celebrating our accomplishments and recognizing our personal growth will help us cultivate a sense of pride and confidence in our forties.

Embracing a Holistic Approach to Well-being

Aging with confidence in our forties also involves taking a holistic approach to our well-being. This includes nurturing our physical, mental, and emotional health. By prioritizing self-care practices such as regular exercise, healthy eating, and adequate rest, we can enhance our overall well-being and feel more confident in our own skin.

Additionally, nurturing our mental and emotional well-being is essential. Engaging in activities that bring us joy, practicing mindfulness and gratitude, and surrounding ourselves with positive support systems can help us cultivate a positive mindset and boost our self-confidence.

Change and Growth: Two Keys

Getting older entails change and growth. Hobbies might change. New skills could be learned. Goals may evolve. Stepping out of comfort zones uncovers fresh interests. It also develops resilience. Plus, it boosts self-esteem and acceptance.

Fears and insecurities often come with aging. But, if we accept the changes and build confidence, we see the forties differently. A new perspective, a sense of joy, and a feeling of fulfillment emerge.

A Forty-year-old's Milestone

The big four-oh is an important landmark. It's where life introspection often happens. It's a celebration of one's personal journey. It's also a time to recognize the experiences that mould us.

Upon reaching forty, it's vital to cherish the gained wisdom. This is more than just a birthday. It's about acknowledging hurdles conquered. It's also about the life lessons imbibed.

Celebrations can range from intimate ones to grand bashes. Regardless, a milestone like this is a tribute to the past and a toast to the future. It's the perfect moment to be with loved ones who have been with us through thick and thin. It's a chance to show appreciation for their love and support. And, it's a time to celebrate the person we've become.

Chapter 2
Midlife Crisis Myth Busting

Welcome to Chapter 2 on the midlife crisis. In this chapter, we delve into what really happens during this stage and dispel myths while revealing opportunities that lie beneath the surface for people in middle age. Let's separate fact from fiction and embrace the positive changes that can come with it.

Midlife crises have long been misunderstood, sensationalized as a time of imprudent acts and dissatisfaction. Yet, there is more to this phase of life than meets the eye. In this section, we will expose what a mid-life crisis is about, shatter some common misconceptions, and outline possible transitions one can make at this point for self-improvement.

By countering stereotypes and examining what makes up this stage, we aim to make clearer sense of what a midlife crisis truly is. Along the way, we will discuss common signs & symptoms; cultural influences affecting individuals; & relationship transitions that may occur.

But it does not end there. We shall also explore coping mechanisms, highlighting the importance of seeking professional help when necessary. Here together, we find good, if not great, among all hurdles as we embrace the journey through midlife, yearning for its possibilities.

So if you are ready to explode these misconceptions, unraveling their truth, and unlocking potentiality within, then let us start on this transformative quest together.

What's a Mid-Life Crisis?

A mid-life crisis is simply a term frequently used to describe certain upheavals in personal life combined with self-search which mostly take place during someone's middle adulthood between 40-60 years old. However, it is important to debunk these myths associated with it because such experiences are not universal.

Contrary to popular belief, a person doesn't necessarily pass through a mid-life crisis just like everyone else does. People do not go through an obligatory phase they must pass through in their lifetime. Rather, it represents a period of transition characterized by unique challenges and growth opportunities.

Many factors can lead to the onset of midlife crises. Some of these factors may include job dissatisfaction, problems with relationships, realization of mortality, need for self-fulfillment, and re-evaluation of life goals & ambitions.

Dispelling Misconceptions

It is important to note that middle age does not give one the right to reckless behavior or impulsive decision-making. It should not be seen as a negative phenomenon but rather as an opportunity for individuals to reassess their lives, make meaningful changes, and discover new possibilities.

Contrary to common belief, not only men experience mid-life crises. Women also go through significant shifts in their middle adulthood stage, and it should be well accepted and respected.

By getting rid of myths surrounding midlife crises, we can better understand this stage and appreciate its transformative potential. Instead, it represents a time for soul-searching, personal development, newfound happiness & fulfillment that one needs in life.

Debunking the Stereotypes

In most cases, when people think about a midlife crisis, there are some misconceptions attached to them which paint a wrong picture about what individuals really go through. This section aims at demystifying such notions while focusing on the reality concerning midlife changes.

Challenging the Crisis Label

Most people think midlife is a time of crisis, but this is not always true. In fact, many people see it as a chance for personal growth and self-discovery. It is essential to recognize that transitioning into midlife can be positive and empowering rather than exclusively negative and chaotic.

The Myth of Age-Related Regret

Another stereotype holds that midlife crises are occasioned by regrets or dissatisfaction about decisions in the past. However, although reflection comes naturally with age, one must understand that other motives like the desire for personal satisfaction could fuel this transition stage in life when priorities are reviewed.

Embracing Change and Transformation

Midlife crises should not be seen as a tragic event but an opportunity to grow and change. At this point, everything changes; goals need to be reassessed, while new interests are pursued, and change is embraced. This does not indicate a lack of strength or failure; it rather signifies a departure from known tracks so as to give more meaning to one's existence.

By dispelling these myths about middle-aged crises and understanding their intricate nature, we can provide better support for those going through them.

The Opportunity for Growth

When it comes to midlife crises, there is a common misconception that it is solely a negative experience. Nevertheless, it should also be noted that such transitions also present opportunities for personal growth and transformation. Instead of being scared or fighting off these changes, embracing such periods may bring about significant improvements in different spheres of existence.

Midlife crises provide an opportunity for self-reflection and re-evaluation unlike any other periods in life. They give you an opportunity to assess your own personal goals vis-a-vis your values and priorities. By reflecting on where you currently stand versus where you would want to go in life, making deliberate choices consistent with your innermost desires becomes possible.

This period often causes individuals to question whether they're still happy with their current career choices, relationships, or life in general. Through this introspection, hidden talents and passions that were never before explored might be uncovered. It is not too late to follow uncharted routes and indulge in things that make you happy.

Further still, midlife crises can act as a catalyst for growth and self-improvement. The challenges and uncertainties associated with this stage could build resilience and inner strength. By overcoming obstacles, one can develop a stronger sense of self, which results in higher levels of confidence and adaptability.

During midlife crises, people have an opportunity to rediscover themselves by creating lives that reflect their true nature. It gives room for abandoning old roles as well as societal expectations and explores the freedom of being real.

Looking at midlife crises as an opportunity instead of a crisis in life will help you to unlock your potential for growth and transformation. This section of your life should be embraced with an open mind and readiness to explore other better things. Midlife crises can become stepping stones towards a more fulfilling and purposeful life through the right mindset and personal development commitment.

Common Signs and Symptoms

Midlife crisis can occur in different ways. The common symptoms or signs people may experience during this turning point are discussed here. Understanding these clues about oneself can help in actively navigating the difficulties and opportunities brought by midlife.

1. Self-Reflection and Existential Questions

A feeling of self-reflection and contemplation on what life is all about characterizes a mid-life crisis. Individuals going through this stage might question their accomplishments, goals, and overall happiness in relation to their current path.

2. Desire for Change

In addition, an overwhelming desire for change is among the primary indications that one is having a midlife crisis. It could take various forms, such as exploring new hobbies, career shifts, or fulfilling long-standing dreams that seemed off track initially.

3. Increased Restlessness and Discontentment

During this time, individuals usually feel restless, bored, or discontent with themselves, which are normal indicators of a mid-life crisis. In other words, one starts yearning for something else; they are not satisfied with how things are or just doing the same routine every day.

4. Mood Swings and Emotional Turmoil

Most of the time, there are emotional ups and downs associated with the middle age transition period. Mood swings, increased irritability, as well as feeling raw, may happen when one undergoes internal changes accompanying external pressures during this season of his/her life.

5. Crises Triggered by Life Events

Divorce cases, loss of loved ones, or setbacks in careers could trigger more severe instances in these conditions. Midlife crises can be caused or escalated by certain occurrences in our lives. Such factors may make people take a whole new look at their lives in the search for deeper meanings and fulfillments.

Identifying these symptoms is the initial step to effectively dealing with a mid-life crisis. This transition period, therefore, offers opportunities for self-development and finding lasting contentment.

Cultural Influences on Midlife Crises

However, midlife crises are not only individualized but also have cultural influences. Different societies and cultural expectations shape the experiences and perceptions of individuals going through midlife, adding another layer of complexity to this transitional phase.

There are several ways in which cultural influences manifest during middle adulthood crises. These societal norms and expectations about success in career, relationship statuses, or personal gains may contribute to feelings of pressure and frustration. Comparison to societal ideals or cultural standards can fuel self-doubt and a sense of falling short during this stage of life.

Additionally, attitudes towards aging in different cultures, as well as the definition of success in society, play a major role in the way people experience and deal with middle age crises. In some cultures, old age is associated with wisdom, while others view it as a decline or loss of vigor. This could help individuals understand how they see themselves and whether they would like to embrace change so that they can get better chances.

To have more comprehensive knowledge about this stage of life, it is important to consider and acknowledge cultural factors that affect midlife crisis. If people recognize the cultural influences, they can weave their way through this period in a way that considers societal expectations at large.

Changing Relationships

Relationships often change during a mid-life crisis. This transformative moment may be an opportunity for growth or forging stronger bonds with our loved ones.

Open communication, understanding, and empathy are crucial in navigating these transitions. It's vital to understand that both you and your partner are undergoing personal turmoil and fears. Allowing each other to express their feelings while listening attentively allows mutual support as well as strengthening the bond between you two.

You should think about your values as individuals and as a couple on this journey. Through self-reflection, we can engage in meaningful conversations about what lies ahead of us and the kind of relationship both partners want. It is also a good time to explore shared interests, set new goals, and find common ground that might reign it a spark or deepen intimacy.

Embrace Change and Growth

Midlife crises serve as opportunities for personal development within relationships too. It's an opportunity to embrace change with fresh eyes full of curiosity and adventure towards life ahead. Trying out new activities together, rekindling old passions, or engaging in shared experiences may result in lifelong memories.

Both partners need to encourage each other as they grow into different versions of themselves over time. Encourage your spouse to pursue new hobbies or career paths while being open-minded about their shifting tastes and dreams. Consequently, cultivating a relationship based on personal fulfillment will require embracing change together.

Striking A Balance And Seeking Help

In order to successfully navigate midlife crises within relationships, there is a need for striking a balance between personal growth and keeping strong ties together. Maintaining self-care habits can help preserve individual well-being without necessarily disengaging from the partnership.

Seeking professional help will be very beneficial if you are finding it difficult to navigate through the transitions or if the changes have caused conflicts within your relationship. Couples therapy, relationship coaching are some of the avenues that provide guidance and tools for effective communication, conflict management, as well as rebuilding trust.

Remember that midlife crises can be a catalyst for growth and positive transformation. By opening up yourselves through these transitions, you and your partner could create richer bonds, love more deeply, and find satisfaction in life.

Coping Strategies During Middle Age Crisis

There is so much going on when experiencing a midlife crisis, but at the same time, an opportunity for personal development and life-changing experience. People who accept change while also using certain techniques to get over this phase will be able to find new ways of happiness and fulfillment.

Accept Change

One way of dealing with this period is through accepting change rather than running away from it. Acceptance of change being part of nature's cycle can lead to exciting prospects. Such changes may offer an opportunity to take different paths in life by trying new hobbies or following long-held dreams. In this way, one can face midlife age with optimism once they embrace change without fear.

Take Care of Mental and Emotional Health

The midlife crises are often accompanied by different feelings and thus, it's important to pay attention to your mental and emotional welfare. Practice self-soothing activities that will help reduce anxiety and improve your overall well-being. Engage in practices like mindfulness, workouts, taking a walk through the woods, or contacting people you love. Consider visiting a therapist or counselor who could direct and help in managing your emotions during this difficult period.

Discovering Your Purpose In New Endeavors

Midlife crises can also be used as an opportunity to find new meaning in other spheres of existence. Identify areas where you derive satisfaction from and engage in such activities as meet your interests. It may mean learning a new hobby, helping others without getting paid for that, or even changing one's profession altogether. Find out what you are passionate about at this point in life and go after them with gusto so that you may feel renewed purpose and fulfillment.

Remember that experiencing a midlife crisis is not always something negative about yourself; these coping skills will enable survival during this change period for those who put them into practice. Use this time as a jump-off for personal development because someday it may be the turning point of positive transformation on yourself.

Looking for Professional Help

Sometimes it becomes overwhelming during such transitions as a midlife crisis; hence professional guidance is very necessary while dealing with it. There are many resources available for overcoming midlife difficulties.

Counseling is another resource in which individuals can explore their feelings, gain insights, and develop strategies for overcoming problems in a supportive atmosphere provided by trained therapists who help people suffering from mid-life crisis realize its causes thereby enabling informed decision-making.

Another form of assistance that proves vital when one encounters issues related to middle adulthood is coaching. Coaches specialize in empowering individuals to create meaningful and fulfilling lives. They can assist in setting goals, identifying strengths, and guiding individuals through the process of self-discovery and personal growth.

Support groups and online communities can also foster a sense of belonging and togetherness during the middle age crisis. Sharing experiences with others in similar situations can offer solace, confirmation, and advice.

Remember that asking for professional help does not show weakness but strength as individuals are committed to personal growth that necessitates seeking guidance given unfamiliar territories. With proper support, people acquire understanding, develop resilience, and come out stronger from their midlife crisis.

The Journey of Midlife

As it is a journey rather than a crisis, midlife is nearing us. Embrace the transformations and difficulties involved in this period to realize one's full potential for growth and gratification. Instead of dreading the moment, let us explore ways we can take advantage of this transition stage.

Midlife crises may be thought of as turning points when people get an opportunity to look back on their lives, reassess priorities, and take new paths. It's a time for self-examination and identifying hidden potentials. By accepting the journey and being open to opportunities that come up, we expose ourselves to a new journey, one that is both rewarding and fulfiling.

It is worth noting that this journey is different for everyone and there is no one-size-fits-all-solution. However, by looking at it with an open mind and being ready to try new things, we can be strong enough to go through the midlife crises and come out stronger than ever. It's time to explore new passions, set new goals, and embrace the unknown.

So let's change our outlook. Instead of seeing midlife crises as something scary, let us consider them as opportunities for personal development and self-discovery. Accept the changes, take action right away and have a positive attitude towards this transforming experience. The way ahead may be unclear but the possibilities are infinite.

Chapter 3

Self-Assessment at Forty

Welcome to Chapter 3 of our series, where we embark on a journey of personal reflection and growth at the age of forty. In this chapter, we delve into the intricacies of self-assessment, exploring the realms of self-evaluation and identifying key areas for development for continued personal and professional growth.

At forty years old, many people pause to look back on their lives and reevaluate where they have been and what dreams still remain unfulfilled. These moments provide us with real insights about ourselves that pave the way for transformation and improvement.

Together, let's traverse a wide range of introspection. We will discuss how important it is to embrace self-reflection when evaluating life milestones, knowing strengths and weaknesses, among others. The role of personal reflection in career development, fostering relationships, seeking satisfaction from oneself, and conquering difficulties will also be highlighted.

Throughout this chapter, you will receive practical hints, exercises, and aids to ensure your successful self-evaluation journey with us. If you seek clarity regarding your job, want more fulfillment in your life, or just hope to understand yourself better, then read this section designed to guide you on this journey.

Thus, let's begin together a discovery trip towards one's own self, where reflective thoughts are hidden treasures; hence, we shall explore such values in terms of self-reflection, evaluation, and developmental areas. Prepare yourself for the power that comes from learning how to assess yourself so that you may maximize your potential at forty!

Embracing Self-Reflection

In today's fast-paced world, it's easy to get caught up in the whirlwind of daily tasks and commitments. However, amidst the chaos, personal reflection holds the key to achieving a more fulfilling and purposeful life. Taking the time to introspect and delve deep into our thoughts and emotions allows us to gain a clearer understanding of ourselves and our desires.

Personal reflection is powerful because it helps us understand ourselves better, make informed choices, and grow in our personal lives. It also helps us identify our strengths and develop our weaknesses, implying that one must continue improving to keep on living. Thus, by embracing self-reflection, we can align our actions and decisions with the values we cherish most, resulting in greater happiness and contentment.

Personal reflection can be used as a tool to discover patterns, behaviors, and beliefs that limit our potential for optimal performance. This calls for self-reflection where one questions existing belief systems within themselves; they discard false mindsets which limit them from achieving their full potential (Barnett, 2010). The right knowledge about oneself makes the process of facing life challenges with strength and dignity less challenging.

Again, it is through personal reflection that a deep connection happens between emotion and intuition activated within us. Hence, when we critically listen to ourselves, it allows for inner wisdom to ensure decisions made come from our real selves. Listening to my intuition gives me clarity about what I really need in terms of direction, hence enabling me to choose what will lead me towards my goals and desires.

Ultimately, self-reflection tells us how well we take care of ourselves or empowers us as individuals. In this case, an opportunity is given for one's happiness or well-being importance comes first. To thrive, we must invest by sparing some time doing silent meditation as well as evaluating and considering these thoughts deeply.

Assessing Life Milestones

Reaching forty years is a significant moment in life. It reaches a point where we take breaks, think deeply, and estimate our accomplishments, objectives, and passions. This reflection enables us to know better about all that has happened and allows us time for introspection.

This part presents different types of self-evaluation that can help us reassess our lives at this stage. We can identify our areas of growth and development through thinking about what we have done so far. Life milestones can be assessed by reflecting upon one's career, relationship, or personal growth to make informed decisions on reigniting them.

Personal reflections enable us to see how much we have achieved as well as appreciate the important milestones covered so far. Moreover, it helps one see clearly the area(s) they would wish to change or improve. Through this process of self-appraisal, individuals are able to take back their future from its fate and make choices that are intentional.

Consequently, the assessment of life milestones through writing journals or seeking the counsel of mentors or therapists among others provides an opportunity for reflection on what has passed in our past, present, and then setting ourselves towards a defined destiny. Through exploring into dreams; desires as well as purposes self-discovery occurs including growth.

Methods of Self-Evaluation

Different methods for assessing life milestones are presented here that can help us evaluate ourselves at this moment. Reflective exercises like creating a timeline of major events in your life, writing a personal manifesto, or conducting a SWOT analysis (Strengths, Weaknesses, Opportunities, Threats) give useful insights into our journey.

Additionally, feedback from trusted friends, family members, colleagues may offer new perspectives which

could show some weaknesses that we might not notice alone, even in terms of strengths. Life coaches or mentors can also be involved in helping one go through such an introspective quest.

Instead of being too harsh with ourselves while dwelling on past mistakes; self-evaluation is meant to be an opportunity where one can learn from past experiences, celebrate achievements, and look at areas for growth in the future.

Identifying Strengths and Weaknesses

In this part, we are going to examine how personal reflection helps us to identify our strengths as well as weaknesses. Self-appraisal is a powerful way of understanding what we can do better while ascertaining our limitations. By genuinely looking into ourselves, we can determine our unique talents that will enable us to achieve the highest level of success.

Personal reflection is like a mirror which shows the things that you have done well and those that you need to work on. It lets us understand better where we excel and optimize them. Our strengths become visible through self-assessment; hence, they should be used to chase after dreams and ambitions.

Yet, self-examination requires courage because it makes someone face their weak points. This allows one to admit their mistakes, know the areas they lag behind, and rectify them. The recognition of personal flaws opens up ways for personal growth and development.

This implies that there are several techniques and tools that can support self-evaluation. One effective approach is self-reflection, setting aside dedicated time to introspect and analyze our thoughts and actions. Journaling, meditating, or soliciting comments from trusted people help us understand ourselves better in terms of weaknesses as well as strengths.

Personal reflection encourages the recognition of our personal strengths and limitations that serve as a solid foundation for personal and professional growth. Our weaknesses can be addressed by taking self-evaluation into consideration, therefore, this is a means of leveraging our strengths while charting a way towards continuous improvement. As individuals, we are able to develop continuously through self-assessment.

Exploring Career Growth

In our career journeys, it is important to engage in personal reflection. Valuable insights into our career trajectory and areas for development can be gained through self-assessment. This introspective process enables us to navigate careers effectively and attain long-term success.

Our professional capabilities become clearer when we reflect on ourselves, thereby revealing our strengths and weaknesses at work. Therefore, if we identify what we must do better at work, then we shall definitely improve on skills and knowledge necessary for progress within one's industry.

Additionally, with the help of personal reflection, individuals can connect their career goals to their values and passions. Finding fulfillment in our current roles by critically analyzing them while at the same time exploring other opportunities is essential.

Again, using reflective methods will reveal more possibilities for both growth and learning that all of us should take. By evaluating experiences gained before now or what we do best, we shall always have new challenges hence expanding more about what is under study.

When exploring career growth; thus, it becomes vital to adopt self-reflection as an ongoing process because as professionals evolve so should they keep reassessing themselves regarding areas they need to develop further in the future.

Nurturing Relationships

Today's fast-paced life makes people forget about relationships between each other so easily. However, without personal reflection, meaningful relationships cannot be fostered.

We gain a deeper understanding of how we relate with others if only we would take some time for self-assessment. It helps us look back at who we were in terms of strength and weakness, making us open up even more to those close by whom or around whom we interact.

By reflecting on our communication style, we can identify areas where we might need to improve. For instance, active listening or expressing empathy more effectively may be areas that need improvement. These developmental areas can easily be identified through self-reflection, thus enabling us to reach out to others at a much deeper level.

Additionally, personal reflection improves our capability of addressing conflicts and resolving difficult situations in relationships. By examining one's own reactions and behaviors, it is possible to pinpoint contributing factors to conflicts and address them. Having such self-awareness makes it easier for people involved in the conversation to develop productive dialogue, leading to both sides benefiting from the outcome.

Furthermore, by reflecting upon ourselves better, we are able to celebrate and understand each individual's uniqueness in nurturing relationships. We come into contact with diverse perspectives and qualities exhibited by others as a result of comprehending ourselves better. This means that self-assessment helps us become more empathetic towards others and also making us more compassionate, thereby promoting harmonious connections.

In conclusion, personal reflection is key in nurturing relationships. It leads to self-awareness which eventually enables individuals to develop their communication skills, hence becoming good conflict solvers in relationship matters who appreciate different qualities possessed among people around them. Connections that enrich our lives are formed only when individuals engage in self-assessment coupled with an unending commitment towards their growth.

Seeking Personal Fulfillment

In the process of self-actualization, personal reflection holds a sublime place. Through self-assessment, we

are able to know our true passions, dreams, and ambitions. This self-consciousness underlies the areas for improvement that will make our lives more complete and fulfilling.

Self-reflection is an opportunity to discover our deepest desires and convictions that are leading us to live a life congruent with our authentic selves. We become conscious about what brings us the most joy, purpose, and fulfillment by reflecting on our thoughts, feelings, and experiences. These insights serve as compasses which guide us into living in line with ourselves deeply.

When conducting a self-evaluation, it is vital to consider every aspect of our lives such as relationships, career development, personal development, as well as health. Admitting these limitations, fears, and difficulties only opens doors to personal growth since they represent where we want to be at the end.

Gaining insight into our identity through personal reflection enables us to consciously decide on how we want to act. What necessary steps must one take so as to accomplish his or her goals? Therefore, with this knowledge on where you stand in terms of self-improvement, it becomes easy for you to set up your goals' paths hence not acting blindly despite your naivety on the issue regarding maturity.

Developing self-awareness through personal reflection is a transformative process that empowers us to make conscious choices and take intentional actions. It allows us to determine which steps need to be taken for one's aspirations to come true. By identifying those aspects of ourselves that require improvement, we can create a plan that aligns with who we are at heart, ultimately resulting in greater happiness and meaning in life.

Thus, when one begins reflecting personally coupled with evaluating themselves, they embark upon an inner journey of transformation towards their better future selves. Our ongoing commitment toward a deeper understanding of who we really are opens doorways toward fulfillment otherwise unthought of before now when all of this is taken into account. In doing so, we are able to steer through the puzzles within life with lucidity and purpose, which will not only nurture our good state but also shine over other people.

Overcoming Challenges and Setting Goals

This segment discusses how self-assessment can be used as a tool for overcoming challenges and setting goals. Personal reflection and self-evaluation play a vital role in identifying one's strengths, weaknesses, and areas that need further development.

As we do personal reflection, it is possible to gain more insight about ourselves and know what may be stopping us. Therefore, by assessing our progress, we can establish where we stand currently as well as determine appropriate actions that must be taken to achieve their aspirations in life.

One effective method of self-assessment is to set specific, measurable, attainable, relevant, and time-bound (SMART) goals. By using this format, you can make sure that your objectives have value to you personally as they relate to your passions or dreams.

Evaluating Progress and Identifying Obstacles

For mapping our own growth, it is necessary for us to regularly look back on how far we have come while taking stock of any necessary adjustments. Through careful examination of ourselves, we are able to notice barriers standing in the way of our growth, hence making strategies for defeating such challenges needed.

By honestly reflecting on the outcomes of both successes and failures, one acknowledges those areas where he/she performs better than others and also identifies problems which hinder them from achieving success. At times, they reveal their development needs besides showing the invisible patterns responsible for restraining them from reaching their full potential.

Creating a Roadmap for Personal Growth and Achievement

Once an individual has gone through personal reflection coupled with self-evaluation leading them toward clarity, it becomes essential to create a roadmap towards personal growth and achievement. This roadmap helps individuals align their choices with their targets as well as keep track of their actions throughout life.

Smaller steps can be taken in order to achieve our goals incrementally. Having milestones will help us celebrate and inspire us.

In setting up goals, it will also be significant to remain adaptable and flexible. Life is unpredictable and full of surprises. Instead of looking at them as problems, having a growth mindset makes it possible to see opportunities for learning and self-improvement during such times.

To sum up, personal reflection, self-evaluation, and development areas are essential in overcoming challenges and making realistic goals. These are the practices that enable one to overcome obstacles, embrace growth, and succeed in his/her life.

Embracing Growth in the Next Chapter

The process of personal reflection has brought us here; we have reached a stage where we can begin again with a firm footing on the ground. Assimilation from our self-assessments has laid a foundation for continuous improvement (Laureate Education (Producer), 2013). At this point, we can do away with what we have been doing before so that we can go forward into new possibilities where there is room for further nurturing.

Personal reflection has served as the compass guiding us through the complexities of self-evaluation. It enables an individual to identify areas needed for improvement which would mean developing particular traits or skills (Laureate Education (Producer), 2013). We open ourselves up to new opportunities for personal growth and achievement by acknowledging these areas.

As we prepare ourselves for the unknown future territory, this journey becomes invaluable because continuous self-assessment processes become crucial tools that shape individuals' destiny (Hunt et al., 2005). Through maintaining deep-seated personal reflections, human beings can adjust to their ever-changing landscapes thereby continually refining their aspirations or objectives. Embracing growth demands daring oneself beyond limits set earlier, hence allowing oneself to step out of comfort zones upon which one's development areas lie.

As we say goodbye to introspection on our part; let us now say hello to the road ahead with renewed enthusiasm and purpose. With the knowledge from personal reflection, we can therefore meet it head-on and be sure about ourselves because we know who or what we are and that is what we want for our future.

Chapter 4
Shaping Success for You

This chapter examines subjective success. It'll help you draft your unique success definition that lines up with your aims. Redefining success your way may lead to greater joy as you strive for your visions.

Grasping Subjective Success

Subjective success means that success doesn't have one universal meaning. It alters with each person's values, conditions, and dreams. Let go of society's canned success concept and accept your very own.

Success isn't the same for everyone. It's subjective. One person's victory may seem insignificant to another. By accepting subjective success, you script your own satisfaction journey.

"Subjective success syncs your goals and steps with your values and dreams - independent of outside pressures."

Shaping your own success definition, you focus on what matters to you. You set goals that fit your unique life, promising a more fulfilling existence.

By welcoming subjective success, you equip yourself to live genuinely and make decisions that fulfill your success vision. You carve out a path that's authentically yours, free from societal sway or outside elements.

In the following sections, we will guide you through the process of crafting your personalized success statement, reflecting on priorities and trade-offs, overcoming societal expectations and external influences, setting measurable goals, embracing failure, nurturing a growth mindset, and sustaining success. Each step will help you further understand and embody the notion of subjective success, enabling you to live a fulfilling, purpose-driven life.

Crafting Your Personalized Success Statement

In today's society, success is often defined by external metrics such as money, status, or power. However, true fulfillment and happiness can only be achieved when we define success on our own terms. Crafting a personalized success statement is the first step towards living a purpose-driven life.

By taking the time to reflect on your core values, passions, and long-term goals, you can create a clear vision of what success means to you. This personalized success statement becomes your compass, guiding your actions and decisions.

 "Your success statement should reflect your authentic self and align with your deepest desires. It is the roadmap to creating a life that brings you true satisfaction and fulfillment."

Defining your own success allows you to focus on what truly matters to you, rather than chasing after society's expectations. It empowers you to set your own standards of achievement, embracing a holistic view of success that encompasses personal growth, meaningful relationships, and overall well-being.

Don't forget, being successful is very personal. It's a journey that constantly changes. A custom success statement clears any confusion and gives you direction in life, helping you stay true to you.

Thinking Over Your Needs and Compromises

On the path to success, we sometimes face tough choices. We have to make decisions and it's important to think about what really matters. Understand the compromises you need to meet your success.

Each action is a trade-off – we give up something to give time to something else. Knowing priorities helps you make clever choices that suits your long-term aim.

Compromises are part of decision-making. They need thought. You need to balance the wins and losses in each choice, consider the long-term results, and decide what you're ready to give up.

Compromises are part of seeking success. It's about sticking to your beliefs even if it means giving up something now. Remember, every decision you make gets you closer to your aim.

Decision-making is a skill that improves over time. In this part, we give useful tips to help you make smart choices while dealing with compromises. Points to think about include:

Know your goals and values: What makes you tick? And what are you aiming for? These ideas guide your choices. Ponder the results: Think about each choice's ups and downs. How do they affect your future and present? Gauge the win-lose: For each choice, figure out what's gained and lost. What can you give up for what matters most? Ask for help: Turn to trusted ones for varied perspectives on each choice's win-lose.

Making choices isn't always a cakewalk. But, looking at your wants and weighing the cost-benefit will brush away doubts and set clear intentions.

Rising above Society's Expectations and Outside Forces

In our world today, societal norms and outer influences can mess with our idea of success. From kid age, the messages about success and goals surround us. From chatting, cruising social media to advertisements, the urge to fit in is strong.

But sticking to who you are and your success idea is key to living genuinely. It's about balancing these outside forces and staying close to your values, dreams, and aims. "Success should be measured by your own yardstick, not society's ruler." - Oprah Winfrey

To overcome societal expectations and external influences, it's important to first reflect on what truly matters to you. Take the time to identify your own values and priorities. What are the things that bring you joy and fulfillment? What are your unique abilities and passions?

Once you have a clear understanding of what success means to you, it becomes easier to resist the pressures of society. Surround yourself with like-minded individuals who support your goals and aspirations. Seek out role models who have achieved success on their own terms and learn from their experiences.

Remember, societal expectations are often fleeting and ever-changing, but staying true to yourself and your own path is what leads to long-lasting happiness and fulfillment.

It's important to set boundaries and not let the opinions and judgments of others define your worth. Embrace your uniqueness and make choices that align with your values, even if they go against the grain.

When you stay true to yourself, you will find that success becomes more meaningful and fulfilling. It's about finding harmony between societal expectations and your own personal growth.

So, let go of the need for validation from external sources and focus on what truly matters to you. Embrace your own journey and define success on your own terms. Only then can you live a life that is truly authentic and meaningful.

How to Set Goals that Lead to Success

Setting goals is key for success. It plots out your journey to reach your dreams. Concrete goals allow you to check your growth and fine tune your path.

Ensure your goals can be measured. This clarity aids in keeping track of your progress, with measurable goals acting as stepping stones to success. "Think of goals as road signs directing you towards success." For achievable goals, divide your dream into smaller, practical tasks. This plan gives you a clear process to follow and a more accurate progress check. Each goal must be dedicated, reachable, applicable, and time-bound (SMART goals).

Identifying your goals is just step one. Next, decide the success benchmarks. These indicators let you see if you've reached your mark. With exact benchmarks, you can fairly assess your growth and modify your strategy when needed.

Monitoring your growth keeps you focused and validates your path. It lets you check your achievements against your benchmarks and make modifications to your plan if necessary. Celebrating milestones boosts your confidence and energizes your journey to success.

Don't forget, success isn't a straight shot. It needs adaptability, flexibility. While you measure your progress, stay open to new info and adjust your goals and plans as necessary. View the hiccups and hurdles as growth opportunities, they help fine-tune your route to victory.

Creating clear goals, defining victory rules, and watching your progress keeps your success journey filled with purpose and joy. It helps keep you dialed in, inspired, and responsible, boosting your odds of reaching your unique taste of triumph.

Welcoming Mistakes and Learning from Stumbles

Tripping and detours are parts of the road to victory. Instead of roadblocks, view them as learning experiences. By doing this, you grow your resolve and rebound even stronger.

When you trip up, it's easy to feel dispirited and disheartened. But, these moments can be launch pads towards our aims. They nudge us to reconsider our plans, learn from our slip-ups, and tweak things to advance. "Mistakes aren't against success; they're part of it." - Arianna Huffington Check out some tips to help your welcome mistakes and learn from missteps:

Change your view: Don't view falling down as a measure of your skills or worth, see it as a growth chance. Realize that roadblocks are short-term and offer crucial clues for future victories.

Learn and adjust: Look closely at what didn't go as planned. Uncover the reasons and think of ways to do better. Change your strategy and add improvements that up your chance to win. In the words of Henry Ford, "The only true error is the one we gain nothing from."

Grow resilience: Bouncing back is what resilience means. Start viewing setbacks as steps forward in building your toughness. Remember, the point is not falling, but the number of times you rise.

Find support: Build a circle of encouraging friends, mentors, or coaches. Their advice and morale-boosting words can aid you through tough times. They offer lessons from their own experiences to help you face obstacles.

Gain from successful people: Learn from those who resiliently faced failures and setbacks. Their narratives are motivational and share great teaching on resilience and determination.

Remember, setbacks are temporary, not permanent hindrances. They're chances for growth and betterment. Embrace troubles, build resilience, and see setbacks as stepping stones to your goals. Success comes not from a lack of failure but by the power to overcome it.

Fostering a Growth Attitude for Ongoing Prosperity

To consistently make progress, having a growth mindset is vital. With a mentality that accepts challenges and promotes frequent improvement, you'll empower yourself to maneuver through barriers and reach success.

Believing in a growth mindset means you think hard work, commitment, and tenacity can boost your skills and smarts. This thinking turns failures into launch pads for growth, not dead ends. It lets you tackle problems head-on, ready to adapt.

Quote: "The only limit to your success is the extent of your growth mindset." - Carol Dweck

With a growth mindset, failure isn't saying you're not good enough. It's a stepping stone to get better. Setbacks become lessons, not barriers. This mindset keeps you improving and stepping out of the familiar.

Diving Into Challenges and Keeping the Learning Going

Welcoming challenges is key to a growth mindset. Don't avoid tough tasks or situations. See them as growth chances. Every challenge is a new learning opportunity. By always embracing challenges, your skills and knowledge grow, paving the way to ongoing success.

Never-ending learning is another growth mindset part. Develop a hunger for new knowledge and exploration of fresh ideas. Make it a habit to find ways to learn, whether in a class, reading books, going to workshops, or having deep talks. More learning makes you adaptable and versatile. That's essential in our fast-moving world.

Making Yourself Stronger and Adaptable

Resilience means getting back up after life knocks you down. We all face tough times, and bouncing back is key. A positive outlook helps during these times. Learn from your experience and come out stronger.

Being adaptable is like resilience. It involves changing and thriving despite new circumstances. Today's world changes quickly, and being adaptable helps us succeed. An open mind leads to embracing changes. Flexibility in thought allows us to handle uncertainties and embrace the chance to grow.

Overall, developing a growth mindset helps us succeed. Meeting challenges head-on, learning continuously, growing stronger, and staying adaptable are ways to improve. They help us overcome hurdles on the path to success.

Continuing Success and Celebrating the Little Wins

Success isn't just a goal, it's a lifelong journey. After reaching a goal, a new one appears: maintaining success and finding joy in it. In this last section, we'll talk about ways to keep your success going and how to celebrate achieving small and big milestones.

To sustain success, it is essential to prioritize self-care and maintain a healthy work-life balance. Remember, sustainable success requires not only hard work but also taking care of your physical, mental, and emotional well-being. By nurturing all aspects of your life, you can avoid burnout and find long-term satisfaction in your accomplishments.

Celebrating milestones is crucial for staying motivated and recognizing your progress. It provides an opportunity to reflect on your achievements, acknowledge your growth, and appreciate the journey.

Whether it's a small milestone or a significant achievement, take the time to celebrate and reward yourself. These celebrations will fuel your ongoing commitment to success.

Sustaining success goes beyond reaching a specific goal; it involves continuous growth, fulfillment, and finding joy in your journey. By prioritizing self-care, celebrating milestones, and embracing the process of defining and redefining success on your own terms, you can create a sustainable and fulfilling life of success.

Chapter 5

Understanding the Benefits of Lifelong Learning

Welcome to Chapter 5 which is on personal growth and development. This chapter will focus on the magic of lifelong learning. Lifelong learning is more than just acquiring knowledge; it is about cultivating an attitude toward constant growth that can result in personal growth and unlocking new paths to success.

Are you ready to embark on a journey of self-discovery and exploration? In this chapter, we will explore numerous enriching resources that could support your lifelong learning voyage. With online courses and educational platforms, libraries, mentorship programs, there are many avenues through which you can expand your horizons.

Therefore, lifelong learning unlocks professional skills growth, broadens horizons, or allows one to develop a hobby or interest. Continue with us as we highlight how perpetual education affects personal improvements concerning our lives at offices or any working place and in general mental health.

Get ready to embrace the power of lifelong learning and unlock your true potential. Let's dive in!

What does Lifelong Learning mean?

During this section, we shall examine what it takes for something to be described as lifelong learning. It refers to the continuous acquisition of knowledge throughout one's life beyond formal schooling. This thinking supports anybody's own development at whatever age he or she might be.

Hence, other than being part-time education, it comprises things like reading books, attending seminars needed by specific jobs, participating in online courses during summer holidays, and taking part in experiential training schedules among others (Reference). Clearly stated, these facts depict how this kind of self-enhancement helps individuals toward achieving intellectual stimulation, adaptability, while having a sense of satisfaction that comes along with it.

Unlike traditional education where there are set timelines and syllabi – Juma et al., (2018) explain that...

The approach allows for people who are interested in various subjects enabling them to identify their passions as well as a deeper understanding of their world.

A mindset of lifelong learning can unlock many benefits for an individual. Not only does lifelong learning contribute to personal growth, but it also enhances cognitive abilities, critical thinking skills, and creativity. It fosters adaptability and resilience, enabling individuals to thrive in an ever-changing world.

Furthermore, the advantages of continuous learning are huge. It boosts chances on the job market. Additionally, it helps people broaden their minds and become more understanding of others from different cultures or backgrounds as well as open doors people would never have thought about.

In conclusion, lifelong learning is a journey of continuous personal growth and exploration. It is a valuable resource for individuals seeking personal development, professional advancement, and a fulfilling life. By embracing lifelong learning, individuals can embark on a path of personal growth that knows no limits.

The Key to Lifelong Learning: Curiosity

Curiosity motivates perpetual education. This curiosity creates interest and drives constant development hence makes us curious so that we look for new knowledge and experience outside our existing knowledge boundary. In this way, one will be able to embark on a journey of continuing learning out of curiosity.

Nurturing Curiosity

To develop curiosity, it is essential that we nurture an open and inquisitive mindset. We can embrace the unknown, ask questions, and venture into new ideas. Curiosity fuels interest in knowledge; it prompts us to dig deeper for answers over our own assumptions. It requires creating a climate that encourages questioning thereby unlocking personal growth.

Embracing the Unknown

Embracing curiosity implies stepping outside our comfort zones and embracing what is not known. This means being willing to go where other people refuse to tread. There are endless possibilities for personal growth and development if we learn how to embrace the unknown.

Expanding Horizons

Learning with curiosity widens the horizon of life. We discover new interests, passions, and talents that may be dormant within us. As we keep on exploring and enhancing our skills and knowledge throughout our lives, lifelong learning becomes a thrilling adventure of self-discovery as well as personal growth. Curiosity is the key to lifelong learning because it drives us forward, helps us look for understanding, and accepts the change of ourselves. In this regard, therefore, cultivate your curiosity by embracing uncertainty at best which will lead you into a journey of lifelong learning that you thought could never have existed before now.

Resources for Lifelong Learning

Taking up a lifelong learning program opens up opportunities for personal growth. Within this part, we provide you with selected resources from diverse sources crafted towards quenching your quest for knowledge across various subjects such as online course platforms like edX, Coursera, Udemy, LinkedIn Learning, library services, or mentorship programs.

Online courses offer convenience and flexibility thus allowing you to study at home during your free time pace yourself just as much as you want whenever you feel low energy or tiredness kicks in. For instance, there are numerous courses available on Coursera, Udemy, LinkedIn-Learning, etc., each dealing with different topics from all areas of life.

Moreover, educational platforms like Khan Academy, Skillshare, edX have curated content available from leading institutions and professionals for those who need a more structured learning environment. They offer you courses, tutorials, and workshops to improve your skills and knowledge.

Libraries are valuable sources of lifelong learning that often get overlooked. Libraries provide numerous books, audiobooks, and digital resources. Besides the vast choice of topics for reading, libraries hold workshops, lectures, and discussion groups to boost your education experience.

Mentorship programs can also play a crucial role in your lifelong learning apart from formal education. You can reach out to experienced mentors in your field of interest to gain knowledge, receive guidance, or even expand your contacts.

Remember it's essential to find resources that best suit your interests as well as goals when it comes down to lifelong learning. Look into these various ways of acquiring knowledge let alone your personality development journey will begin.

Benefits of Lifelong Learning on Personal Growth

Lifelong learning has significant implications for personal growth if taken seriously. Thinking over one's life as a continuous process of education leads to new insights, abilities, and experiences that can transform various aspects of life itself at large. In this part, however, we discuss how lifelong learning shapes personal growth profoundly.

Enhanced Critical Thinking Skills:

Having a culture of continuous learning in the workplace encourages critical thinking, questioning, analysing, and evaluating information. As you advance in your lifelong learning journey, this helps you to become a critical thinker who is able to make well-informed decisions. This invaluable skill can be applied both at personal and professional levels allowing one to confidently navigate through complex situations.

Enhanced Confidence:

Confidence comes out when an employee attains new knowledge and skills through lifelong learning. Your self-assurance grows as you achieve personal goals and overcome obstacles such that you can face new opportunities or challenges with a powerful mindset. In essence, lifelong learning offers an opportunity for constant self-development and growth on an individual basis.

Widened Perspectives:

Committing to lifelong learning means getting exposed to various ideas, cultures, and perspectives. In so doing, learners develop a deeper understanding of their environment by studying different courses. Ultimately, this broadened perspective enhances one's empathy level towards other people's plight and allows them to accommodate alternate opinions. By welcoming the idea of lifelong study into your life, you become more open-minded as well as a rounded person.

Adaptability amid Changing Circumstances

Personal success demands that one remains adaptable in a rapidly changing world. Through learning for life, we acquire skills needed to cope with changes as they come our way. Continuous improvement of your competency base ensures that you remain relevant even with technological advancements and other alterations that take place within the job market arena. The continuous process of updating oneself enables a person to remain agile and adaptable no matter how many times things change around him/her. So then it is clear that lifetime education is not merely about acquiring knowledge; it is something much more profound than that – it is about personal development. From improving critical thinking capacity by boosting confidence levels, extending horizons while adjusting to transformation can fully highlight why continuous development holds considerable benefits for all individuals no matter their age group. Enjoy the path leading toward eternal training which will make possible unveiling all human potential.

Lifelong Learning in the Age of Digital

The digital age has revolutionized access to educational resources, offering a world of possibilities for lifelong learning. Technology and online platforms have changed the way we learn, helping us grow at personal levels and opening up new opportunities.

Learning in the Digital Era:

Today, with numerous resources available through technology like never before, learning during this era has become more convenient. Flexible learning options are provided for individuals by courses that are online, educational websites, and interactive platforms which can fit into any kind of busy lifestyle they may lead. These resources will come in handy when one wants to learn a different language, acquire some technical skills, or follow up on various interests he or she might have developed.

However, every technological progress comes with its own challenges despite its benefits. In this digital age, it is important to navigate through oceans of information to identify credible sources from non-reliable ones. Additionally, distractions and excessive information can impede the process of knowledge acquisition thus requiring the development of mechanisms that ensure concentration is maintained as well as making good use of resources available within these tools and platforms.

Incorporating Lifelong Learning into the Digital Age Demands Adaptability:

This means being open-minded enough to explore new horizons while embracing lifelong learning. Utilizing such a mindset with proper resource employment implies unlimited opportunities for self-improvement and personal growth during present times. Therefore, go into the digital today; there is no limit to your lifelong education capacity!

Building a Lifelong Learning Mindset within Organizations

Not only does lifelong learning involve personal pursuits, but it also has a significant impact on workplaces. Both organizations and employees can benefit from embracing a culture of continuous learning. By fostering a lifelong learning mindset, these firms can keep up with current market changes and be ahead of other competitors. Workers, on the other hand, grow personally; they build their capacity as well as future career prospects.

There are several effective strategies that you can implement to promote lifelong learning in your workplace. Firstly, create opportunities for training programs, workshops, and seminars tailored to employees' professional development. These resources provide helpful knowledge and skills that contribute to individual growth and improve overall team performance.

Another useful approach is creating mentorship programs where seasoned workers share their expertise with juniors. Mentorship relationships build a culture of knowledge transfer, collaboration, and personal growth. When this happens, enterprises become able to tap into the collective wisdom of their staff thereby promoting lifelong learning.

Moreover, companies may use technology to support lifelong learning initiatives. Online platforms for studying and e-learning courses present flexible options for employees who would like to advance their skills at their own pace. Such digital tools allow for continuous learning and give access to a wealth of information that is beneficial both within individuals and organizations.

Through encouraging lifelong learning in workplaces; many advantages are experienced by firms involved in this practice. A culture of continuous learning leads to higher levels of innovation as well as encourages experimentation among employees regarding new ideas or approaches. In addition, it increases employee engagement and satisfaction since they feel valued when supported through professional growth stages such as these ones discussed above. Moreover, it nurtures adaptability which is important in an organization so as to make it navigate through change processes while identifying emerging opportunities.

To sum up, building a lifelong mentality towards learning at the workplace is vital both at the individual level as well as organizational success story. Organizations may therefore develop supportive environments for continuous trainings where individuals thrive best while contributing maximally. Embrace lifelong learning in your workplace and unlock the countless benefits it brings.

Lifelong Learning and Personal Well-being

Lifelong learning is also indispensable for personal development in terms of well-being. Within this chapter, we shall look at the deep connection between continuing education and mental, emotional, and physical wellness, bringing into focus how it can improve our lives overall thereby enhancing personal satisfaction.

When we engage in lifelong learning, we are embarking on a journey of self-discovery and personal growth. By acquiring new knowledge, developing new skills, and expanding our horizons we stimulate not only our minds but also nourish our souls. Lifelong learning arouses curiosity; builds creativity as well as provides direction and fulfillment.

Keeping on learning throughout life can have a good effect on mental health. It helps keep us alert and thinking clearly which help prevent cognitive decline like dementia. Besides that, lifelong learning fosters critical thinking skills as well as problem-solving abilities towards adapting to change situations with ease or flexing muscles when faced by life's challenges with resilience.

Indeed, the most productive response to any situation is to embrace lifelong learning. This subject of knowledge brings us closer to other people's thoughts and opinions as well as makes us more accepting and kinder towards others. On the other hand, it fills one with a sense of self-worth that only comes from gaining new information thereby making someone feel good about themselves.

Also, lifelong learning plays an important role in our being physically healthy. However, research has shown that exercising our minds through intellectual activities like acquiring new skills or knowledge can actually improve brain health and even reduce the risk of age-related conditions. Then again, this tends to be associated with engagement in physical activities such as dancing or outdoor exploration which in turn encourages exercise and promotes good health.

Lifelong Learning: A Strength for Self-Growth and Wellbeing in a Fast-Paced World

Lifelong learning serves as a powerful tool in an ever rapidly changing world where personal growth and well-being are increasingly emphasized upon. It is also intended to enable persons to develop fulfilling careers while at the same time promoting their overall health. By embarking on this lifelong journey, one goes through transformational experiences that lead to self-fulfilments among other things.

Lifelong Learning for Those in Their 40's

Learning never stops regardless of how old you may be since there is no limit when it comes to this process. There are numerous advantages associated with continuing education even at an advanced age thus making it very suitable for those in their 40's . We will consider some peculiar benefits which lifelong education provides those in their 40's within the scopes of personal development and welfare. In fact, if those in their 40's engage in lifelong learning, they will enhance their cognitive abilities significantly. Further research also shows that practicing mental exercises like; learning new skills, attaining knowledge as well as involving oneself in educational activities might contribute to keeping ones' mind alert hence preventing cognitive impairments.

Additionally, by engaging in lifelong learning, those in their 40's can maintain their social connections. In this case, older adults can learn by joining community classes, educational workshops, or even participating in online learning communities thus creating new relationships with people who are like-minded.

Various Platforms Are Available for Accessing Lifelong Learning Resources Aimed at Those in Their 40's . At a local level, there are a number of resources available to older learners including courses and activities offered by community centers and senior organizations. Therefore, they have been created to enable those in their 40's to take part in meaningful learning experiences according to their abilities and preferences.

It is important for those in their 40's to be proactive in embracing lifelong learning so that they can continue to develop and find fulfilment during this phase of their lives. The only limitation is one's own imagination; so, it is never too late to become involved in continuous education. Start your own lifelong journey of exploring today so as to open up yourself for more personal growth opportunities!

Lifelong Learning: Embrace the Journey

As we wind up this chapter, we have to bear in mind how powerful lifelong learning can be. Lifelong education does not merely seek information but it creates room for self-growth and opens various doors for us. Thus, when you embrace this as an ongoing process of acquiring knowledge, then you will realize how many ways you can enrich your life and reach the pinnacle of your potential through it.

We have been able to unravel the various aspects of lifelong learning from its definition and importance to its benefits. We have looked at how curiosity drives this adventure, and we provided a great number of resources to aid you in your search for knowledge. However, that's not the end of the story; it is just the beginning.

Now is your time to take ideas from what you've learned and apply them in every aspect of your life. Lifelong learning has no boundaries when it comes to classrooms or offices as it is an all-round process that involves personal interests, relationships, health among others. It means growing, grabbing opportunities, and always broadening one's mind.

Hence, let this be the start of a journey into lifelong learning. Get curious to know more; provide available materials for further growth while never settling down. It implies investing in your personal development by committing yourself to continual education thus being capable of adjusting in an ever-changing world thereby shaping a future filled with infinite possibilities. So let us go then, you and I…

Chapter **6**

Keeping Fit After 40

Being in your 40s means it's more important than ever to stay healthy. Age brings changes and caring for those changes involves a mix of a juggled diet, exercise, good habits, and regular doctor visits.
With this plan, you'll be able to live a full life. Ready to learn about fitness advice, food choices, changes to your routine, mental health, screenings, controlling your weight, heart health, and graceful aging? Come with us on this exciting journey, and we will learn about a bright, wholesome life at 40.

Why Health Matters at 40

Hitting your 40s means it's time to place health at the top of your list. There will be physical changes. Tackling these with care can maintain the rich life you deserve.

The reason health matters more after 40? Simply put, it's ageing. Our bodies change. There might be less strength in our muscles, bones might not be as dense, metabolism might slow. The danger of some medical issues like heart disease and inflammation can also rise.

However, by adopting healthy habits and making conscious choices, you can minimize these age-related effects on your health. Taking proactive steps to maintain physical fitness, improve your diet, and adopt a healthier lifestyle can significantly impact your overall well-being.

Investing in your health at 40 not only helps with your physical well-being but also has a positive impact on your mental and emotional health. By staying active, eating nutritious foods, and managing stress effectively, you can experience increased energy levels, improved mood, and enhanced cognitive function.

Remember, your health is your most valuable asset, and by taking care of yourself, you are setting the foundation for a vibrant and fulfilling life beyond your 40s. So, make your health a priority and embrace the journey towards optimal well-being.

Fitness Tips for Over 40s

As we age, maintaining a healthy and active lifestyle becomes increasingly important. For individuals over 40, incorporating fitness routines tailored to their specific needs can make a significant difference in their overall well-being. Here are some practical fitness tips to consider:

1. Strength Training

Include regular strength training exercises in your fitness regimen. This helps maintain muscle mass and bone density, which tend to decline with age. Focus on exercises that target major muscle groups, such as squats, lunges, and push-ups.

2. Cardiovascular Exercise

Do cardio like fast-walking, jogging or biking. It helps your heart and boosts stamina. Try to do 150 minutes of moderate or 75 minutes of intense aerobic workout every week.

3. Bend and Stretch

Remember to do exercises to increase your flex and stretch. It keeps joints moving and less stiff. Think about yoga or Pilates for this.

4. Listen to Yourself

Stay aware of your body's messages and pick the right workout intensity and length. It's important to find a balance between pushing hard and avoiding hurt. If needed, ask a fitness expert for advice.

5. Take Breaks

Give yourself enough rest between workouts for your body to repair. It's especially important while getting older to avoid injuries and support overall wellness.

Follow these tips and you'll maintain your muscle, boost your heart health, and stay fit as you move through your 40s and onward. Keep up with your health goals, always remember that sticking to it is key.

Food Tips for Top Health at 40

When you reach your 40s, what you eat becomes more important for your health. By eating smarter, you can maintain energy, control weight, and lower disease risks. Here are top food tips to feel your best in your 40s:

Incorporate Nutrient-Dense Foods

Focus on consuming nutrient-dense foods that provide essential vitamins, minerals, and antioxidants. Include a variety of fruits, vegetables, whole grains, and lean proteins in your daily meals. These foods have lower calorie density and higher nutritional value, helping you achieve a balanced diet.

Practice Portion Control

Pay attention to portion sizes to avoid overeating. Use smaller plates and bowls to help you visualize appropriate serving sizes. Listen to your body's hunger and fullness cues and aim for balanced meals that include proteins, carbohydrates, and healthy fats.

Stay Hydrated

Proper hydration is essential for maintaining optimal health. Drink an adequate amount of water throughout the day to support digestion, nutrient absorption, and overall bodily functions. Consider carrying a water bottle with you to ensure you stay hydrated while on the go.

Limit Processed and Sugary Foods

Avoid or limit your intake of processed foods, sugary snacks, and beverages high in added sugars. These foods often lack essential nutrients and can contribute to weight gain, inflammation, and an increased risk of chronic diseases. Opt for whole, unprocessed foods whenever possible.

Plan and Prepare Meals Ahead

By planning and preparing your meals ahead of time, you can make healthier choices and avoid relying on convenience foods. Set aside some time each week to plan your meals, create a shopping list, and prepare nutritious meals that you can easily grab and enjoy throughout the week.

By incorporating these diet tips into your daily routine, you can support optimal health and well-being, ensuring you thrive throughout your 40s and beyond.

Lifestyle Changes for Long-Term Health

As you enter your 40s, making positive lifestyle changes becomes key to ensuring long-term health and wellness. By incorporating simple but effective habits into your routine, you can significantly improve your overall well-being. Here are some essential lifestyle changes that can have a profound impact on your health:

Stress Management Techniques

Managing stress is crucial for maintaining good health, especially as you age. Practice relaxation techniques such as deep breathing exercises, meditation, or yoga to reduce stress levels. Engaging in hobbies, spending time in nature, and connecting with loved ones can also help alleviate stress and promote a sense of well-being.

Sufficient Sleep

Getting adequate sleep is essential for your physical and mental health. Aim for 7-9 hours of quality sleep each night. Establish a calming bedtime routine, create a comfortable sleep environment, and prioritize sleep hygiene practices such as avoiding electronic devices before bed and keeping a consistent sleep schedule.

Tobacco Cessation

If you are a smoker, quitting smoking is one of the most impactful changes you can make for your health. Seek professional support and explore smoking cessation resources to help you overcome nicotine addiction and reduce the risk of various health issues, including heart disease, lung cancer, and respiratory problems.

Alcohol: Less is Best

Drink less alcohol to stay healthy. One drink daily for women, two for men is okay. Try out non-alcoholic drinks. Choose what's best for your health.

These everyday changes boost your health for the long run. Live healthier and happier in your 40s and further.

Mental Health Matters After 40

When we're in our 40s, mental health becomes super important. Taking care of our mind is just as necessary as our body. This balance leads to more pleasure in life, better problem-solving, and overall good health.

Less stress means better mental health. Getting older comes with new stress triggers. Techniques like meditation, deep breaths, or mindfulness help calm your mind and control stress.

Having strong relationships helps our mind too. Keep close ties with family, mates, and local community. These connections give emotional aid and make us feel a part of something. Being social regularly and setting healthy limits benefits mental health.

Engaging in cognitive exercises

Engaging in cognitive exercises can also play a beneficial role in maintaining mental health at 40 and beyond. This includes activities such as puzzles, memory games, reading, and learning new skills. These activities help keep our minds sharp, improve cognitive functions, and promote overall brain health.

Seeking professional support when needed is essential. If you are experiencing persistent feelings of sadness, anxiety, or other mental health concerns, it is important to reach out to a mental health professional. They can provide expert guidance, support, and customized treatment options tailored to your specific needs.

Remember, prioritizing your mental health is not a sign of weakness, but rather a sign of strength and self-care. By taking steps to maintain your mental well-being, you are investing in a healthier and happier future.

Preventive Screenings and Health Check-ups

Regular preventive screenings and health check-ups play a crucial role in maintaining optimal health at 40 and beyond. These proactive measures help detect and address potential health issues before they become serious, ensuring early intervention and prevention.

For individuals in their 40s, several screenings and tests are recommended to monitor various aspects of health. These include:

Blood Pressure

Regular blood pressure checks are essential to assess cardiovascular health. High blood pressure, also known as hypertension, often goes undetected but can significantly increase the risk of heart disease and other complications.

Cholesterol Levels

Monitoring cholesterol levels is crucial for assessing the risk of heart disease. Elevated cholesterol levels can contribute to the development of plaque in the arteries, increasing the risk of heart attacks and strokes.

Diabetes Screening

Diabetes is a common chronic condition that can lead to various complications if left untreated. Regular screening allows for early detection and proper management, helping to reduce the risk of complications.

Colonoscopy

Colonoscopies are recommended for individuals in their 40s to screen for colorectal cancer. Early detection can significantly increase the chances of successful treatment and improved outcomes.

Mammogram

Women should continue to undergo regular mammograms in their 40s to screen for breast cancer. Early detection plays a vital role in successful treatment and improved survival rates.

Prostate-Specific Antigen (PSA) Test

Men in their 40s should consider discussing the potential benefits and risks of prostate-specific antigen (PSA) testing with their healthcare provider. This screening test can help detect prostate cancer at an early stage.

Remember to consult with a healthcare professional to determine the appropriate schedule and frequency for these screenings and tests based on your individual health history and risk factors. By prioritizing preventive screenings and health check-ups, you can stay proactive in managing your health and ensure a healthier future.

Keeping a Good Weight

Getting older? Past 40? Keep your weight in check. It's key for your health. Weight, metabolism, and health are all linked. You want simple, doable plans. They'll keep your weight just right. You'll feel better, live better.

Why Manage Weight?

Weight matters. It connects to heart disease, Type 2 diabetes, some cancer types. A good weight can pep you up! Put that pep in your step! Enjoy life more as you grow older. Mind clearer, body nimble, life full.

Simple Tips for Good Weight

Weight loss begins with small steps. Find balance in your eating. Try fruit, veggies, whole grains, lean proteins. Watch your portions. Don't supersize your meals.

Moving is key too. Stay active. Aim for a couple of hours of moderate workout each week. Do you like brisk walks? Cycling? Perfect! Try strength workouts too. Lift weights. Use resistance bands. More muscles mean faster metabolism. And that's a big plus!

It's also important to prioritize adequate sleep, as lack of sleep can disrupt hormone regulation and affect weight control. Additionally, managing stress levels and finding healthy ways to cope with stress can prevent emotional eating or overeating, both of which can contribute to weight gain.

Lastly, staying hydrated is essential for weight management. Drinking plenty of water can keep you feeling full, prevent overeating, and support optimal body function.

In conclusion, maintaining a healthy weight plays a vital role in promoting overall health and well-being as you enter your 40s and beyond. By implementing practical strategies, such as adopting a balanced diet, incorporating regular physical activity, managing stress, prioritizing sleep, and staying hydrated, you can achieve and sustain a healthy body weight, enhancing your quality of life.

Ensuring Heart Health After 40

As you enter your 40s and beyond, prioritizing your heart health becomes imperative. Cardiovascular diseases can pose significant risks, but with key lifestyle modifications, you can reduce these risks and maintain a healthy heart.

Regular physical activity is essential for maintaining heart health. Engaging in activities such as brisk walking, cycling, swimming, or dancing for at least 30 minutes a day can help improve cardiovascular fitness, strengthen the heart muscles, and regulate blood pressure.

Heart-healthy eating habits

Adopting a heart-healthy diet can significantly benefit your cardiovascular health. Include plenty of fruits, vegetables, whole grains, and lean proteins in your meals. Limit the intake of saturated and trans fats, cholesterol, and sodium. Opt for healthier cooking methods like grilling, baking, or steaming, and avoid excessive consumption of processed foods and sugary beverages.

Handling Stress

Continual stress can damage your heart. Mix stress relief methods into your daily life. These can be meditating, practicing deep breaths, enjoying yoga, or hobbies that unwind you. Self-care is essential, so take breaks and sleep adequately.

Actively safeguarding your heart health reduces the chances of heart issues. Regular exercise, a heart-friendly diet, and stress reduction can help. You can then stay healthy throughout your 40s and onwards.

Getting Old: Enjoying the Adventure

40's Getting older is a normal part of life. Being in your 40s is a chance to age gracefully and keep your vitality. During this stage, keep your health a top priority. Taking care of your body and mind can keep you feeling positive as you age.

Aging gracefully involves accepting yourself. Be open to changes that come with ageing and value your life lessons. Self-acceptance leads to self-love, building confidence for life's journey.

Thankfulness is also key to aging with grace. Appreciate life's good parts regularly. Being grateful can alter your viewpoint adding joy and satisfaction into your daily life.

Being healthy at 40 needs good habits too. Do workouts often, have varied meals, and sleep nicely. Self-care is also good. This can mean calming your mind, enjoying the outdoors, or doing things you love.

Chapter 7

The Journey to Mental
Strength and Happiness

You're now in Chapter 7 of our book. Here we will discover different methods that boost mental strength and augment happiness. Regardless if you're searching for ways to think sharper, endure challenges or control stress, we're here for you.

Having mental strength is key to a rewarding life and we recognize how vital it is to maintain our mental health. In this chapter, we'll dive into the impact of sharp thinking, why resilience matters, smart ways to manage stress, exercise's role on your mental health, how to foster positive connections, creating a wholesome environment, getting help, and practicing mindfulness.

Once you're done with this chapter, you'll have a complete set of tactics to improve your mental strength and nurture a higher level of happiness. Ready? Let's plunge in and experience the profound effect of these tactics, together!

Grasping Mental Health

Mental health plays a key role in living a content and meaningful life. It includes our emotional, psychological, and social health, and affects how we think, feel, and behave. It's vital to comprehend mental health to sustain a balanced and healthy living.

One central aspect of mental health is recognizing how important it is. Just like we give importance to physical health, mental health equally matters. Prioritizing our mental health helps us become resilient, manage stress efficiently, form nurturing relationships, and improve our life's overall quality.

The Importance of Mental Well-being

Having good mental well-being is crucial as it allows us to navigate life's challenges with greater ease and flexibility. It promotes positive self-esteem and a sense of purpose, enabling us to develop healthy coping mechanisms and maintain overall happiness.

When we prioritize our mental well-being, we are better equipped to manage stress, reduce the risk of mental health disorders, and experience improved clarity and focus. Mental well-being empowers us to make better decisions, form strong relationships, and achieve our goals.

Factors Influencing Mental Well-being

Mental well-being is influenced by various factors, including genetics, environment, and lifestyle choices. Some individuals may be predisposed to certain mental health conditions due to their genetic makeup. However, it is important to remember that genetics alone do not determine our mental well-being. Environmental factors such as upbringing, culture, and socioeconomic status also play a significant role.

Lifestyle choices, including exercise, diet, sleep, and stress management, greatly impact mental well-being. Engaging in regular physical activity, consuming a balanced diet, getting sufficient rest, and developing effective stress management techniques are all conducive to positive mental health.

Furthermore, social connections and support systems contribute to our mental well-being. Nurturing relationships, maintaining a healthy work-life balance, and seeking support when needed enhance our overall mental well-being.

The key to living a satisfying life lies in understanding mental well-being. Once we know its importance and what affects it, we can give mental health priority and make decisions that nurture a positive and thriving outlook.

Mental Sharpness' Power

Living in our fast-paced globe, mental sharpness becomes vital for tackling everyday difficulties. It defines our efficiency in thinking, reasoning, and processing data. Peak cognitive abilities are important for brain health and overall well-being.

With a sharp mind, we excel at decision-making and problem-solving, and handle complex tasks smoothly. It helps us keep focus and attention, boosting our productivity in life's diverse aspects.

Cognitive Abilities' Impact

Our cognitive abilities are directly affected by our mental sharpness. These abilities encompass memory, focus, learning, and problem-solving. Sharpening our minds, we can enrich these cognitive functions, fostering overall brain health.

A bright mind assists in storing and retrieving information. As a result, learning improves. It lets us concentrate on subtleties and minimize distractions, leading to heightened productivity and efficiency.

Improving Mental Sharpness' Techniques

What's the good news? Techniques are available to whisper power into our mental sharpness and bolster brain health. One useful tactic is doing activities that strain our cognitive abilities - like puzzles, crosswords, or acquiring a new talent.

Working out regularly is a valuable means to boost brain power. Exercising enhances blood circulation in the brain, supplying it with essential nourishment and oxygen for ideal cognitive performance.

Moreover, embracing a lifestyle rich in balanced eating, proper sleep, and stress handling methods helps preserve brain power and overall cognitive health.

With setting brain power as a priority and incorporating these strategies into our daily routines, we can tap into our entire cognitive capacity and relish an enhanced, focused brain function.

Fortifying Resilience for Enhanced Mental Fortitude

Resilience is an important trait enabling individuals to tackle and endure the trials and tests life puts them through. It is significant in sustaining mental robustness and wellness. Cultivating resilience involves not just surviving adversities but also evolving, blossoming, and rebounding even stronger than before.

In this part, we will delve into efficient methods to nurture resilience and promote a formidable mindset. These strategies can empower individuals to tap into their inner power and confront hardships with resilience and tenacity.

Importance of Optimistic Attitude

A method to cultivate resilience is fostering a positive attitude. Optimism allows individuals to perceive troubles as gateways for expansion and education. By highlighting on their strong points, accomplishments, and probable solutions, individuals can improve their mental resilience and effectively sail through tough periods.

Change and Flexibility: Key Traits

Those who bounce back from hardship know that change is normal. They welcome it, adjusting to fresh situations while seeking ways to grow. Openness to change boosts mental toughness, helping folks steer through life's murky patches with ease and speed.

Creating Reliable Support Circles

Having a sturdy support network simplifies resilience-building. Encircle yourself with caring, understanding pals, relatives, and advisors. These bonds offer emotional backing and cheer during testing periods. They instill in people the boldness and affirmations needed to confront problems directly.

Fostering Kindness Towards Self

Instead of harsh self-blame, realizing self-compassion is crucial in growing resilience. A gentle, understanding approach to oneself helps carve a resilient self-view, bouncing back from falls more efficiently.

Embracing Mindful Presence

Practicing mindfulness can boost resilience. Being fully present, recognizing feelings, and accepting them without self-rebuke aids in forging emotional resilience, keeping one anchored during challenging periods.

Applying these methods and nurturing a resilient mindset can augment mental toughness. It aids people in traversing the storms they face. The process of building resilience, though continual, leads to personal evolution and enhanced wellness with grit and resolve.

How to Handle Stress for Good Mental Health

Our minds can suffer if stress gets too heavy. So, we must learn how to deal with it well. This will help our mental health and make life feel more balanced. Forgotten stress can cause problems in our minds and bodies. This messes up our day-to-day activities and life quality.

Having stress-handling methods is key to stay safe. These methods help us deal with hard times, making us stronger and healthier. The techniques could be hobbies or relaxing practices. You could also talk to those close to you or professionals for support.

Why Stress-Handling Methods Help

Healthy stress-handling methods give us ways to ditch stress. Using good strategies allows us to lessen the bad effects stress has on our mental health. Stress-handling methods help us take back control of our feelings and thoughts. Then we can have a more positive, balanced view of things.

Not everyone's stress methods will be the same. What works well for one might not work for another. So, try out different methods. See what clicks for you. Some common methods include:

Participating in physical exercise or any type of activity that brings happiness and relaxation Practicing mindfulness and meditation to foster a state of calmness and self-awareness Engaging in creative outlets such as painting, journaling, or playing a musical instrument Seeking support from friends, family, or a mental health professional to help navigate challenging situations

Regardless of the coping mechanisms we choose, it is important to prioritize self-care and make time for activities that promote mental well-being. By actively managing stress through coping mechanisms, we can cultivate a healthier and more balanced life.

The Role of Exercise in Mental Well-being

Regular physical activity and exercise have a significant impact on our mental well-being. Engaging in exercise not only benefits our physical health but also has positive effects on our mental health.

Exercise helps to reduce symptoms of stress, anxiety, and depression, while promoting feelings of happiness and well-being. Physical activity stimulates the release of endorphins, also known as the "feel-good" hormones, which contribute to improved mood and overall mental state.

Incorporating exercise into your routine can also help you manage and cope with daily stresses. Engaging in physical activity provides a healthy outlet for pent-up emotions and tension, allowing you to clear your mind and focus on the present moment.

Furthermore, exercise enhances cognitive function and boosts mental sharpness. It improves blood flow to the brain, supplying it with essential oxygen and nutrients, which promotes better concentration, memory, and overall cognitive abilities.

There are various forms of exercise that you can explore to improve your mental well-being. Cardiovascular exercises like running, swimming, and cycling can elevate your heart rate and release endorphins. Strength training exercises, such as weightlifting or resistance training, help build muscle and improve overall physical fitness.

The key is to find activities that you enjoy and make them a regular part of your routine. Incorporating physical activity into your day can be as simple as incorporating brisk walks, stretching breaks, or taking the stairs instead of the elevator. Small, consistent steps towards making exercise a habit can have a significant impact on your mental well-being over time.

Remember, always consult with a healthcare professional before starting any exercise program, especially if you have any pre-existing medical conditions or concerns.

Nurturing Relationships for Mental Wellness

When it comes to mental wellness, our relationships and social connections have a significant impact. Nurturing positive relationships and maintaining healthy social connections are crucial for improved mental well-being.

Strong relationships provide emotional support, encouragement, and a sense of belonging. They can help reduce feelings of loneliness, anxiety, and depression. By fostering meaningful connections with family, friends, and community members, we create a support system that positively impacts our mental health.

Making and keeping good friendships takes work and talking. It means sharing feelings, hearing actively, and saying thank you. If we speak openly and truthfully, we can make our ties stronger, solve problems, and understand better.

How Friends and Family Matter

Being with others gives chances for learning, doing things together, and feeling good inside. Joining in hobbies, fun events, and community groups can make us feel we belong and give us people who care when times are tough.

It's good to look for quality, not quantity in friendships. Sure, knowing a lot of people can help, but giving time and care to a few good friends can really make our minds healthier. These close friends give us safety, trust, and emotional help which make us feel better overall.

Also, being part of a group or community lets us give back to something bigger than ourselves. Through taking part, helping out, or sharing hobbies, we find purpose, fulfillment, and connection which make our mental health better.

To sum up, friendships and being with others are very important for our mental health. Taking care of positive friendships, staying involved with others, and joining supportive communities let us build a strong group of helpers and make us feel much better overall.

Creating a Healthy Environment for Mental Well-being

Creating a healthy environment is essential for promoting mental well-being and fostering a positive mindset. The environment we surround ourselves with can significantly impact our emotional and psychological state.

One crucial aspect of creating a healthy environment is practicing self-care. Self-care involves prioritizing your mental and physical well-being by engaging in activities that bring you joy and relaxation. This can include activities such as reading, practicing mindfulness, taking baths, or engaging in hobbies that you love. By taking care of yourself, you can cultivate a nurturing environment that supports your mental well-being.

Setting boundaries is another important aspect of creating a healthy environment. Boundaries help protect your mental health by establishing limits on what you are willing to tolerate in your personal and professional relationships. This can involve saying "no" when you feel overwhelmed or setting aside dedicated time for yourself without any distractions.

Additionally, fostering a positive and optimistic mindset can contribute to a healthy environment. Surround yourself with uplifting and positive influences, such as supportive friends and family, inspirational literature, or engaging in activities that boost your mood. Remember, negativity can drain your mental energy, so focus on cultivating positivity in your surroundings.

Eliminating toxins and promoting cleanliness

Maintaining a clean and orderly home or workspace can massively improve your mental health. Mess and confusion can create stress and can be a hurdle while concentrating or chilling. Make sure to invest some time in tidying up your area, aiming for a neat, clutter-free, and distraction-free environment.

40's For a healthier living space, keeping away from harmful substances is imperative. Make sure there is good air circulation in your living areas, avoid any risky materials, and select organic cleaning items. These measures will boost air quality and minimize potential health risks that could affect your mental health.

The creation of a healthful environment for your mental health is a continuous procedure that necessitates steady effort and introspection. By integrating self-care habits, setting limitations, promoting optimism, and adopting cleanliness, you can build a positive atmosphere that advocates mental health and enhances your life quality.

Reaching Out for Mental Health Support

Looking for help is a prerequisite to manage mental health properly. Nobody should tackle life's hurdles alone, asking for support is both a courageous and necessary move.

Many ways to find support exist. However, professional help holds significant value. Mental health experts specialized in advice, aid, and targeted actions to better one's mental health.

Different types of professional assistance are available. One choice is to look for therapy from a certified therapist or counsellor. They will offer a confidential and secure area for you to express your feelings, manage tough experiences, and learn handy strategies for managing your mental health.

Do you need help? Think about seeing a psychiatrist. They are special doctors for mental health. They can tell you what's wrong, give you medicines, and work out a plan just for you.

If you feel really bad or need to talk to someone straight away, there are special phone lines. Trained people answer these. They can help you, tell you who else can help you, and make sure you are safe.

It's good to ask for help, not bad. It means you want to feel better. You could talk to a therapist, see a psychiatrist, or call a phone line. Asking for help shows you're brave and want to be healthier.

Using Mindfulness for your Mental Health

Being mindful can really help how you feel. This means thinking about the here and now. Mindfulness gives you a strong idea of your thoughts, feelings, and what is happening around you. This can help you cope better with tough times.

To be more mindful, find some time just for you. Do things that make you feel calm and happy, like meditation or deep breathing. Be in the moment and forget about everything else. Don't worry about doing things right or wrong. The more you do this, the calmer you'll feel, and your stress will go down. Bring mindfulness into your daily routines. Simply feel each moment; taste your food, admire nature on a walk, genuinely listen to people. By living fully right now, you can develop deep thankfulness and happiness.

Add mindfulness to your life to help your mind and find more peace, understanding, and general joy. Use the now, explore yourself, and grow from within.

Chapter 8

Knowing Your Emotions
and Growing Up

Welcome to Chapter 8. Here, we'll talk about why empathy matters in knowing your emotions and growing up. Are you ready, let's dive right into knowing why empathy is vital, how it can help with self-awareness, and boost your emotional know-how. Let's go on this adventure of knowing the impact of empathy on our growth.

Why is Developing Empathy for Emotional Understanding Important?

Eager to grow? Then, realize why empathy in understanding emotions is key. It helps us feel and understand what others go through. This makes us better at handling our feelings and becoming more self-aware.

As empathy grows, we get better at acknowledging others' feelings. This strengthens our bonds, helps us see through their eyes, and promotes understanding.

Just so you know, empathy is a major player in developing emotional understanding. With growing empathy comes growing awareness. We get to know our feelings and how they affect our actions. This makes us handle our feelings wisely and respond with more empathy and understanding.

Polishing our empathy skills improves how we converse, settles fights, and cultivates deep connections. Developing empathy is a journey that needs real practice and a heart that wants to truly connect with people.

This piece will delve into how empathy significantly benefits our emotional intelligence and personal growth. Empathy serves various roles, from boosting self-understanding to improving relationships and solving disputes. It's a vital tool that enhances all areas of our lives.

Understanding Self through Others' Feelings

Empathy and self-awareness work together, enhancing personal growth and emotional intelligence. As we work on empathy, we enhance our grasp of others' experiences, feelings. This helps us to recognize and better understand our emotions and responses.

Applying empathy lets us see different viewpoints. Attentive listening and acceptance of others' feelings heightens sensitivity to our emotional sphere. This boosts our ability to spot patterns, triggers, and biases in our thought process.

Reflective questioning is a powerful tool for nurturing self-awareness through empathy. A tricky situation might prompt us to ask, "What if I were in their position?" This question pushes self-examination and closer investigation of our feelings and view.

The Power of Paying Attention

Another helpful method is active listening. Being fully present in conversations and focusing deeply on others, we can better perceive subtle signs and emotions. This not only enhances empathy towards the speaker but also offers precious insights into our reactions and thinking.

Journaling is a strong method for growing self-awareness with empathy. Reflecting on life's events helps us discover hidden feelings and thoughts. Writing lets us explore deeply, linking our empathy and self-awareness.

40's Continued practice in empathy strengthens our emotional intelligence. Knowing our own feelings aids in solving problems and showing compassion.

Empathy's Role in Emotional Maturity

Emotional maturity helps people tackle challenges with grace. This section focuses on how empathy aids in emotional maturity, boosting personal progress and emotional health.

Empathy is comprehending and sharing others' feelings. It lays a firm base for emotional maturity. Through empathy, we understand ourselves and others better, which helps us handle emotional situations with compassion and insight.

Practicing empathy helps to control our emotions and empathize with others' feelings. This emotional management and empathy are parts of emotional maturity. They help us handle our feelings and provide support and understanding to others.

Empathy plays a big role in resolving disagreements and effective communication. By putting ourselves in others' shoes, we improve our ability to understand their views. It helps us find win-win solutions to problems.

When we improve our empathy, we boost our emotional smarts. This is key for our own growth and success in life. Emotional smarts include self-awareness, self-control, empathy, and social skills. These elements help our emotional maturity.

To wrap it up, empathy and emotional maturity are tied together. Improving empathy can increase your emotional smarts. It helps you tackle tough situations with understanding, empathy, and emotional maturity.

Making Empathy Better for Stronger Relations

Empathy is the basic skill needed for sound, fruitful relationships. By improving empathy, we can establish a better connection with others. This allows mutual understanding. We will now discuss some ways to improve empathy. We'll also see how it can positively affect our contacts with others.

A useful method to boost empathy involves active listening. Be sure to really listen when in a discussion, without judging or interrupting. This helps you grasp the other person's ideas, feelings, and experiences. It also shows you're ready to connect deeply.

Another strategy is to put yourself in someone else's shoes. This practice, often known as perspective-taking, involves imagining yourself in their position and considering how you would feel and react. By doing so, you gain insight into their emotions and can respond with more empathy and compassion.

Engaging in activities that promote empathy development can also be beneficial. For example, participating in volunteer work or community service exposes you to different perspectives and challenges, helping you develop greater empathy for others.

Furthermore, being mindful of your nonverbal cues and body language is essential for empathetic communication. Maintain eye contact, display open body posture, and offer validating gestures such as nodding or a reassuring touch. These actions demonstrate your attentiveness and convey that you genuinely care about the other person's emotions.

In conclusion, developing empathy skills is crucial for establishing and maintaining fulfilling relationships. By actively practicing empathy through strategies such as active listening, perspective-taking, and engaging in empathy-promoting activities, we can foster stronger connections and enhance our overall emotional intelligence. Empathy is a powerful tool that can transform our relationships and contribute to a more empathetic and compassionate world.

Empathy in Conflict Resolution

Conflict resolution is a complex process that often requires bridging gaps and building understanding among individuals. One crucial element in this process is empathy. Empathy allows us to put ourselves in someone else's shoes, understand their perspective, and validate their emotions.

Applying empathy in conflict resolution changes how we deal with disagreements. Active listening and empathy make both parties feel respected. This encourages open talks and a joint effort to find a solution that benefits everyone.

Empathy pushes us to consider others' feelings and concerns, not just our own. This helps us to understand the real issues that cause the conflict. Then, we can find solutions that address these causes.

Empathy: The Key to Peaceful Solutions

Conflict resolution without empathy just gives short-term solutions or leaves issues to reappear in the future. Empathy builds a deep understanding of others' emotions and needs. This leads to resolutions that last and create peace.

Using empathy in conflicts makes it easier to find solutions where everyone is happy with the result. Being able to see other perspectives helps us find what we have in common. From there, we can find shared goals and solutions that improve relationships.

Finally, empathy creates trust and strengthens bonds in conflict resolution. Feeling heard encourages open, honest talks. This trust makes resolving conflicts respectfully and constructively possible.

Adding empathy to how we solve conflicts can lower tension, build understanding, and help relationships grow. Not only does empathy help us solve problems, it helps us grow as people and understand feelings better.

Empathy in Leadership

Empathy is super important for leaders. It helps them connect with their team and make smarter decisions. Good leaders aren't just about power and pointing the way-- they also understand and support their people.

Leaders with empathy can create trust with their team. They encourage openness and teamwork. By seeing things from their team's viewpoint, these leaders can understand their thoughts, struggles, and needs better.

Also, empathy helps leaders make choices that take care of their team. By thinking about how their decisions affect feelings, empathetic leaders can make work places that support growth and success.

Plus, empathy helps leaders meet their team's emotional needs. By recognizing their feelings and providing a safe and understanding place, these leaders can create positive and effective work cultures.

To foster empathy in leadership, we need to listen, understand feelings, and appreciate different viewpoints. By promoting empathy, leaders can inspire and motivate their team. This can lead to a more successful team and a growing organization.

Building Better Feelings: Empathy Exercises

We boost emotional smarts with empathy workouts. It lets us understand ourselves and others deeper. By joining in, we can grow our empathy and emotional smarts.

A great workout for growing empathy is seeing from others' view. Imagine being in their shoes. Think the world looks like from their place. We'd know more about their feelings, life, and aims. Effectively creating empathy and emotional intelligence.

Active listening is also a valuable exercise. Pay full attention to a speaker, don't judge or disrupt. Listen, understand their points of view. This method strengthens empathy and emotional smarts.

Being mindful boosts empathy too. Be aware of your feelings at the moment. You'll empathize with others' emotions better. Mindfulness leads to more empathy and stronger links, boosting emotional intelligence.

Exposure to various experiences is a helpful empathy workout. Diving into different cultures and views makes us understand the world more. We grow empathy for different individuals. This can promote major emotional intelligence growth.

Understanding Empathy as a Path to Self-Improvement

Empathy strengthens us. It helps us connect better, to feel more, and to understand ourselves more. It's like a magic key that opens doors to deeper friendships and self-awareness. So when we choose empathy, we win. And so do the people around us. They feel understood and cared about. And that feels really good.

How to be more empathetic every day? Pay real attention when people share their lives with you. Listen to them. Show them that their tales matter to you. It's one way to build strong bonds with others. Also, walking in their shoes for a moment helps us see the world in new ways. That's another win.

But hey, don't forget about you! Show yourself the same kindness you show others. Accept your feelings. Understand them. It's called self-empathy. It helps us love ourselves more and know what we need. It's another key to unlocking personal growth.

In closing, empathy isn't just for making friends. It's key to our own growth and emotional smarts. So let's get out there, be an active listener, and remember to be kind to yourself too. It's a journey to becoming more emotionally intelligent. Let's take it together.

Chapter 9

Your Career at
a Crossroads

Welcome to Chapter 9 it is here that we will look at the obstacles and opportunities associated with job transitions. Today's rapidly evolving employment landscape requires adaptability and upskilling for success. This chapter is designed to guide you through the unknown in your professional journey whether this means a change in career, new industry exploration or growth within your current field.

Would you like to see new possibilities? Would you like it if you could steer your career towards things that are in line with what you love and dream about? Let us get started on the key methods of making a successful transition such as assessing one's skills and abilities, exploring other paths, developing a plan for change, and creating support networks.

So as we begin this journey together, remember that adaptability to changes as well as embracing upskilling are among the most critical skills for success at work today. So let us enter into this fantastic arena known as career shifts whose path is an important part of your professional satisfaction.

Knowing Why People Shift Careers

In today's fast-paced and ever-changing job market there has been an increase in career shifting cases. Whether it's due to advancements in technology, trends within industries people belong in or personal growth people go through periods where they have to decide whether or not they should switch careers. The dynamic nature of the world of work is one reason why professionals may need to make changes from their current positions. This is because industries are always changing given that new technologies come up while customer tastes keep changing as well hence businesses have also changed their operations accordingly leading some roles or even skills becoming irrelevant over time while others gain prominence.

These adjustments help individuals grow and develop themselves towards better career prospects later on. In order to remain ahead while still being open-minded enough towards adopting new opportunities, when learning institutions develop courses concerning such areas they want students willing to explore them as soon as possible. For example, adapting enables one to avoid stagnation and the vulnerabilities associated with becoming obsolete in a certain role.

Additionally, career development involves emotional and professional growth. While trying to develop new competencies or interests individuals may realize that their current line of work does not align with what they want to achieve in life anymore. Often this realization motivates them to search for alternative options in order for them to discover themselves anew.

Furthermore, it is also true that job changes can increase people's happiness and satisfaction levels at work. When someone decides on pursuing a passion-related profession, he feels more fulfilled thus enhancing his general well-being. For instance, professionals find motivation in achieving their personal goals by connecting them with their jobs.

It is necessary for career stability and future success that people remain open minded regarding the shifting dynamics of the labor market so that they will be able to respond when there is need for change. As discussed below we shall explain how one can identify crossroads in careers, such as signs indicating career confusion; techniques used in evaluating skills & interests of a person; and strategies employed while designing effective plans meant for successful transition into any given job.

Professionals often find themselves at crossroads in their careers, uncertain about what to do next. Identifying these signs is critical as it creates room for growth and transformation.

When you Feel Stagnant or Unfulfilled

One of the main indications that one is at a career crossroad is when one feels stuck or unfulfilled by his/her current job. You might lose interest in work or lack motivation and enthusiasm. These feelings are a clear sign that you need to think about changing your career.

Industry Changes

Another telltale sign is massive changes taking place within your industry. This can include technological advancements, market disruptions, or shifts in consumer preferences that make certain jobs or skills redundant. By recognizing these changes, you will be able to pivot proactively and stay ahead of the game.

Seeking Fresh Challenges

Do you constantly crave fresh challenges and learning opportunities? The desire to expand your skill set and handle new exciting projects suggests that it's time for a career shift. Embracing change and looking for new challenges may enable you to enjoy more professional fulfillment than ever before.

Importance of Upskilling

When an individual reaches a juncture where they have to make the decision on what to do with their career, upskilling becomes essential if they are going to remain relevant in their respective fields of work and increase their chances of success in different positions. By obtaining new competencies and knowledge, one enhances his/her worthiness in his/her profession as well as opens doors into various professions.

Recognizing the Signs of Career Crossroads: An Opportunity for Self-Reflection and Growth:

However, accepting this meaning entails considering other options such as continuing education through retraining particularly through online courses which allow flexibility in terms of schedules thus enabling people who can no longer keep pace with the traditional way of teaching due to personal responsibilities appreciate distance mode education which allows them learn while carrying out other responsibilities at home and workplace.".

Assessing your Skills and Interests

At this point, you ought to evaluate your skills, interests, and strengths before making a career change. This self-assessment will help you determine where to go with your career shift and what skills you need to learn. Through understanding your ability and passion, it will enable you to make an informed decision on the path to choose.

Begin by assessing the skills that are already acquired and find out if they can be relevant in the field of interest. Look for transferable skills that may be useful in other areas as well as those that require more development. It is through this assessment that you can pinpoint the gaps and how to fill them.

Also consider those interests which actually motivate you. Find out what tasks or activities give you energy and fulfillment. By exploring new careers that correspond with one's desires as well as values would enhance one's opportunities of gaining satisfaction from their work.

After determining your skills set along with interests, formulate a plan for up skilling yourself by acquiring necessary information hence knowledge based competencies about the job market needs. Identify where exactly you should develop your talents further then try finding relevant training programs such as courses or certifications in those respective fields plus embrace continuous learning together with adaptability as one commences on his/her new career journey."

Always remember that if you want to make a successful career transition, then evaluating your skills and interests is very crucial. By knowing what you are good at, where you need improvement and the steps required for upskilling, one can easily move into a rewarding career with confidence.

Different Career Paths to Think About

To have an effective shift in your career, it's prudent to consider various job alternatives available in your field. You should be able to explore other options before making up your mind on which direction to take as far as changing careers is concerned.

The first step is conducting extensive research on different industries or job roles. Look out for opportunities that build upon your existing skill set, but also provide room for growth and development. Consider how your career has unfolded and relate these skills and experiences to new fields full of excitement.

Networking and speaking with professionals already working in the sectors of interest can give you invaluable insights about such careers. Reach out to industry experts, attend career fairs, and join relevant professional groups to expand your knowledge base while collecting firsthand information regarding potential career paths ahead.

Your horizons will widen when you begin thinking outside of the box concerning other jobs or careers. Don't limit yourself; instead embrace this opportunity by discovering new avenues worth exploring leading towards a passionate experience in life.

Creating a Career Transition Plan

When considering a change of occupation, it is important to have an elaborate plan that will ease the shifting process from one profession to another. This way, setting clear goals; creating a realistic timeline; and seeking support will help you navigate through challenges faced so far while moving forward with purpose.

Begin by setting goals that are specific when making a move towards another profession. Consider what expertise needs developing – sectors that seem interesting – compelling opportunities noticed. Defining goals becomes a roadmap guiding changes made during this time.

Equally vital is having a timeline. Divide the process into smaller parts or steps giving yourself due dates on each stage. This will help you to remain focused as well as maintain momentum in your progression. Also, don't forget to be flexible so that if there are unforeseen changes that need to be done in your timelines, you can adjust accordingly.

Getting Support

While transitioning into a new career might seem difficult, it does not mean that it is a journey that one must take alone. Get mentors who have done this before or career coaches and professionals who have gone through the same shifts successfully. Their guidance and insights can provide valuable advice and help you avoid common pitfalls.

You should also consider taking up some training related to your new job. Besides attending online lessons, workshops and getting industry certifications may increase one's competencies necessary for staying relevant in an ever-changing labor market. This helps in consolidating a better position during the time of transition as well as making you more competitive.

Remember; change of occupation is characterized by growth and dynamism. It is important to embrace challenges, refine your plan whenever necessary and celebrate milestones achieved along the way. By developing a comprehensive career transition plan and seeking the necessary support, you can confidently navigate the evolving professional landscape and embrace new opportunities.

Challenges & Obstacles Faced and How to Overcome Them

Entering into a career shift can be a thrilling but scary experience as well. It is important though to acknowledge and address the struggles and difficulties that one may encounter when entering this phase of their lives. By recognizing these stumbling blocks, you will be able to develop effective methods for dealing with them and keep on track while navigating through this new path.

When making a career change, fear and uncertainty are natural emotions. The idea of leaving your comfort zone and starting afresh can be daunting. Nevertheless, fear must be dealt away with by concentrating on the possibilities ahead. Continuous education is a way of boosting your confidence which provides you with the necessary tools for adapting to any changes in industry conditions.

Building resilience is another attribute to overcome challenges associated with career shifts. Resilience enables you to bounce back from failures, denials, or obstacles that come on your way. Inculcating a growth mindset, celebrating small wins, engaging mentors or experts in your interested profession would assist you in developing resilience that would see you through hard times.

Bear in mind; others have walked the same journey before thus don't give up easily (persistence). Seeking guidance from professionals who have gone through similar career changes might provide useful insights for those making such decisions for their lives. For example, they may tell their stories, advise or enhance our understanding in various aspects of our life choices. Moreover, connecting online platforms with fellow switchers during events could also form an encouraging network where motivation can be found.

You will overtly take actions to overcome these barriers and challenges along your transition process in Career Shifts if you recognize them first. With determination and dedication coupled with the right attitude however it becomes possible to sail through this transformative journey towards accomplishing what we want.

Transformation Through Upskilling and Continuous Learning

Career shifts have become quite frequent given today's ever-innovating job market scenario. Thus professionals need to adapt as industries evolve due to new technologies. One of the strategies for handling these transitions is upskilling and continuous learning.

Technology moves fast, and employers' requirements evolve rapidly as well so they need to be continuously upgraded. It is important to keep updating your skills due to technological advancements and use of different tools in workplaces. Upskilling helps an individual acquire knowledge on new things happening within an industry thus, locating them at a better position when seeking employment opportunities.

By investing in up-skilling you show your commitment towards personal and professional development. Employers appreciate those individuals who are willing to learn because one can easily change into someone else whom the company needs at any particular time thus making it possible for him/her being recruited easily. There are numerous ways that people can use today to gain more skills besides just going back to class which include taking online courses, attending workshops or even participating in industry conferences.

Adapting to The Changing Job Market

Upskilling does not only help with your career shift but also enables you navigate through the dynamic job market. An individual can effectively change with the demands of employers or modifications taking place in jobs by acquiring new skills as well as keeping updated on what is happening in an industry.

The rapid development of technology and automation has led to obsolescence of certain job roles while giving rise to new ones. Thus, through upskilling oneself they can be positioned for such emerging opportunities thereby enhancing their employability. Adapting to a fluid labour market is essential if you want your career path to sustain long time goals.

Moreover, continuous development is a way to stay ahead of the competition. As more professionals discover the significance of lifelong learning, there is a need for differentiation by acquiring highly demanded skills. Staying current with industry trends will make you marketable in your new career path and outstanding to potential employers.

Building up Professional Network

One of the most important things when changing careers is having a good professional network. Creating and utilizing connections can help you expand your horizons, gain insights and receive support during this transformational stage.

Similarly, adjusting to another career often means entering uncharted waters. In reaching out to professionals in their chosen field or desired sectors, they are able to find out what they know or have experienced. Hunt for suitable networking gatherings, meetings on the web, conferences and speak with people who may advise them.

Professional network growth does not only mean increasing one's prospects but also helping others in their journeys too. By creating reciprocal relationships, one can cooperate together or exchange ideas as well as being supported by a collection of like-minded individuals going through parallel career changes.

Networking nowadays is not confined to face-to-face meetings alone though it involves social media interaction as well as online platforms. Utilize online platforms such as social media sites so that you can engage with experts within your field. Participate in various discussions occurring within groups that revolve around different industries thereby extending your networks and keeping yourself updated about emerging issues or concerns regarding those networks.

Looking for Right Connections

Ensure that when building your professional network you focus on quality rather than quantity. Look for those who share similar goals, values and desires with you .Search for mentors who offer guidance and advice while peers become accountability partners throughout the journey of your career life.

Network genuinely because all relationships start from somewhere eventually leading towards something better. Be a genuine listener having an authentic voice; realize when someone needs help so assist them accordingly since networking begins through nurturing relationships other than packing business cards.

A strong professional network can be a great asset as one navigates through their career change. When building relationships and looking for opportunities to interact with people, you develop a supportive community that will help you succeed in your endeavors.

Dealing with Personal and Financial Considerations

There is more to think about when making this decision of switching careers as it affects the person's life both personally and financially. Switching careers implies careful preparation where various aspects are taken care in order to ensure that successful transition takes place.

The initial step while navigating personal concerns is evaluating how the shift will affect an individual's lifestyle, daily routine and work-life balance. Take time out to think about your priorities, check if the new job corresponds to personal goals set or values reflected on.

In addition, there are financial considerations which play a crucial role in determining whether to switch careers or not. The assessment of one's current financial condition alongside the knowledge of what economic consequences might follow from changing career should not be omitted here. Reflect upon aspects such as changes in earnings, expenses and monetary stability.

Developing a Financial Plan

Create an effective financial plan so that you can minimize any financial risks during transition periods. This involves budgeting, identifying possible sources of income and starting a saving plan that caters for all the first costs or any alteration in revenue to come up with cash flows for each month throughout this time.

It may be helpful to consult a financial planner or consultant who can provide you with advice about your situation and guide you through this process.

Moreover, seek for other alternative ways of earning money or part-time jobs which may assist you stabilize yourself financially during this time when shifting career lines.

Emotional Support and Mindset

Significant personal and emotional challenges come with a career shift. Let friends, family members and mentors who can guide, inspire and offer emotional support to you be part of your life during this period.

A Positive Mindset

It is vital that one remains upbeat and strong-willed in the course of transition. Take advantage of the benefits brought about by a change in careers; recognize those aspects that make you feel fearful or unsure as well as concentrate on self-improvement.

Work-Life Integration

The professional goals should not supersede family considerations or vice versa as a result of financial decisions made at a time when someone is shifting careers. Come up with strategies for integrating work and personal lives such that after starting on new vocational paths, it will still be possible to relate well with people, keep up with interests and take care of oneself.

Personal journey through which I would have to weigh personal and financial considerations while changing careers requires maintaining balance between my professional objectives versus my private life. Develop an integrated plan for bridging your occupational goals into the realization thereof, but at the same time allowing you to engage yourself in friendships, hobbies, and self-pampering.

Embracing Your New Career Path

Once you have overcome the trials associated with switching careers successfully, don't hesitate to take your new direction with high spirits. At this point of your career path it is important that you are adaptive enough to learn new things as we move along the dynamic world towards newer changes.

Transitioning into a new career requires a growth mindset and willingness to learn. Embrace the lifelong learning mentality that will help you gain relevant skills throughout your life from any available sources whether it's colleges or online platforms. For instance, in current dynamic job markets today being constantly trained with additional skills development enhances competitive edge hence employees need to upskill frequently

Take time out, celebrate milestones along the way; give credit to your hard work, determination and resilience, which got you through this shift in profession; reflect on the journey and benefits of that experience; recognize what you have achieved thus far to move forward and embrace a new beginning.

Chapter 10

Entrepreneurial Spirit in the Middle Years

Chapter 10 unwraps the world of entrepreneurship in middle age - a fearless move against the tide! It's about folks who dared to start their own ventures later in life.

Wondering why people kick-off businesses in their later years? Or fancy giving it a shot? This chapter brims with invigorating success tales, packed with useful tips and tactics to overcome hurdles and seize chances that midlife business initiation brings.

Age is never a barrier for entrepreneurial spirit. Plenty discover true purpose post reaching a life milestone. Let's cheer for these valiant souls whose passion for business blooms into blooming ventures. So, if you harbor entrepreneurial dreams or yearn to learn about the journeys of middle-aged entrepreneurs, this chapter aims to ignite your spirit. Let's recognize the might of the entrepreneurial spirit while uncovering triumphant tales and lessons from late bloomers.

Midlife Entrepreneurs: A Growing Trend

The trend of diving into entrepreneurship is picking up among the middle-aged, making them a rising cohort of entrepreneurs. We delve into why this trend is gaining momentum and spotlight those who found satisfaction and success in establishing their own firms during their mid years.

Middle age often prompts folks to ponder and unearth themselves better. It urges them to take up new quests that resonate with their interests. Starting a business at this stage helps them use their rich experience, skills, and contacts.

A strong craving for personal satisfaction and purpose fuels these midlife entrepreneurs. Many mid-aged individuals long for work that matches their principles and lets them contribute to their societies.

Entrepreneurial Triumphs

In this part, we'll discover how some midlife entrepreneurs toppled norms and launched outstanding entrepreneurial journeys. These stories aim to inspire readers and disprove the myth that starting a business late in life is daunting.

Take Jane Peterson who spun her love for cooking into a successful bakery, or Mark Johnson who created a thriving marketing firm. These amazing journeys show the boundless possibilities of midlife entrepreneurs.

These stories are to inspire those thinking of starting a business during their middle years. Pursuing a dream, achieving financial autonomy, or creating a lasting heritage, the midlife entrepreneurs' paths show that it's never too late to achieve success.

Middle Aged? It's Your Time to Shine as an Entrepreneur

People in their middle years often discover an Entrepreneurial Spirit, and it might be a perfect time to pursue some ambitious projects. But, it's not always easy. You need to kindle and nurture that spirit. Here's how.

1. First, have a good think. Recognize your talents, keen interests, and past experiences. Spot an area that lights a fire in you. Could this passion become a sound business? Knowing your distinctive value can fuel your Entrepreneurial Spirit.

2. Secondly, knowledge is power. To set up shop, you need to be on top of your game. Never stop learning. Attend workshops or join webinars to gain insights. Build a skillset to crush every hurdle along the way.

3. Lastly, surround yourself with positivity. Share your aspirations with like-minded folks. Connect with vibrant entrepreneurial communities. Seek assistance from those who've been there and done that. Such networks can provide the guidance, inspiration, and accountability you need.

4. See Mistakes as Lessons: In business, failures are inevitable. Take them as chances to grow and learn. Know that not all efforts may win, but each mistake gets you closer to your goal. Let these push you to continue and sharpen your business ideas.

5. Stay Flexible and Welcome Change: Business is always changing. As an older entrepreneur, flexibility is key. Keep up with business trends and new tech. Be ready to shift your methods as needed. This will let you grab new chances and keep you moving forward.

6. Tackle Hurdles: Starting a business later in life can bring unique hurdles, like money worries or risk aversion. Turn these hurdles into chances to grow and find ways to beat them. Get advice from pros or financial experts who can guide you through the money matters of starting a business in your middle years.

Encouraging your business spirit in your middle years is thrilling and life-changing. Through following your interests, learning from others, creating a support team, learning from mistakes, and staying flexible, you can develop the business mentality needed to kick off a successful venture later in life.

Overcoming Age-Related Obstacles

Starting a business later in life as a midlife entrepreneur may present unique challenges related to age. However, numerous success stories prove that these obstacles can be conquered with determination and perseverance.

One common concern for midlife entrepreneurs is the fear of not being taken seriously in a competitive business landscape. The myth that entrepreneurship is only for the young can be discouraging. However, it's important to remember that success is not determined by age, but by passion, dedication, and expertise.

Age can also bring with it a set of responsibilities, such as caring for aging parents or supporting children. Finding the right balance between family obligations and business pursuits becomes crucial. This may require managing time effectively, seeking support from loved ones, and leveraging technology to streamline operations.

In addition, midlife entrepreneurs might face technological challenges or feel unfamiliar with the rapidly evolving digital landscape. Embracing continuous learning and seeking assistance from experts and mentors can help bridge the gap and ensure success in the digital age.

It's inspiring to see midlife entrepreneurs who have overcome these age-related obstacles to achieve remarkable success. Take, for example, Mary Johnson, who started her e-commerce business at the age of 55 and built it into a thriving online marketplace. Her story demonstrates that age is not a barrier to entrepreneurial success, but rather a wellspring of wisdom and experience to draw upon. Tackling challenges related to age, midlife entrepreneurs can create their own victories in commerce.

Good Reasons to Begin a Venture When Older

Jumping into business later can have great outcomes. Entrepreneurs at this age bring much to the table, setting them up for wins. Now, let's look at the special perks of launching ventures when older.

1. Plenty of Know-how

Biz folks at this age carry loads of skills, knowledge, and proficiency. They have lots more industry experience which aids in making crucial choices and solving issues. This advantage can give them an edge and help their ventures succeed.

2. Wide Ranging Connections

Throughout their years, these folks have collected a lot of valuable contacts. Having this crowd is handy when starting up, giving them access to possible clients, vendors, partners, and advisors. Using these networks can speed up growth and assist in navigating difficulties.

3. More Purpose

At this age, many find a yearning to do something meaningful or to make a difference. Now, by launching a business, they can align their values and interests with their work. This purpose can stoke motivation and botch up resilience, making them more successful in the end.

4. Balance and Flexibility in Work

Once people reach middle age, they often enjoy more financial freedom, which gives them control over their time. They can freely allocate their time between work, family, hobbies, and self-care while running a business. This flexibility enhances their satisfaction and makes running a business during midlife rewarding.

Exciting Midlife Entrepreneurial Journeys

Let's learn about some folks who, during their middle years, ignored age norms and chased their entrepreneurial dreams. Their success shows the mettle and achievements of midlife entrepreneurs, proving that age is no barrier to starting a new business.

Consider Susan Adams as an example. She was an executive and at the ripe age of 50, she chose to swap her high-paying job for her own business. She launched a sustainable fashion brand. Thanks to her vast industry knowledge and her commitment to sustainable practices, Susan created Green Threads.

It's a clothing line combining fashion with environmentally friendly practices. Nowadays, her brand is doing great. She's not only preserving the environment but also takes pleasure in running a flourishing enterprise.

Let's look at Michael Carter as well. He spent his whole career teaching and then developed a love for woodcraft. At 55, he started Carter Creations, his own handmade furniture company. His top-notch artisan skills and novel design swiftly brought his furniture fame among the choosy buyers. His success demonstrates the potential of chasing your true calling at any age and making a successful business out of it.

Midlife folks are starting businesses and succeeding everywhere. From tech firms to bakeries, these entrepreneurs prove you can achieve greatness at any age.

Their success shines a light for others, showing age doesn't limit dreams. With tenacity, drive, and love for their work, they've accomplished amazing things. Age doesn't discourage them; rather, it fuels their legacy.

How to Find What Makes You Tick

If you're a midlife person looking to start a business, it's crucial to identify what you love. Here are tips that might help you find what thrills you:

1. Think About What You Enjoy

Contemplate your hobbies and skills. What makes you happy? What are you good at? These might direct you towards a business idea you adore.

2. Dip Your Toes in Varied Waters

Delve into industries that spark curiosity. Hunt for chances where your skills matter. Think about areas compatible with your skill set or sectors you've yearned to investigate.

3. Learn from Success Stories

Gather encouragement from the success stories of entrepreneurs who found their calling in their middle years. Studying their paths can help you see the various journeys you might emulate for valuable insight.

4. Leverage Your Network

Utilize your network of friends, colleagues, and mentors. Seek wisdom from people who've been successful in their businesses. Their support and connections can help you find your passion.

5. Check Your Ideas

Once you've spotted a prospective business idea, try it. Begin small with offering your goods or service to a few people or doing market research. See the responses to fine-tune your concept and ensure it matches your passion.

With these tips, start your business with a clear mind and belief. Remember, locating your passion is an ongoing process that's doable at middle age. Armed with resolve and vision, your business can prosper and your life can be very fulfilling in later years.

Meeting Financial Obstacles and Risks

Setting up a business in your middle years is both thrilling and rewarding. However, it's equally key to note the financial risks involved. In this part, strategies to navigate these obstacles will be shared, along with uplifting success stories of entrepreneurs who hurdled these financial risks to run profitable businesses.

Money Saving Tips for Business

If you begin a venture when older, a firm money plan is key. Here's advice to help seasoned business folks dodge money hurdles:

Research your market well: Knowing your aimed market helps make smarter money choices and distribute resources wisely. Form an achievable budget: A clear budget helps control spending and avert money mishaps on your journey. Find monetary sources: Look at a range of sources for funds. Try small business loans, grants, or even outside investments. Form a solid money advice group: Surrounding yourself with monetary advisors helps in making strong financial decisions in your venture.

Uplifting Tales of Triumph

Mature business people show that money setbacks shouldn't hold back triumph. Read about a few who faced money hurdles and created flourishing ventures:

Sharon Thompson, a prosperous online clothing brand creator, started her venture with scarce cash. She tapped into her contacts and used social media well. Robert Johnson, a mature businessman, transformed his love for woodcraft into a lucrative venture. He began on a small scale and put profits back into broadening his product range. After climbing the corporate ladder, Michelle Rodriguez moved on. She founded her consultancy without significant debt. She achieved this by managing her finances and saving keenly.

Tales of success like Michelle's show us something. With smart financial planning and determination, you can start a prosperous business in midlife. Learn from these success stories. You'll gain insights into overcoming financial obstacles for late-life business ventures.

Support Circles for Midlife Start-ups

Midlife business founders need strong support networks. They're vital for hurdling problems, gaining insights, and finding inspiration along the way. Let's look at the value of such networks. We'll provide tips for connecting with resources, mentors, and like-minded people for a favorable outcome.

These entrepreneurs encounter unique challenges. With the backing of peers who have been there, navigating these hurdles becomes easier. Surround yourself with those who understand your journey and share your goals. Networking events, specialized industry forums, and online groups are excellent places to connect.

Mentor Search

Mentors are golden for entrepreneurs hitting midlife. They offer wisdom from first-hand experiences and offer guidance for late starters in business. Trying to link with business experts, joining professional groups, or going for mentorship schemes can help you find these vital individuals.

Also, you must actively search for midlife entrepreneur-specific resources. Search for platforms, read-ups, and online hubs that offer support crafted for midlife entrepreneurs. These resources give useful tips, tools, and chances to network to make the business start-up journey smoother.

Another encouragement is the success tales of midlife entrepreneurs who created booming businesses. Reading about their journey can give valuable insights and wipe away self-doubt. The internet, books, and podcasts give numerous success stories and teach lessons from people achieving business success later in life.

To conclude, a strong support system is a game-changer for midlife entrepreneurs starting a business. By networking with like-minded folks, mentors, and using resources at hand, entrepreneurs can gather valuable tips, tackle hurdles, and share in successes. Remember, in this exciting journey of entrepreneurship, you're not alone.

Finding the Right Mix: Work, Family, and You

Running a business as a mid-life entrepreneur? It's tough to juggle that, family and personal time. But don't worry! There's a way to keep it all in check. We're here to share some handy tips on getting everything in order.

1. Sort and Share tasks

Mid-life and starting a business? You need to order your tasks. Know what's important. Spend time on those. Also, don't do everything. Give some tasks to other people. This will let you focus on the real issues.

2. Draw the Line

Make sure work doesn't eat into your time. Set work hours and stick to them! Share your schedule with your team, clients, and family. With set times for work and life, you'll be less stressed. You'll give quality time to work and folks at home.

3. Make Time Work for You

Time management works wonders for mid-life entrepreneurs. Handle tasks wisely. Break them into small, doable parts. Use productivity tools and apps to help you keep track. Manage your time well, get work done and enjoy time with family and hobbies too.

4. Bring Family into the Mix

Engage your family in your entrepreneurial journey by involving them in business discussions, seeking their input, and communicating your goals and challenges. By fostering a supportive and understanding environment, you can build stronger relationships and ensure that your family remains an essential part of your journey.

5. Take Care of Yourself

Self-care is crucial for midlife entrepreneurs to maintain a healthy work-life balance. Prioritize your physical and mental well-being by nurturing your hobbies, engaging in regular exercise, practicing mindfulness, and seeking support from peers and mentors. By taking care of yourself, you'll be better equipped to handle the demands of entrepreneurship and maintain a fulfilling personal life.

Balancing work, family, and personal life is an ongoing process that requires continuous evaluation and adjustments. By implementing these strategies and incorporating your own unique approaches, you can successfully navigate the challenges and enjoy a fulfilling and rewarding entrepreneurial journey in midlife.

Embracing the Entrepreneurial Spirit in Midlife

As we conclude our exploration of Entrepreneurial Spirit in the middle years, we cannot underestimate the significance of embracing this spirit as a catalyst for success. The stories we've shared throughout this section attest to the remarkable achievements of midlife entrepreneurs who dared to start their own businesses.

These success stories serve as a testament to the boundless possibilities that await those who choose to embark on their entrepreneurial journey later in life. From transforming hobbies into thriving ventures to pursuing long-held passions, midlife entrepreneurs have proven that age is no hindrance to success. Launching a company in your prime years gives you the shot to draw upon your hard-earned wisdom and skills. At the same time, it offers a stage to create a substantial change. As we honor these notable people, we desire their tales to motivate you. After all, you might discover your Entrepreneurial Spark and seize the endless possibilities out there.

Chapter 11

Financial Security
for the Future

Welcome to Chapter 11 here we'll be exploring retirement planning, the path to complete financial freedom, and investment strategies to secure your future. Retirement planning is the starting point for securing a stable financial future. By setting goals and having an exit strategy you can confidently navigate the golden years of your life. In this section you will get tips from professionals on creating a personalized retirement plan.

Financial freedom is also an important objective that we will go over in this chapter. By building a strong foundation, managing debt, and establishing an emergency fund you can free yourself from financial stress.

Investment strategies are another key component to securing your financial future. In this section you will explore different saving methods that can help build wealth over time.

Book along with us as we take steps towards unlocking all these possibilities together!

Understanding Retirement Planning

Retirement planning is one of the first steps in securing your financial future. It involves setting clear goals, understanding various types of accounts, and exploring investments that align with your aspirations.

One size doesn't fit all when it comes to retirement plans. Creating a personalized plan starts by taking into account three main things; your current financial situation, what lifestyle you want after retiring, and risks that may come up along the way.

To set clear goals you need something that's easy to work towards. For some people it's retiring at a certain age while others may have never ending dreams like traveling the world or maintaining income levels.

Understanding Retirement Accounts

A big part of building a nest egg for your future is knowing about different types of retirement accounts. There are many different options out there so getting familiar with each ones contribution limits and tax implications will help make sure you're making informed decisions on how they can best be utilized in your plan.

Exploring Investment Options

Growing savings happens through careful selection of suitable investment options over time which increases chances of achieving your financial goals. Here are a few that we'll provide more information on:

Stocks and bonds
Mutual funds
Exchange-Traded Funds (ETFs)
Real estate

Each of these investment options carries unique risks and potential rewards. Diversification is key to managing risk and maximizing return, so spreading your investments across different asset classes will help reduce the impact of market volatility.

To sum it all up, understanding retirement planning basics is essential for securing your financial future. By setting clear financial goals, familiarizing yourself with retirement accounts, and exploring suitable investment options, you can create a personalized retirement plan that aligns with your dreams and helps you achieve a comfortable and prosperous retirement.

Laying a Solid Financial Foundation

Building a strong financial foundation is crucial for attaining long-term financial freedom. It requires careful planning and diligent execution. In this section, we'll discuss three key components that will help you lay the groundwork for a secure financial future.

Budgeting

The first step to taking control of your finances is to create a budget. By monitoring your income and expenses, you can learn where you're spending excessive money and how to allocate it more effectively.

A well-constructed budget helps you prioritize spending, save up for future goals, and avoid unnecessary debt.

Begin by listing all sources of income as well as fixed expenses like rent or mortgage payments, utilities, insurance etc. Then track discretionary expenses like dining out or entertainment. This helps identify areas where you can cut back in order to add more towards savings and investments. Regularly reviewing your budget ensures it remains aligned with your financial goals.

Debt Management

Another key element in establishing a strong financial foundation is managing debt. Large amounts of debt can hinder savings abilities which leads to an inability in achieving financial freedom. Start by understanding current debt levels including outstanding balances, interest rates etc.

Creating a repayment plan allows quicker payoff while avoiding interest charges on higher-interest debts such as credit card balances first. Interest rates should be kept at minimum payment levels on other debts such as loans or mortgages etc. Debt consolidation or refinancing can provide lower interest rates which help simplify repayment plans.

Saving for Emergencies

Life is unpredictable and unforeseen expenses can halt financial progress. This is why establishing an emergency fund is vital. An account that's dedicated to these circumstances allows easier access during difficult times without halting long-term financial goals.

Aim to have saved 3-6 months' worth of living expenses in this fund. It's a safety net that saves you from relying on credit cards or loans when dealing with financial hardships. Ensuring you're able to cover unexpected bills, repairs or even job losses brings peace of mind while chasing your dreams.

By focusing on these three things - budgeting, debt management and emergency funds - you'll be able to lay a strong foundation towards long-term financial freedom.

The Power of Saving and Investing

Long-term financial security and wealth-building are heavily affected by saving and investing. This section will focus on various strategies as well as investment options that'll help strengthen your future financially. So let's get into it!

Why Save

When it comes to financial security, saving is the first step toward your goals. By simply putting some of your income away on a regular basis you can start building a safety net for emergencies and unexpected expenses. It also helps you save money that can be invested to generate additional income.

The Secret Formula

Saving has one of the most powerful factors behind it: compound interest. Through compounding, your money will grow exponentially over time. By reinvesting the interest earned, you'll accelerate your wealth-building journey and achieve your financial goals sooner.

Diversification: Minimizing Risk and Maximizing Returns

In this world, you have to understand that diversification is crucial in investing. The more diverse your investment portfolio is across different sectors and industries, the lower risk there is. Makes sense right? With a well-diversified portfolio, market volatility won't hit as hard and you're more likely to secure a stable financial future.

Choosing the Right Investment Vehicles

Investment options are endless! So make sure to carefully select the ones that align with your goals and risk tolerance when it comes to investing. Stocks, bonds, mutual funds or real estate all come with their own set of benefits and considerations so take some time to do thorough research or even consult experts if needed!

By combining these two - saving plus investing - you'll be able to make huge strides in securing a nice financial foundation for yourself. In our next sections we're going to dive into retirement planning, social security, constructing an investment portfolio and much more!

Navigating Retirement Accounts

We know retirement seems far away but trust us when we say it's never too early! Understanding different types of retirement accounts plays a vital role when it comes down to planning for yours.

Different Types of Accounts

401(k)s: These are employer-sponsored retirement plans that allows contributors pre-tax salary contributions. Some employers even allow matching contributions which boosts savings potential.

IRAs (Traditional and Roth): Individual Retirement Accounts (IRAs) are self-directed accounts that provide tax advantages. Traditional IRAs offer potential tax deductions on contributions, while Roth IRAs allow for tax-free withdrawals in retirement.

Benefits and Contribution Limits

Each type of account offers its own benefits and contribution limits. For example, 401(k)s often have higher limits compared to IRAs which you must understand so you're able to maximize your savings.

Tax Implications

When it comes to taxes, different types of retirement accounts come with varying implications. Contributions made into traditional 401(k) and IRA's are usually tax-deductible which reduces taxable income. On the flip side, contributions made into Roth IRA's are made with after-tax dollars - providing tax-free withdrawals in retirement.

By utilizing these accounts strategically you'll be able to optimize your savings for when the time comes and also use their unique benefits. In case you need help deciding what works best for you, consult with a financial advisor or retirement planning professional!

Social Security is the backbone of any retirement plan. Knowing how to qualify for it, how to claim it, and the effect that early or late retirement can have on your benefits is a must. And incorporating Social Security into your overall retirement plan is crucial if you want to ensure maximum financial protection.

Building A Diversified Investment Portfolio

A well-constructed investment portfolio is one that doesn't put all its eggs in one basket. It's a strategy used by investors to manage risks and boost returns. Diversification helps minimize investment weaknesses by spreading funds across various asset classes, risk levels, and investment vehicles.

In doing so, you capture gains from different sectors while reducing the negative impact of market fluctuations on your assets. By investing in multiple asset classes such as stocks, bonds, commodities, and real estate; you give yourself a chance at making money no matter what kind of market conditions arise.

By diversifying investments through mutual funds and exchange-traded funds (ETFs), investors who might not have the time or knowledge to oversee their investments receive instant diversification without having to do much work.

Different types of investments are made via mutual funds. Depending on the type of fund you invest in - be it stock, bond or real estate - your money will be spread out accordingly among those sectors. In ETFs we can see similar behavior but usually with index tracking funds where they invest in stocks from an index like S&P 500.

Diversifying also means investing in different risk levels and vehicles such as individual stocks or bonds. Different options come with different rates of return with accompanying risks ranging from low-risk low-reward corporate bonds to high-risk high-reward penny stocks.

Further managing risk involves things like regular rebalancing which ensures that your portfolio remains aligned with your goals regardless of how certain investments perform over time as well as allocating amounts based on risk tolerance.

All this combined constructs an effective diversified investment portfolio that yields maximum returns while mitigating risks.

Retirement Income Planning

Planning your income for retirement revolves around ensuring you can maintain a comfortable and sustainable lifestyle as well as covering important expenses. In this section, we will go over strategies that may help you generate consistent income during your golden years.

Annuities are the most popular choice when it comes to guaranteed lifetime or fixed-term income. With an annuity, you will be able to create a steady stream of money that will cover all your essential expenses and grant you longevity in terms of savings.

One effective way to generate income during retirement is systematic withdrawals from your retirement accounts. This method allows you to withdraw a fixed amount regularly from your investments and ensures consistent cash flow while maintaining your portfolio.

Apart from annuities and systematic withdrawals, there are other investment options available. Dividend-paying stocks, bonds, real estate investment trusts (REITs), and other income-generating assets are among the alternatives that investors can consider. Diversifying income sources will help reduce risks and maximize potential earnings.

To optimize one's retirement income streams, one needs to carefully evaluate their expenses, investment returns, tax liabilities. Adjustments may need to be made along the way to make sure that income aligns with lifestyle goals and financial needs.

The next section of this guide will tackle tax considerations in retirement planning as well as strategies on how to minimize tax burdens.

Tax Considerations in Retirement

Taxes play a vital role in planning for retirement. The amount of money spent on taxes can have a huge impact on savings and overall income when retired. So we've compiled some key things regarding taxes that retirees should look into:

Roth Conversions

Converting traditional accounts like an IRA or 401(k) into a Roth IRA can save you money by reducing future tax liabilities. However, keep in mind that the conversion will affect this year's taxable income but qualified distributions from a Roth IRA are tax-free which makes for a great source of funds upon retiring.

Tax-efficient Withdrawal Strategies

Another important aspect of retiree tax planning is finding the most efficient way of withdrawing funds from your retirement accounts. By managing withdrawals right you can potentially minimize taxable income and maximize overall savings.

A good example would be taking out money both in taxable and non-taxable accounts like Roth IRAs or health savings accounts (HSAs).

Charitable Contributions

It's not just about giving back but also getting more back through credits on charity donations.

Donating to qualified organizations can earn you tax deductions that will in turn reduce your overall tax liabilities.

Medicare and Social Security Taxation

Remember that some income sources will be subject to taxation. For example, social security benefits and medicare premiums.

Knowing the rules and thresholds for these taxes can help you plan better and potentially mitigate their impact on your retirement income.

Being intelligent with money now that you don't need to spend it all will lead to a wealthier future.

Long-term care can be a menace to retirement savings. It's critical that you consider the cost while planning for your golden years. We're gonna teach you in this section how to plan for long-term care, protect your assets and secure a financially stable future.

One of the most key things when it comes to long-term care is insurance options. They cover services from nursing home care all the way down to assisted living facilities and in-home care. Here we'll go over different types of insurance policies along with their benefits in order to make sure your retirement savings are safe.

Alternative funding sources can be another route if insurance isn't ideal for you. By using financial tools such as health savings accounts (HSAs) or annuities, you might be able to cover these costs on top of what you already have saved up. In this section we'll also go over these options and how they can be integrated into your retirement plan.

In case you didn't know, there are steps and strategies out there that individuals like yourself can take in order to shield their wealth from potential long-term care expenses. You should really consider some Medicaid planning along with creating trusts and engaging in appropriate estate planning measures.

If all else fails, always remember that understanding the importance of long-term care planning while taking proactive steps to prepare yourself is almost fool proof.

Now let's get into market volatility

Wouldn't it be nice if investing was easy? Well unfortunately folks it's not that simple. Market volatility makes it hard for even the most experienced investors to make good decisions at times. However, don't worry because this section will help with all of that stress by giving you valuable insights and strategies so that even throughout turbulent times, sticking through it will eventually give big rewards.

Mitigating Risk

Understandably a lot of people like spreading their investments across different areas because just having one run bad would absolutely suck right? Right! So instead of just letting that happen, you should really consider working with a professional to manage your risk in order to limit potential loss.

Staying Disciplined

Oh boy here's the fun part. Market volatility can make people panic and make impulsive decisions that might not work at all in their favor, which is why it's absolutely crucial to remain disciplined and avoid making any knee-jerk reactions.

Opportunities Amidst Volatility

As we've mentioned before, volatility brings uncertainty but it also presents opportunities for savvy investors like yourselves. By staying informed and doing some thorough research, you'll be able to find those holes in the market where some good investments are hiding.

Chapter 12

Cultivating Meaningful Relationships

Welcome to Chapter 12 of our journey to personal and professional growth. In this chapter, we explore the art of cultivating meaningful relationships. Whether it's building strong personal connections or fostering professional networks, the key lies in honing your communication skills.

Personal connections are a vital source of happiness and fulfillment in our lives. By nurturing relationships with family, friends, and loved ones, we create a support system that adds richness to our experiences. Additionally, building strong professional connections is crucial for career growth and success, opening doors to opportunities and collaborations.

Within these sections, we will delve into the importance of effective communication skills. By fine-tuning your ability to listen actively, express empathy, and assert yourself, you can deepen personal connections and build rapport with colleagues, mentors, and industry professionals.

Moreover, we will discuss the challenges that can arise in communication and provide strategies to overcome them. Conflict resolution, emotional management, and navigating difficult conversations will become easier when armed with the right tools.

As technology continues to shape our world, we cannot ignore its impact on relationships. We will explore how leveraging social media, online networking platforms, and digital communication tools can enhance personal and professional connections.

Emotional intelligence plays a significant role in navigating relationships. By developing self-awareness, empathy, and emotional regulation, we enhance our ability to create meaningful connections.

Lastly, we understand that maintaining relationships can be challenging in today's busy world. We will discuss strategies for effective time management, prioritization, and setting boundaries to ensure the sustainability of your personal and professional connections.

Through this chapter, we hope to empower you with the knowledge and skills to cultivate meaningful relationships that contribute to your overall well-being and success.

The Power of Personal Connections

Personal connections are an essential component of our overall well-being and happiness. Nurturing and cultivating strong relationships with family, friends, and loved ones can bring immense joy and fulfillment to our lives. These personal connections provide a support system, a sense of belonging, and a source of emotional support during both good and challenging times.

Improving your communication skills is key to fostering meaningful personal connections. Effective communication allows you to truly connect with others, understand their needs, and express your own thoughts and feelings openly and honestly. By actively listening, demonstrating empathy, and practicing clear and assertive communication, you can enhance your relationships and deepen personal connections.

When we invest time and effort into building personal connections, we create a network of support that enriches our lives. We can celebrate successes together, navigate through difficult times, and create unforgettable memories. These personal connections become the foundation of our social support system, providing a sense of belonging and community.

Strong personal connections also contribute to our overall mental and emotional well-being. They offer an outlet for self-expression, a safe space to share our thoughts and emotions without judgment. Having someone to confide in and lean on during challenging times can help alleviate stress, anxiety, and feelings of loneliness.

In the next section, we will explore the benefits of building strong professional connections, looking at how they can enhance our careers and open doors to new opportunities.

Building Strong Professional Connections

In today's competitive professional landscape, building strong connections is crucial for career growth and success. The ability to establish meaningful relationships with colleagues, mentors, and industry professionals can open doors to new opportunities, knowledge sharing, and collaborations.

Networking strategies play a vital role in developing professional connections. Attending industry events, conferences, and seminars allow individuals to meet like-minded professionals, exchange ideas, and forge valuable partnerships. Additionally, utilizing online networking platforms, such as LinkedIn, can expand your professional network beyond geographical boundaries.

However, developing professional connections goes beyond mere networking. Effective communication is key to building rapport and fostering trust with your peers. Active listening, expressing ideas clearly and concisely, and demonstrating empathy are essential communication skills to establish strong professional connections.

Applying Effective Communication Techniques

One of the most impactful ways to build professional connections is through effective communication techniques. Active listening involves giving full attention to the speaker, maintaining eye contact, and providing thoughtful responses. This not only shows respect but also enhances understanding and strengthens relationships.

Moreover, expressing ideas clearly and articulately is crucial in professional settings. Using concise and persuasive language, emphasizing key points, and tailoring your message to the audience can leave a lasting impression and facilitate effective communication.

Lastly, empathy plays a significant role in building professional connections. Understanding others' perspectives, acknowledging their experiences, and showing genuine interest in their work create an environment of trust and mutual support.

By applying these strategies and honing your communication skills, you can build strong professional connections that not only enhance your career prospects but also provide valuable insight and support throughout your professional journey.

Effective Communication Skills in Personal Relationships

Effective communication serves as the bedrock of any successful personal relationship. It lays the groundwork for understanding, trust, and connection. In this section, we will explore various essential communication skills that can promote healthier and more meaningful personal connections.

Active Listening

Active listening involves fully engaging with the speaker and demonstrating genuine interest in what they have to say. It requires focusing on the speaker's words, body language, and emotions, while also providing verbal and nonverbal cues to show understanding and empathy. By practicing active listening, you can foster deeper connections and enhance your relationships.

Empathy

Empathy is the ability to understand and share the feelings of another person. It involves putting yourself in someone else's shoes and experiencing their perspective. By cultivating empathy, you can create a safe and supportive environment in your personal relationships, allowing for open and honest communication.

Assertiveness

Assertiveness is the ability to express your thoughts, feelings, and needs in a respectful and confident manner. It involves setting boundaries, conveying your opinions, and standing up for yourself while also considering the feelings and perspectives of others. Developing assertiveness allows for effective communication, promoting mutual understanding and strengthening personal connections.

These are just a few examples of the essential communication skills that play a significant role in fostering healthier personal connections. By honing these skills, you can build stronger relationships based on trust, empathy, and effective communication.

Mastering Communication Skills in the Professional Sphere

Effective communication is a critical skill to master in the professional world. It forms the foundation of building strong relationships and establishing professional connections. By honing your communication skills, you can effectively convey your ideas, build rapport, and navigate different professional settings with ease.

One of the key techniques in professional communication is clear and concise communication. Being able to express your thoughts in a succinct and organized manner can greatly enhance your credibility and ensure that your message is understood by others.

In addition to verbal communication, nonverbal cues also play a significant role in professional interactions. Paying attention to body language, facial expressions, and tone of voice can help you effectively convey your intentions and emotions.

Adapting your communication style to different professional settings is another essential aspect of mastering communication skills. Being mindful of cultural differences, hierarchies, and professional norms allows you to navigate various environments and connect with individuals from diverse backgrounds.

Overall, perfecting your communication skills in the professional sphere is vital for establishing and maintaining professional connections. By mastering techniques such as clear and concise communication, paying attention to nonverbal cues, and adapting your style, you can enhance your professional relationships and excel in your chosen field.

The Art of Building Lasting Relationships

Building lasting relationships requires more than just initial connections. It entails cultivating trust, authenticity, and mutual support. Whether in our personal or professional lives, nurturing meaningful and long-lasting connections is vital for our overall well-being and success.

In personal connections, genuine trust and authenticity form the foundation of strong relationships. By being open and vulnerable, we create the space for deeper connections with family, friends, and loved ones. Effective communication skills play a significant role in strengthening personal connections, allowing us to understand and empathize with others on a deeper level.

When it comes to professional connections, trust is equally important. By building rapport with colleagues, mentors, and industry professionals, we create a network that can support us in our career endeavors. Effective communication skills such as active listening and clear, concise communication are crucial in fostering healthy professional relationships.

Understanding and honing our communication skills is a key aspect of building lasting connections. Active listening helps us truly understand others' needs and perspectives, opening the door to empathy and mutual support. Additionally, being assertive allows us to express ourselves honestly and respectfully, leading to more authentic and genuine connections.

By prioritizing personal connections, professional connections, and continuously developing our communication skills, we can build lasting relationships that enrich our lives both personally and professionally.

Overcoming Communication Challenges

Communication plays a vital role in our personal and professional lives. However, effective communication can sometimes face obstacles and challenges that hinder understanding and connection. In this section, we will explore strategies to overcome these common communication barriers, enabling you to engage in more meaningful and productive conversations.

Conflict Resolution

Conflicts are a natural part of relationships, both personal and professional. Learning how to navigate conflicts and resolve them amicably is an essential communication skill. This section will provide practical tips and techniques for effectively addressing conflicts, promoting understanding, and reaching mutually agreeable solutions.

Managing Emotions

Emotions can significantly impact our communication and the way we interact with others. To overcome communication challenges, it is crucial to learn how to manage and express emotions effectively. In this section, we will explore strategies to regulate emotions, enhance emotional intelligence, and create a more conducive environment for open and honest communication.

Navigating Difficult Conversations

Difficult conversations can be uncomfortable and challenging, but they are often necessary for resolution and growth. This section will provide guidance on how to approach difficult conversations with empathy, active listening, and assertiveness. You will learn how to express your thoughts and concerns effectively while maintaining a respectful and constructive dialogue.

By implementing these strategies, you can enhance your communication skills and overcome the challenges that may arise in your personal and professional relationships. The ability to navigate conflicts, manage emotions, and engage in difficult conversations will ultimately strengthen your connections and foster healthier and more meaningful interactions.

Leveraging Technology for Enhanced Connections

In today's digital age, technology has revolutionized the way we connect with others. From personal relationships to professional networks, leveraging technology can help enhance and strengthen our connections. By harnessing the power of social media, online networking platforms, and digital communication tools, we can overcome geographical barriers and stay connected with our loved ones and colleagues.

Social media platforms like Facebook, Instagram, and Twitter have become an integral part of our lives, offering us a convenient way to connect and share our experiences with others. They provide a platform for staying updated on the lives of friends and family, and for sharing our own photos, thoughts, and moments. Through these platforms, we can nurture personal connections by engaging in meaningful conversations, celebrating milestones, and offering support during challenging times.

Additionally, online networking platforms like LinkedIn are invaluable resources for building professional connections. By creating a compelling profile and showcasing our skills and achievements, we can connect with like-minded professionals, mentors, and potential employers. These platforms facilitate networking opportunities, job hunting, and knowledge-sharing, thereby enhancing our professional growth and success.

The Role of Digital Communication Tools

Digital communication tools such as email, instant messaging, and video conferencing have transformed the way we communicate professionally. Email provides a quick and efficient way to exchange information and collaborate with colleagues, clients, and partners regardless of geographical constraints. Instant messaging platforms like Slack and Microsoft Teams enable real-time communication, fostering efficient teamwork and collaboration.

Furthermore, video conferencing tools like Zoom and Microsoft Teams have become indispensable in our professional lives, especially in a world where remote work is increasingly prevalent. These platforms enable face-to-face interactions, fostering a sense of connection and facilitating effective communication even when physical proximity is not possible.

While technology offers numerous benefits in enhancing personal and professional connections, it is essential to use it mindfully and strike a balance between virtual and in-person interactions. Nonetheless, by leveraging technology wisely, we can bridge distances, maintain relationships, and strengthen our personal and professional connections.

The Role of Emotional Intelligence in Relationships

Emotional intelligence plays a significant role in nurturing and strengthening personal connections and professional relationships. By developing self-awareness, empathy, and emotional regulation, individuals can foster meaningful and authentic connections with others.

In personal relationships, emotional intelligence allows individuals to understand and manage their own emotions, as well as empathize with the emotions of their loved ones. This understanding and empathy create a foundation of trust and open communication, enabling deeper connections and stronger bonds.

Similarly, emotional intelligence plays a crucial role in professional connections. By being aware of their own emotions, individuals can effectively navigate workplace dynamics, manage stress, and build positive relationships with colleagues, clients, and superiors. Empathy and emotional regulation also contribute to effective teamwork, conflict resolution, and collaboration.

Developing emotional intelligence requires self-reflection and a willingness to understand and empathize with others. By actively practicing self-awareness, individuals can identify their emotional triggers and patterns, leading to better decision-making and improved communication skills.

Furthermore, emotional intelligence allows individuals to tune into the emotions of those around them, fostering empathy and understanding. This ability to empathize not only improves relationships but also enhances problem-solving, negotiation, and the ability to lead and inspire others.

In conclusion, emotional intelligence plays a pivotal role in nurturing both personal connections and professional relationships. By honing self-awareness, empathy, and emotional regulation, individuals can create deeper, more meaningful connections, leading to greater personal fulfillment and professional success.

Maintaining Relationships in a Busy World

In today's fast-paced world, it can be challenging to prioritize and nurture our personal and professional connections. However, maintaining these relationships is crucial for our overall well-being and success.

In this section, we will explore effective strategies to navigate the busyness of life while ensuring the sustainability of our personal and professional connections.

Time Management

One of the key aspects of maintaining relationships in a busy world is efficient time management. By prioritizing and allocating dedicated time for our loved ones and professional contacts, we can ensure that these connections remain strong and meaningful. Utilize tools and techniques like calendars, schedules, and to-do lists to organize your time effectively.

Prioritization

In a world filled with numerous responsibilities and commitments, it is crucial to prioritize our relationships. Recognize the importance of personal connections and professional networks in your life and make them a priority. By consciously choosing to invest time and effort in these relationships, you can strengthen the bonds and create a sense of fulfillment and support.

Maintaining Boundaries

Setting and maintaining boundaries is essential for maintaining relationships in a busy world. Learn to say no when necessary and avoid overextending yourself. By establishing clear boundaries, you can manage your time and energy more effectively, ensuring that you have the capacity to nurture your connections without feeling overwhelmed.

In conclusion, despite the hustle and bustle of our lives, it is vital to prioritize and maintain our personal and professional connections. Through effective time management, prioritization, and maintaining boundaries, we can foster lasting and fulfilling relationships that enrich our lives both personally and professionally.

The Impact of Mindfulness on Relationships

Mindfulness is a powerful practice that can have a profound impact on our personal and professional connections. By cultivating awareness and being present in the moment, we can deepen our relationships and enhance our communication skills.

In our fast-paced world, it is easy to get caught up in the demands of daily life, leaving little room for genuine connection. Mindfulness allows us to slow down, tune in to ourselves, and truly engage with others. When we are mindful in our interactions, we listen actively, offer our full attention, and respond empathetically. This level of presence fosters deeper personal connections and helps build trust and understanding.

Furthermore, incorporating mindfulness into our professional connections can lead to more meaningful collaborations and improved teamwork. By being fully present and attuned to the needs and perspectives of our colleagues, we can enhance communication, promote effective decision-making, and cultivate a positive work environment.

Practicing mindfulness also enables us to manage stress and emotions more effectively, which is crucial for maintaining healthy relationships. By developing self-awareness and emotional regulation skills, we can respond to challenges with clarity and compassion, rather than reacting impulsively. This not only benefits our personal connections but also allows us to navigate professional conflicts with grace and professionalism.

Chapter 13

Time Management Masterclass

Welcome to Chapter 13 on time management. We'll delve into time management secrets for balanced living. In this module, we'll learn top-notch techniques of organizing tasks for better time control and life satisfaction.

Ever felt swamped with an endless task list? Ever battled with squeezing time for yourself or balancing work and life? If yes, you're in good company. Many today are yearning for ways to use their time better for balance.

The good news is, mastering the art of task organization, you can command your time and have work-life coordination. This doesn't only rev up your productivity, it also improves your general wellness.

In this section, we'll uncover strategies such as understanding task organization, achieving work-life accord, crafting a personal time control system, and setting goals effectively for a harmonious life. We'll also tackle common hurdles like time killers and diversions, and underscore the role of self-care in maintaining work-life health.

So, if you're set to rule your time and build a more balanced and rewarding life, let's navigate the realm of excellent time control together!

Grasping How to Prioritize

Running your time well is a must for a level life and balance between work and personal time. One major part of managing time is ranking tasks. Prioritizing them helps you see and focus on what's really key. This makes your time usage super-efficient.

There are many ways to rank tasks depending on which to do first. People often think about how urgent, important, and impactful each task is to their big goals. Tasks that need doing now because of deadlines need quick focus. But important jobs related to your long-term aims get higher ranks.

One way to rank tasks is Eisenhower's Matrix, otherwise known as the Urgent-Important Matrix. This way breaks tasks into four parts using urgency and importance. Categorizing tasks lets you spend your time effectively. You can focus on the most critical, delegate or leave tasks that are less important.

The ABC method is another quick and practical way to rank tasks. Giving tasks an A, B, or C based on priority helps you decide which to do first. Splitting your task list into smaller bits and giving them ranks helps you keep it clear and avoid distraction.

Including ways to rank your tasks in how you manage time can help you feel more in control and increase your results. Good ranking uses your time wisely. It makes sure your focus is on what matters most. This helps you achieve a life that's better balanced in the end.

Work-Life Harmony: Making It Happen

Many of us struggle to find equilibrium between work and personal life. It's like a high-wire act, balancing work duties and personal happenings. But with smart strategies, a satisfying work-life harmony is achievable.

One effective way is to manage our tasks wisely. Prioritize what matters most and focus. This strategy makes sure our time isn't wasted. It may mean a regular review of work, sharing tasks, and refusing unnecessary obligations.

Besides, keeping stress in check is vital. Practicing self-care daily is the key. Maybe exercise, some quiet meditation, or pursuing a hobby. Such activities recharge us, lower stress. Blurring work-life lines? Avoid it. Ensure there's time to unwind, to spend quality moments with family, to do activities we enjoy.

Putting these strategies to use, making mindful choices, we can have work-life harmony, leading to a more rewarding life overall. Keep this in mind-it's not about perfect balance daily, but a sustainable rhythm that enables personal and professional success.

Building Your Own Time Management Plan

We live in a fast-moving world. Everyone needs good time management skills to stay productive without feeling overwhelmed. Organizing your tasks, setting priorities and goals helps to boost your productivity. Let's explore these elements of a personal time management plan.

Ranking Tasks

A strong time management plan focuses on task prioritization. Consider the urgency and importance of your tasks. By doing this, you can use your time and energy on high-impact tasks. That way, you'll focus on things that truly advance your goals.

Reasonable Deadlines

Setting achievable deadlines for tasks is another vital part of time management. Guage the time each activity may need. This way, you can create a doable schedule without stress. Reasonable deadlines can fight procrastination and keep you on the right path.

Sharing Tasks

Delegation is an useful tool. It can automate your efficiency and effectiveness. Spot tasks that others can handle. Spare yourself for priority activities. Delegation is teamwork. It lets you tap into other's skills and expertise. This ultimately gives you the best results.

Efficient time management builds a solid foundation that lets you get the most from your hours. Prioritizing, setting doable deadlines, and sharing tasks heightens your productivity and gives you balance.

Your Goals, Your Life Balanced

Goal setting guides you towards a balanced, fulfilling life. SMART (Specific, Measurable, Achievable, Relevant and Time-bound) goals offer direction. Breaking goals into small doable tasks lets you move forward step by step.

Let your goals reflect your vision of a balanced life. Make sure your goals are measurable for tracking and motivation. Keep them achievable to avoid being overwhelmed.

Your goals need to reflect what matters to you. This way, you find purpose and your actions align with your values. Making your goals time-bound adds urgency and accountability.

Keep Score and Adjust

Regularly check how you're doing. This lets you celebrate wins and identify where changes are needed. Tracking your progress keeps you motivated and your momentum up.

Always be ready to tweak your goals. Life changes, and so do circumstances. By checking on your goals from time to time, you ensure they match up with your changing priorities. This helps keep your life balanced.

Bear in mind, setting goals isn't just about the end results. It's also about the process. Accept the journey and treat yourself kindly. When your goals are on point and you stick to them, it will guide you towards the balanced life you want.

Tackling Time Drains and Distractions

Time drains and distractions can greatly reduce your productivity and disrupt your work-life balance. It's important to spot and resolve these. Establish lines, handle tech use wisely, and work mindfully, to take back control of your time and make every second count.

Spotting Common Time Drains

First, try to figure out which activities or habits suck up your time but don't add value to your work or private life. These time drains could be excessive social media use, pointless internet surfing, unnecessary meetings, or multitasking. Once you've identified these activities, you can work on reducing or eradicating them.

Creating Boundaries

Boundaries are key to managing your time wisely. Be clear on your priorities, and set limits on tasks that can turn into time pits. Build the habit of saying "no" when needed and offload tasks when others can do them. When you set boundaries, you make room for activities that align with your goals and help you live a balanced life.

Control Your Tech

All those gadgets? They're useful but can be attention-grabbers too. It's time to take charge. Set times for checking emails. Put aside uninterrupted work moments. Say no to that ping of a new notification. Try apps or web tools that block time-wasting sites or social media.

Mindful Work is Key

Ever heard of mindfulness? It's a big help in pushing away the stuff that steals time. Make it a habit. Be all in with each task. Breathe deep. Allocate chunks of time. Quiet your mind. You can stay sharp, get more done. And the bonus? More satisfaction and a work-life balance that feels just right.

Put these skills to work, push away the time-stealers. Set boundaries. Dive into tasks thoughtfully. Value every minute. You got this!

Take Care of Yourself

Balance also means self-care. It's not about being full of yourself. It's about filling yourself up. This is NO extra, it's a MUST. Look for ways to fit self-care into your day-to-day. It helps you refuel, manage stress, and keep feeling good.

Self-care encompasses various activities that focus on nurturing yourself physically, mentally, and emotionally. It can involve anything from engaging in hobbies or exercise, to practicing mindfulness and ensuring you get enough rest. By making self-care a priority, you can enhance your productivity, reduce burnout, and improve your ability to handle challenges both at work and in your personal life.

Explore Various Self-Care Practices

There are numerous self-care practices to choose from, so you can find the ones that resonate with you and suit your lifestyle. Physical self-care can involve activities like regular exercise, healthy eating, and getting enough sleep. Taking care of your mental well-being can include engaging in activities that bring you joy and relaxation, such as reading, practicing meditation, or spending time in nature.

Emotional self-care involves nurturing your emotions and finding healthy ways to cope with stress. This can be achieved through activities like journaling, therapy or counseling, and spending time with loved ones. Remember, self-care is not limited to specific activities and can differ from person to person. The key is to find what rejuvenates and energizes you.

By prioritizing self-care, you are equipping yourself with the tools necessary to create a work-life balance that supports your overall well-being. It allows you to recharge and show up as your best self, both in your personal life and in the workplace. Incorporating self-care into your everyday routine is an investment in your long-term happiness and success.

Efficient Time Blocking Tips

Time blocking can entirely transform your time management, boosting your output. You reserve certain time slots for specific jobs, tasks, or activities. This way, you stay engaged and optimize your day. Here are tips to help you successfully adopt time blocking:

1. Rank Your Tasks

Begin by pinpointing your crucial tasks and give them distinct time slots. Figure out which tasks demand your urgent intervention and provide them extra focused time. Ranking your tasks helps allocate suitable time and focus to each task.

2. Create Feasible Time Assumptions

While assigning time slots, remember to create feasible time assumptions for every task. Reflect on aspects like intricacy, potential hurdles, and your pace. Dodge overcommitments and have flexibility to modify your plan if required.

3. Lessen Distractions

Throughout your time slots, strive to minimize disruptions. Let your colleagues and family know your availability, disable device notifications, and set up a propitious atmosphere for focused work. This will help sustain concentration and boost your output.

4. Rest Periods

Don't forget to slot in short rest periods within your time slots. Regular intervals prevent burnout, enhance focus, and maintain overall health. Utilize these rests to unwind, rejuvenate, or even take a short walk.

5. Evaluate Your Progress

Regularly check how you're doing. If you need to, tweak your time blocks. Look at how well you're managing your time. If it's not optimal, adjust your timing. Being flexible helps you handle things that come up and stay productive.

Using these methods, you can use time blocking effectively. It can help you use your time well, keep focused, and finish your tasks more easily. Begin using time blocking every day. You'll soon see how it boosts your productivity and helps balance work and life.

How to Keep Work-Life Balance Over Time

Work-life balance is an ongoing goal. It takes hard work and the ability to adjust. To keep your personal and work life balanced, you need to stick with strategies that boost work-life balance over time.

Being resilient is key to long-term work-life balance. By having good coping skills and bouncing back from problems, you can manage personal and work demands more effectively. Rest, take care of yourself, and ask for help when you need it. Remember, to have work-life harmony, you have to look after you first.

Setting limits is another key part of keeping work-life balance. Be clear about your work time, set rules for communication, and learn to say no if need be. Express your wants and boundaries to your coworkers, clients, and loved ones so they know and respect your need for balance. By setting and keeping these boundaries, your work won't take over the rest of your life.

The key to juggling work and life is adaptability. As things change and what's important to you changes, your time management strategies should too. Always take a look at your goals, responsibilities and commitments. Make changes when needed. Be flexible. Be open to trying new ways that fit your current situation. Stay focused on maintaining a flow between work and life.

40's Get to Know Eisenhower's Matrix: A Strong Tool for Task Management

Let's explore Eisenhower's Matrix, or as some call it, the Urgent-Important Matrix. Are you in need of something to help you order your tasks? You've come to the right place! Created by Dwight D. Eisenhower, the U.S.' 34th President, this matrix is key for time management and boosting productivity.

40's But, what's Eisenhower's Matrix? In simple terms, it's a system allowing you to sort tasks according to urgency and significance. This lets you focus on things that matter most. It's a great help for using time and energy wisely.

There are four areas on the matrix: Do, Schedule, Delegate, and Delete. The Do space is for tasks needing immediate action, those both urgent and important. Next, the schedule corner is for tasks important, yet not needing immediate action. The Delegate area is for tasks that are urgent but not important-they can be handed off. Finally, The Delete area is for tasks that have zero urgency and importance-they're out of your list.

Making use of Eisenhower's Matrix, will help in sorting tasks efficiently, making sure to focus on the right task at the right time. Let's dive into this amazing task management tool and learn to use it to your advantage!

Understanding the Eisenhower Matrix

Let's talk about the Eisenhower Matrix. It's a handy tool for managing tasks, developed by Dwight D. Eisenhower. This tool sorts tasks based on urgency and importance. It has become popular and is used by many for personal and professional task management.

This matrix has four sections:

Do: These tasks are important and urgent. They need your immediate attention. They sit at the top of your to-do list.Schedule: Tasks here are important but not currently urgent. These can be pencilled in for later and are second in priority to "Do" tasks.Delegate: This group of tasks are urgent but not important. Hand these tasks off to others. This way, you free up time for important duties.Delete: Tasks in this category are neither urgent nor important. These tasks can be removed. They don't add value to your aims or schedule.

The Eisenhower Matrix is a great tool for managing time effectively. It helps you focus on goal-oriented tasks and avoid spending time on lesser priorities. It can be very beneficial in managing both personal and professional duties for better organization and productivity.

Applying the Eisenhower Matrix

Ready to use the Eisenhower Matrix? Here's a simple guide to get you started:

Sort tasks: Use the Eisenhower Matrix to separate tasks into four groups: Do, Schedule, Delegate, and Delete. Do group: Find tasks urgent and important. They need immediate action and sit at the top of your list. Schedule group: Here are tasks important but not urgent. They can wait. Finish 'Do' tasks first. Delegate group: Focus on urgent, but unimportant tasks. Give these tasks to others to free up your time. Delete group: Spot tasks not urgent or important. Remove these from your list to lighten your load.

Use the Eisenhower Matrix to sort tasks. It helps you focus on what's important. It's a tool for time-management and boosting productivity.

Why the Eisenhower Matrix helps

The Eisenhower Matrix is a famous tool for managing tasks. It helps to increase productivity. It organizes tasks by urgency and importance. This gives a clear picture of what needs doing now and what can wait.

A big benefit of the Eisenhower Matrix is focus. It sorts tasks by urgency and importance. This helps you use your time and resources better. It lets you focus on tasks that move you towards your goals.

The Eisenhower Matrix is a tool for prioritizing tasks. It helps people focus on vital tasks by managing time and resources well. It stops people from using energy on tasks that don't match their top concerns. Using the Eisenhower Matrix builds good time management. The matrix provides a system for sorting tasks. It simplifies your to-do list, helps manage workload, and increases productivity, along with the feeling of achievement.

In summary, the Eisenhower Matrix is a boon for guiding you where to spend your time and effort. You'll align your task list with your aims, boost productivity, and reach higher success in work and personal life.

Eisenhower Matrix - How to Get the Best Results

The Eisenhower Matrix works best with a few tips. One, you could color-code tasks according to their importance. When you assign colors to tasks in each square, you create a color map of priorities. This lets you spot at a glance the big-ticket tasks to focus your time and energy on.

Another tip is to keep tasks in each square to a minimum. It's key not to overfill with dozens of tasks. Try for no more than 10 tasks per square. This is to make sure you keep sight of the top tasks. This method stops tasks from getting lost in the crowd and ensures tasks are done efficiently and to your satisfaction.

40's People can make separate task charts for work and life stuff. This way, they can handle time and aims better in all parts of their lives. It keeps things clear, focused, and helps with a good work-life balance.

But, to get the most out of the Eisenhower Chart, you have to drop stuff that's not needed. Not all tasks need your time and focus. By checking tasks for how urgent and important they are, people can find tasks to remove from their list. This makes more room and energy for tasks that really match their goals and top needs.

Chapter 14

Cultivating a
Growth Mindset

Welcome to Chapter 14 in this chapter, we will dive into the topic of having a growth mindset and how it can help transform your life, especially in your 40's when you might be reassessing your career, personal development, and future goals. The power of a growth mindset lies in its ability to turn obstacles into opportunities for success and growth.

A growth mindset is the belief that your abilities and intelligence can be developed through dedication, effort, and learning. It's about adopting the mentality that failures are learning experiences that'll get you closer to achieving your goals. A person with a growth mindset welcomes challenges because they know it expands their knowledge.

By developing a growth mindset, you'll become more resilient when faced with adversity. You'll approach setbacks with a positive attitude, which ultimately helps you learn from your mistakes rather than giving up because it's too hard. With a growth mindset, there's no telling what you can achieve. Your true potential will be unleashed once you unlock all these qualities.

We'll explore various aspects in this chapter such as embracing failures, overcoming the fear of failure, developing resilience, adapting to change, and building an environment around yourself that supports your goals. We'll provide strategies on maintaining this newfound perspective so that it stays ingrained in us for years to come.

So let's get started on this self-discovery journey together. Adopting a new perspective on life may seem tedious but if done right it can take us to new heights both personally and professionally.

The Power of Embracing Failure

In our quest for personal and professional development, accepting failure is key. Instead of viewing them as setbacks or signs of incompetence, we should see them as stepping stones toward success.

Each failure allows us to learn from our mistakes so that we grow stronger each time we fall. When we embrace failure, doors open up everywhere, showing us new opportunities and ways for transformation. But how do we shift from fearing failures to embracing them? It starts with accepting that failure is a natural part of the process. It doesn't mean we're not meant for success or are at a disadvantage compared to others. Failure is necessary; it's how we grow.

By accepting failures, we free ourselves up to take more risks in life. Trying new things and pushing past our comfort zones becomes easier because we know whatever happens, we'll always learn from them.

So embrace failures and all the power they hold in shaping your journey toward success. Rather than moping around and dwelling on them, remember that each failure brings you closer to greatness.

Overcoming Fear of Failure

In this section, we will talk about the common fear of failure and how it affects personal and professional growth. A lot of people avoid failure at all costs but fail to realize that it's the key to success. If we reframe failures as stepping stones for growth and learning experiences, then we can overcome our fear.

The first step is to change how you think about things. Instead of viewing them as a negative outcome, view them as an opportunity for growth and improvement. You can learn valuable lessons from your failures that will lead to your success in the future.

It's important not to take failures personally because they don't reflect on who you are or what you're capable of. Everyone fails in their lifetime, so just know that other people have gone through worse than you. Accepting that failures are part of the process allows us to become more adaptable, resilient, and resourceful.

One way you can overcome the fear of failure is by setting realistic expectations and goals. Putting all your focus on one goal will only make failure feel worse if you don't achieve it. Take smaller steps toward your ultimate goal so every small win feels like an achievement.

Building a network that supports your dreams is another effective strategy for overcoming fear of failure. Find mentors, coaches, or people who've gone through similar experiences as yours so they can provide guidance when needed.

To sum it all up, accepting failure is crucial in order to grow as a person professionally and personally. Look at things from a different perspective, set achievable goals, build supportive networks, then navigate through anything with resilience.

In addition to a support system, fostering resilience can be achieved by surrounding yourself with like-minded people who encourage growth and offer guidance during tough times. Building relationships with mentors, friends, and colleagues that share the same mindset can help you stay resilient, provide valuable insights, and offer support.

Developing a resilient mindset means embracing failure, staying positive, and building a network of supportive individuals. By focusing on personal development and learning from your missteps, you'll be able to go through anything knowing you have the strength to get back up and keep going.

How Being Adaptable Can Help You Grow

Growth is almost always about change. At one point or another in our lives, we've all heard some variation of this saying, but how many of us actually put those words into action? Whether it's in our professional or personal lives, being adaptable allows us to embrace new challenges more effectively than those around us.

With the way things are in today's world, being adaptable is crucial for growth. The moment we stop evolving is the moment we start losing opportunities. This is why cultivating an adaptable mindset is key.

When something unexpected happens or if we're met with a setback, it's easy to give up hope. But those who believe they will grow when faced with change quickly adapt and find new ways to achieve their goals. They view these challenges as learning experiences instead of shortcomings.

Having an adaptable mindset also helps individuals listen to feedback better. Instead of brushing off criticism, they take it to heart so they can learn from it and make improvements faster than before. When we don't allow ourselves to be fixed on certain ideas or beliefs, then our minds become more open, which will lead us toward success-especially when dealing with rapidly developing industries.

So at its core, adaptability means not fearing change but rather welcoming it so we can fully transform ourselves when given the chance.

The Importance of a Supportive Network

While adapting your mind's perspective is important, it won't mean much if you don't surround yourself with people who support you. Finding others who encourage growth and offer guidance is essential for anyone looking to develop a growth mindset.

When we have a supportive network, not only do we get the motivation to overcome obstacles, but we also have a place to share our stories, learn from their mistakes, and celebrate each other's achievements. This in itself already creates an environment where growth can thrive naturally.

Aside from simply being there for you when you need it, being surrounded by others who want to grow just as badly as you do will push you even further. You'll be more inclined to step out of your comfort zone knowing they'd be doing the same if they were in your position.

Building a network doesn't always have to be done through professional connections either. In fact, if anything, having personal relationships with friends and family that believe in your potential can play an even bigger role in nurturing your growth mindset. So make sure those around you encourage you to improve and embrace different challenges that come up along the way.

With enough time spent together struggling, failing, and winning as a group, building this type of network becomes effortless and second nature. The community will continuously work towards their own personal development while pushing everyone else forward too.

Strategies for Developing a Growth Mindset

Developing a growth mindset may seem daunting at first. However, with the right strategies and techniques in place, you'll be well on your way to adopting one. Here are some practical strategies and techniques to help you cultivate a growth mindset:

Embrace challenges

A key aspect of developing a growth mindset is embracing challenges as opportunities for growth. When you face these tests, take them as learning experiences rather than threats. Remember that failing is normal and can be turned into an advantage if you learn from it.

Reframe failure

Instead of letting failure hold you back, use it as motivation to improve and get better next time. Reflect on past failures and identify what went wrong so that you can make adjustments moving forward.

Cultivate a growth-oriented mindset

Success comes when intelligence and abilities are developed through effort and hard work. Understand that there is always room for improvement in anything that we do. So instead of being too focused on the end product, recognize the process of growth itself.

Practice self-reflection

Regularly reflect on your thoughts, emotions, and behaviors to identify whether or not they align with your goals in life. If they don't, identify why this may be the case so that you can change it accordingly.

Seek feedback

Feedback can sometimes make us feel attacked or even discouraged depending on how it's delivered; however, viewing it as constructive criticism will surely help us grow faster.

Set achievable goals:

Setting realistic goals will give us more purpose moving forward because we know that these goals are possible within our limits. Take your time with each step along the way towards reaching them.

Applying a Growth Mindset in Different Areas of Life

A growth mindset goes beyond personal development - It shows positive results across various areas such as relationships, careers, and personal development.

Relationships:

When tough situations arise between two people who have adopted a growth mindset, rather than avoiding conversations that may lead to arguments, the two people will be curious and willing to learn from one another. This focus on open communication, empathy, and adaptability is crucial for growth in a relationship.

Career:

A growth mindset can completely transform a career. It nurtures resilience, adaptability, and a craving for continuous improvement. People who embrace failures as learning opportunities are more likely to bounce back from setbacks and view them as stepping stones to success. They actively seek feedback, embrace challenges, and acquire new skills and knowledge to stay relevant in ever-changing professional landscapes.

Personal Development

When it comes to personal development, a growth mindset is the key to unlocking one's full potential. By embracing failures, individuals can view them as valuable learning experiences that provide valuable insights for self-improvement. This mindset allows for setting realistic goals, embracing challenges outside of one's comfort zone, and persisting in the face of obstacles. It encourages a continuous pursuit of growth and learning in all aspects of life.

By applying a growth mindset in these different areas of life, individuals can cultivate resilience, adaptability, and a passion for personal and professional growth. Embracing failures as valuable learning experiences and approaching challenges with curiosity and a desire to learn can lead to positive outcomes and a more fulfilling life.

Maintaining and Sustaining A Growth Mindset

To sustain this type of thinking, you need to believe that every failure is another step closer to success. You must also be able to recognize each setback's opportunity for learning and self-improvement.

Another crucial aspect is resilience, which can be gained by practicing self-compassion towards yourself when faced with challenges or failure. Instead of being discouraged by failure, think of it as motivation so you want to persevere until you make it work, even if you fail repeatedly along the way. Lastly, keep people around you who understand your goals or who share them because they will help motivate you on your journey towards self-improvement.

Chapter 15

Signature
Strengths and Skills

Welcome to Chapter 15 of our book, where we explore the power of your unique abilities in standing out from the crowd. In this chapter, we delve into the concept of signature strengths and skills and how utilizing them can unlock your full potential in various aspects of your life.

RephraseIt's no secret that everyone possesses their own set of talents and capabilities that differentiate them from others. We all have that certain something that makes us special and enables us to excel in certain areas. These unique abilities, when embraced and harnessed, can be the key to standing out in today's competitive world.

By consciously utilizing your strengths, you can make a remarkable impact in both personal and professional settings. Imagine the satisfaction of knowing you are fully leveraging your talents and making a meaningful contribution to your career, relationships, and personal growth.

This chapter will guide you through the process of understanding your unique abilities, unleashing your signature strengths, and leveraging them for success. We will explore how your strengths can pave the way for outstanding achievements in your career, help you build strong and genuine relationships, and foster personal growth.

Whether you are looking to shine in the workplace, create lasting connections with others, or simply become the best version of yourself, this chapter will provide practical strategies and insights to help you stand out by utilizing your unique abilities.

So, we're starting a self-exploration trip. Here, we'll learn about our key strengths and abilities. We'll learn to embrace our uniqueness, tackle hurdles, build our personal brand, and integrate our special skills into daily life. We'll unlock the strength to be exceptional, just inside us.

Grasping Your Distinctive Skills

To use your strengths effectively, know what makes you special. Your distinctive skills are vital to your identity- they make you different. These are your unique talents, your inherent skills, the aspects of your character that get you noticed.

Finding your unique abilities is step one towards tapping into your full potential. Doing so lets you use your strengths, to benefit yourself and positively influence different life areas. By knowing what makes you unique, you can improve self-awareness and gain the courage to embrace your individuality.

Detecting your unique abilities need self-reflection. Ask yourself what you're naturally good at. Consider the skills or talents you do easily and ones that bring satisfaction. Note down aspects others often value or admire about you. These findings will help you discover your unique abilities and realize why they make you distinctive.

Remember, everyone has their own set of unique abilities. It's not about comparing yourself to others or trying to be better than anyone else. It's about embracing what makes you special and using those strengths to create a positive impact. Understanding your unique abilities is key to unleashing your full potential and living a fulfilling, authentic life.

Unleashing Your Signature Strengths

Now that you have identified your unique abilities, it's time to unleash your signature strengths and utilize them to your advantage. Your signature strengths are the qualities that set you apart from others and can help you stand out in various areas of your life, including your career, relationships, and personal growth.

Utilizing your strengths allows you to tap into your full potential and achieve success. By harnessing these innate abilities, you can make a significant impact in your professional and personal endeavors.

In the workplace, your signature strengths can set you apart from your peers, making you an invaluable asset to your team and employers. Identify how your strengths align with your job responsibilities and find ways to utilize them in your daily tasks. This will not only make your work more fulfilling but also increase your productivity and efficiency.

When it comes to relationships, your signature strengths can help you foster deeper connections and create meaningful bonds with others. By being aware of your unique abilities, you can communicate and showcase them effectively, allowing others to appreciate and benefit from what you bring to the table.

The key to personal development is using your inherent skills effectively. When you use these unique strengths to tackle challenges and explore new opportunities, you can consistently grow and evolve into your best self.

Now, remember, everyone has their own blend of skills. It's crucial to acknowledge yours without comparing or doubting. Release your innate abilities. Stand above the rest. Make positive changes in every aspect of your life.

Use Your Strengths to Excel in Your Job

In the race for good jobs today, it's essential to stand apart. By using your strengths effectively, you can become a priceless resource at work and rise in your profession.

Communicate Your Unique Skills

One of the keys to using your strengths effectively is to convey your unique skills to your potential employers, co-workers, and customers. This means spotlighting your key abilities, showing them how your skills bring extra value to the company.

While updating your resume or CV, adjust it to highlight your strengths and successes. Clearly explain how your unique skills have brought results in your previous roles. Use measurable examples to validate your contributions.

Becoming Essential at Work

Beyond just showcasing those unique skills, it's crucial to become an indispensable part of your office team. This includes proactively seeing how your unique strengths can help your team or company excel. Volunteer for projects or tasks that align with your strengths. Offer your expertise and insights to help solve problems or improve processes. By consistently delivering high-quality work and making a positive impact, you demonstrate your value and become an indispensable member of the team.

Continuous Growth and Improvement

In addition to leveraging your existing strengths, it's essential to continuously grow and improve. Seek out opportunities for professional development and further enhance your unique abilities.

Stay informed about industry trends and developments. Attend conferences, workshops, or webinars that can broaden your skillset. Keep up with the latest technologies and tools that are relevant to your field. By continuously investing in your growth, you can stay ahead of the curve and maintain a competitive edge.

Building Strong Relationships

Networking and building strong relationships are also key components of leveraging your strengths for career success. Foster connections with colleagues, mentors, and industry professionals who can provide guidance, support, and opportunities for growth.

Take the initiative to connect with others, both in person and online. Engage in conversations, share your expertise, and offer assistance whenever possible. By cultivating a strong network, you increase your visibility and open doors to new possibilities.

Conclusion:

Leveraging your strengths for career success requires a strategic approach. By showcasing your unique abilities, becoming an invaluable asset, continuously growing, and building strong relationships, you can position yourself for long-term career growth and fulfillment.

Making a Difference in Personal Relationships

In personal relationships, being distinctive lays the groundwork for establishing robust ties and meaningful, enduring relationships. It's your unique skills that become vitally important in this context, enabling you to highlight your assets and express yourself effectively with others.

A critical part of making a difference in personal relationships is mastering the art of communication regarding your capabilities. Allocate some time to comprehend your distinct skills and understand their significance to your relationships. It could be your empathetic listening capacity, your knack for providing support, or even your ability to infuse humor; these traits can differentiate you and lead to stronger bonds.

Moreover, highlighting your capabilities in personal relationships goes a step further than just effective communication. It's about translating your distinct skills into everyday behaviors and engagements. For instance, if you are known for your excellent listening skills, dive headfirst into conversations, demonstrating undivided focus and sincere interest.

Nurturing these refined connections not only makes you stand out, but also adds to the richness and prolongation of your relationships. Utilizing your distinct skills leads to a nurturing, satisfying circle of friends, family, and the dear ones who value you for being you.

To sum up, making a difference in personal relationships implies effective communication and display of your distinct skills. In doing so, you develop resilient ties and create enduring bonds with people around you.

Nurturing Your Strengths for Personal Growth

Your unique abilities are like seeds waiting to be nurtured and cultivated for personal growth. By harnessing and utilizing your strengths, you have the power to overcome obstacles, embrace opportunities, and become the best version of yourself.

Personal growth is a lifelong journey that requires self-reflection and continuous development. Start by identifying your unique abilities and understanding how they contribute to your overall well-being and success.

Once you have recognized your strengths, focus on nurturing and honing them. Explore ways to apply your unique abilities in different areas of your life, whether it's in your career, relationships, or personal endeavors.

Overcoming Challenges:

Utilizing your strengths can be instrumental in overcoming challenges. When faced with difficulties, tap into your unique abilities to find innovative solutions and think outside the box.

Embrace your strengths and use them as sources of resilience and motivation. Leverage your skills and expertise to navigate obstacles with confidence, knowing that you have the tools to overcome any roadblock that comes your way.

Embracing Opportunities:

As you nurture your strengths, you'll notice new opportunities arising in your life. Recognize these moments as chances to grow and expand your horizons.

Embrace these opportunities and take calculated risks. Your unique abilities give you a competitive edge and can set you apart from others. By utilizing your strengths, you can strive for excellence and achieve success in areas aligned with your true passions and talents.

Becoming the Best Version of Yourself:

Nurturing your strengths is a personal journey of growth and self-discovery. It's about embracing who you are and using your unique abilities to create a meaningful and fulfilling life.

Take the time to reflect on your strengths and the areas where you want to grow. Set goals that align with your values and utilize your unique abilities to work towards them.

Remember, personal growth is a continuous process. Stay committed to nurturing your strengths and exploring new opportunities for development. Embrace the journey and celebrate the progress you make along the way.

By utilizing your strengths and nurturing your unique abilities, you can unlock your full potential and embark on a transformative path of personal growth. Start today and embrace the endless possibilities that await you.

Embracing Your Individuality

Embracing your individuality is essential when it comes to utilizing your unique abilities and standing out from the crowd. In a world that often encourages conformity, it takes courage and self-assurance to fully embrace your true self without fear or hesitation. But when you do, the rewards are remarkable.

By embracing your individuality, you tap into your unique strengths and talents that set you apart. You no longer feel the need to conform to societal expectations or compare yourself to others. Instead, you become confident in your abilities and are able to showcase them authentically.

Being unique helps you see things differently, solve problems creatively, and bring special skills to everything you do. Your uniqueness makes you shine and leaves a lasting mark.

When you're true to your unique self, you inspire others. You become a role model for those trying to find their voice. Your true self and bravery are rays of hope for people wanting to be true to themselves.

So, how do you be true to yourself? Start with looking within and accepting yourself. Discover your special skills and see your own strengths. Believe you have something good to give the world, and show your skills without fear.

When you fully accept your unique self, you'll see chances that match your true self. New paths, bonds, and success will follow. So, be true to yourself. The world is ready for your light.

Beating challenges and self-doubts

Using your strengths and being unique can be hard. Challenges and self-doubts can stop you from accepting your unique gifts and reaching your dreams.

There are ways to knock down problems and tap into your full might. Acknowledge the issues hindering you, and you're on the path to triumph and boosting your strengths.

Spot and Comprehend Problems

To beat hurdles, you must first recognize them. Think about the hang-ups dragging you down. Spotted any recurrent trends or self-defeating actions? Getting the base of these issues will let you craft focused combat strategies.

Fight Negative Mindsets

Negative mindsets can chain you down, keeping you from your full power. They usually sprout from past events or society's pressures. Fight and reshape these thoughts to open up brand new opportunities for growth.

Create Feasible Goals and Chunk Them

Forming feasible goals is key to outdoing setbacks and fully utilizing your strengths. Split your goals into bite-sized tasks and plan to tackle them step by step. This method keeps you alert, driven, and lets you advance despite struggles.

Pursue Help and Direction

Don't shy away from reaching out for help or guidance when grappling with hurdles and negative mindsets. Cultivate a network of supportive pals, guides, or experts who can cheer you on, advise you, and keep you accountable. Their viewpoints and experiences can offer fresh understanding and help you manage hurdles better.

Think of hurdles and limit beliefs as mere bumps, not mountains. Armed with the right tactics, outlook, and help, you can conquer these issues. Harness your rare strengths to make a mark. Enjoy personal growth's voyage and release your full capacity.

Building Your Own Personal Brand

Putting your one-of-a-kind talents on display and making a name for yourself involves personal branding. Your brand mirrors your person, standards, and distinct attributes.

To create an engaging personal brand, you must know your special talents and strengths. Spend moments identifying your uniqueness and how these traits can be beneficial to others.

Once you get a firm grip on your exclusive abilities, show and talk about them efficiently. Design a personal brand statement that tells everyone who you are and all you provide. This statement should be brief, catchy, and a genuine mirror of your strengths.

Uniformity is crucial in building a personal brand. Make sure your brand overlaps on all your digital and physical platforms, like your webpage, social media accounts, and professional networking sites. Stick to the same language, visual trademarks, and message to create a harmonious and widely recognised brand.

Ensure your personal brand mirrors your morals and interests. Expose your unique skills by sharing materials, anecdotes, and encounters that mirror your real persona. This honesty will attract fellow-minded people and possibilities that match your brand.

Personal branding is constant work. You frequently look at and polish your brand as you transform and mature. Stick with your true self while adjusting to new quests and trials.

Next, we dive into the value of crafting a valuable network that can boost your strengths and make you more remarkable.

Forming a Helpful Network

Making your strengths stand out isn't a solo job. Creating a helpful network greatly aids your quest for accomplishment. Engaging with those who respect and value your unique skills prompts new growth and potential paths.

Helpful networks give advice and aid, letting you face rough times with fearlessness. Connecting with people that align with your beliefs and goals encourages inclusion and friendship, sparking your drive and resolve.

Maximize the benefit of teamwork by interacting with people with abilities that complete yours. Team partnerships magnify your positives and make up for negatives, leading to joined wins greater than what you can achieve alone.

Establishing a Helpful Network
Use these tactics to construct a helpful network:
Go to trade meetings and happenings where you can encounter professionals who have similar desires and hobbies. Join online communities and forums related to your field of expertise. Engage in discussions and establish connections with like-minded individuals. Participate in networking events and meetups organized by professional organizations or local communities. These gatherings provide opportunities to build relationships face-to-face. Seek out mentors who can guide you based on their own experiences and expertise. Their insights and advice can be invaluable in your journey. Offer your support and expertise to others. Building a network is a two-way street, and contributing to the success of others helps foster strong and meaningful relationships. Utilize social media platforms to connect with professionals, join relevant groups, and share your insights and expertise.

Remember, building a supportive network is not about quantity but quality. Focus on cultivating genuine relationships based on mutual respect, shared values, and a common desire for growth. Your network should be a trusted circle of individuals who inspire, encourage, and uplift you, enabling you to utilize your strengths and stand out.

Integrating Your Signature Strengths in Everyday Life
Discover the power of integrating your unique abilities into your everyday life and watch as they naturally become a part of who you are and how you navigate the world. By utilizing your signature strengths, you can unlock your full potential and create a life that is aligned with your authentic self.

One practical tip for integrating your unique abilities is to consciously apply them in various situations. Whether it's problem-solving, communication, or decision-making, leverage your strengths to approach challenges and opportunities with confidence and creativity. This not only allows you to excel in different aspects of your life but also reinforces your sense of self and purpose.

Another strategy is to surround yourself with individuals who appreciate and support your unique abilities. Connect with like-minded individuals who value diversity and encourage you to embrace your strengths. By building a supportive network, you can gain valuable insights, collaborate on projects, and create opportunities to further develop and showcase your unique abilities.

Remember, the key to integrating your signature strengths is to be mindful and intentional in your daily life. Recognize moments where you can utilize your strengths and make a conscious effort to apply them. Over time, this will become second nature, allowing you to continuously grow and thrive in all aspects of your life.

Chapter 16

Spiritual
Exploration at Forty

Chapter 16 dives into spirituality. As you hit forty, you may wonder about spirituality's role in your life. This chapter, regardless of where you stand on the spiritual spectrum, will elucidate the correlation between spiritual principles, satisfaction in life, and various practices that can enrich your life and help you in your pursuit of enlightenment.

In Section 2, we dig into spiritual principles. This part helps you comprehend diverse belief systems and how they influence personal development and fulfilment.

When forty, the longing for inner fulfilment becomes potent. Section 3 puts this under the lens, sketching out various routes you can embark on to find happiness and purpose in life.

Next, Section 4 immerses us in methods for spiritual growth. Let's find out how practices like meditation, mindfulness, and yoga can boost your spiritual bond and aid self-exploration.

Mindfulness, a robust process enhancing spiritual consciousness and inner satisfaction, is what we discuss in Section 5. We will look at ways to weave mindfulness into everyday life and make the most out of it.

Lastly, Section 6 shines a light on meditation, another key method for spiritual advancement. Get to know diverse meditation strategies to pick the one that clicks and accentuates your spiritual journey.

Section 7 delves into yoga. This practice impacts body and soul deeply. We'll examine its physical and spiritual boons and various styles.

Section 8 deals with finding serenity in a hectic world. We'll explore rituals and thought changes to cultivate peace when life hits 40's turbulence.

Section 9 guides towards higher consciousness. We'll study practices for connecting with your 'higher self' and accessing universal knowledge.

Feeding your spiritual journey is Section 10's focus. We'll dip into self-care's importance, unity, and ongoing learning in deepening the spiritual bond.

In the last segment, Section 11, we invigorate you to grasp the thrill of spiritual voyage. Get advice, inspiration, and practical how-tos to navigate this life-changing experience at 40.

Keen to start an exceptional spiritual quest? Let's reveal the remarkable insights awaiting in the realms of spiritual beliefs, personal contentment, and practices.

Spiritual Beliefs Deciphered

Spiritual beliefs heavily affect personal growth and satisfaction. They mould our interpretation of the world and determine our role in it.

Diving into spiritual beliefs, we can find a deeper purpose in life. This journey helps us understand ourselves better, changing us profoundly.

People follow various beliefs. Some choose religions like Christianity, Islam, Hinduism, and Buddhism. Others may choose modern practices like New Age, mindfulness, or energy healing. The choices are vast!

Each belief has unique rituals and philosophies to help personal growth. Studying such beliefs gives us a wider view of human life. We discover new possibilities!

How Spiritual Beliefs Shape Us

Spiritual beliefs affect our daily life. They mold our values, relationships, and decisions. By embracing our spirituality, we feel more interconnected, compassionate, and grateful.

During hardships, spiritual beliefs give comfort and strength. They make us ponder about life, existence, and our own consciousness.

Understanding various spiritual beliefs teaches us to value human diversity. It encourages acceptance, empathy, and unity. It blends the barriers that separate us.

Learning about spiritual beliefs can push for personal improvement, satisfaction, and a purposeful life. We can broaden our views, take in new opportunities and realize our boundless potential.

Understanding Personal Satisfaction

Join the search for personal satisfaction. Uncover different routes to joy and purpose. In our busy world, personal satisfaction is a goal for many, who want a life rich in meaning.

Personal satisfaction means matching your actions, beliefs, and objectives with your deepest wants. This grants a strong feeling of happiness. It's more than just physical success. It focuses on complete mental, physical and spiritual well-being.

Several methods can help in your journey to personal satisfaction. Some of these include reflecting on yourself, setting important goals, feeling grateful, improving relationships, and doing activities that bring pleasure.

Examining yourself and thinking deeply play a big role in personal satisfaction. Take time to learn about your thoughts, feelings, and wishes. This helps you lead a life true to yourself. You can journal, meditate, or talk to a life coach.

Meaningful goals that match your beliefs and dreams give you direction. It could be a personal project or improving your health, or growing spiritually. Clear, reachable goals will motivate you in your journey.

Cultivating gratitude for the present moment and all that you have can significantly enhance personal fulfilment. Being appreciative of the small joys in life, practicing mindfulness, and regularly expressing gratitude to yourself and others can shift your focus towards positivity and contentment.

Nurturing relationships with loved ones and creating a supportive network of like-minded individuals can help you feel connected and fulfilled. Surrounding yourself with positive and inspiring individuals who share your values and aspirations will not only bring joy but also provide a sense of belonging and support as you navigate your personal journey.

Engaging in activities that bring you joy and fulfilment is crucial for personal growth and satisfaction. This can include hobbies, creative pursuits, physical exercise, volunteering, or contributing to causes that resonate with your values. Taking time for self-care and pursuing activities that nurture your passions will replenish your energy and bring you closer to personal fulfilment.

By exploring personal fulfilment and incorporating these practices and techniques into your life, you can unlock a deeper sense of purpose, happiness, and contentment. Remember, the path to personal fulfilment is unique to each individual, and it's important to listen to your inner voice and follow your own journey.

Practices for Spiritual Growth

Embarking on a journey of spiritual growth and self-discovery requires dedication and the incorporation of various practices into your daily life. These practices can help you connect with the spiritual realm and enhance your overall well-being. Let's explore some powerful techniques that can support your spiritual journey.

Meditate: Find Peace Within

Ever sit quietly and just breathe? That's meditation. It lets you calm your mind and find a silent spot within you. By focusing on your breath, peace comes. Practice regularly to grow your spiritual side, learn more about yourself, and boost your emotional wellbeing.

Be Mindful: Now is All You Have

Being entirely in the moment is mindfulness. It lets you appreciate life more deeply. Engage fully in every moment, and you'll find gratitude. It'll make you feel more connected with the world. Make it a daily practice, and it can boost your spiritual life and fill your days with more peace and joy.

Yoga: Sync Your Body, Mind, and Spirit

Yoga is more than exercise; it's a mind-body-and-spirit practice. It combines physical poses with deep breathing and meditation to make you stronger, more flexible, and balanced. It releases tension and aids in achieving inner harmony. Practice yoga regularly to boost your physical health and deepen your spiritual connection.

Note-Keeping: Examination and Recognizing Self

Note-keeping is a great habit for personal examination and recognizing oneself. Penning down your feelings, ideas, and happenings helps to unravel mysteries of your soul, probe your psyche's core. Note-keeping aids in sorting your notions and feelings, clarifies any puzzling thoughts, and exposes recurring mind-sets or impressions that might obstruct growth. It also comes handy for setting goals, positive statements, and for cherishing thankfulness on your inner journey.

This introduction to soul-enriching habits only plows the field for your transformative journey. Embed these methods in your day-to-day life and try out more practices to broaden your spiritual bond, enhance self-recognition, and nurture individual and spiritual expansion. Keep your mind open and let these habits steer your course towards a satisfying and purposeful life.

Significance of Mindfulness

Witness the amazing influence of mindfulness in fostering spiritual consciousness and individual satisfaction. Being mindful is all about being absorbed entirely into the current scenario, without forming any preconceived notions. Practicing mindfulness brings you closer to your inner being and the world you are part of.

Make mindfulness an integral part of your everyday life with easy methods like focused breathing, full body contemplation, and conscious eating. These will assist in silencing your chattering mind, enabling you to observe your thoughts and feelings better, and guide you towards tranquility and mental clearness.

Studies have shown that mindfulness can have numerous benefits for both physical and mental well-being. It has been found to reduce stress, anxiety, and depression, improve sleep quality, enhance focus and concentration, and increase overall happiness and life satisfaction.

By embracing mindfulness, you can embark on a journey of self-discovery and inner growth. It allows you to let go of the past and future, and fully embrace the present moment. Through mindfulness, you can develop a deeper understanding of yourself, your feelings, and your relationship with the world.

Start incorporating mindfulness into your daily routine today and experience the profound impact it can have on your spiritual journey and personal fulfillment.

Embracing Meditation

Discover the transformative power of meditation and unlock new depths in your spiritual journey. Meditation has been practiced for centuries and is renowned for its ability to cultivate inner peace, clarity, and spiritual growth. By incorporating meditation into your daily routine, you can embark on a profound exploration of the self and connect with the divine.

Meditation offers a multitude of techniques, allowing you to find the one that resonates with you. Whether it's focused attention, loving-kindness, or transcendental meditation, each technique offers unique benefits and insights. Through regular practice, you can experience decreased stress levels, improved concentration, and heightened self-awareness.

Starting with meditation? Find a quiet, cozy place. Sit or lay down, close your eyes. Breathe deep. Let your body relax. Clear your mind, keep your thoughts on your breathing or on a particular phrase. Got wandering thoughts? Don't fret. Remember, meditation helps to centre your thoughts and foster inner quietness. Keep at it and you'll find peace and clarity, making everyday life smoother.

Once you're comfy with meditating, try out guided versions. These have soft instructions and pictures to draw you deeper. You could focus on feeling grounded, thankful, or work on aligning your energy centers. This will boost your spiritual bonding and personal development.

To fully enjoy the perks of meditating, stick to a regular schedule. Start small. Make each session longer as you get used to it. Doing it every day is key, so choose to meditate each day, feeding your spirit.

Yoga: Good for Body and Soul

Yoga does more than simple exercise. It's a practice with deep changes that are good for your body and soul. By controlling your breath, meditating, and using physical positions, yoga helps create a pleasant balance between mind, body, and spirit.

Regular yoga can boost flexibility, make you stronger, and improve your overall physical health. With different poses and routines, yoga can improve how you stand, increase your muscles, and promote better body understanding.

Yoga does more than just stretching and strength-building. It also promotes mental well-being through the incorporation of mindfulness and meditation. At its core, yoga is about finding inner tranquillity and connecting with the spiritual self.

Different yoga styles exist, each unique in their way. Vinyasa has a dynamic flow, Iyengar emphasizes perfect alignment, and Yin is all about relaxation. Regardless of your interests, there's a yoga style that'll suit you.

Yoga is not just exercise; it's an exploration of the self. It encourages kindness to oneself, accepting imperfections, and living consciously. Be regular with yoga, and you'll find it helps in being resilient, reducing stress, and instilling tranquillity.

Seeking something that covers physical fitness and spiritual growth? Try Yoga. Witness first-hand the transformative ability of this age-old practice and embark on an enriching journey.

Pursuing Tranquility

The forties can be taxing with numerous challenges and duties, leading to stress and disorder. Amid this, it's crucial not to lose sight of achieving tranquility. Inner peace, stemming from within, helps maintain balance and harmony in life.

Finding inner peace might seem complex, but daily actions, like small steps, can guide us. In stormy times, they can anchor us in calmness.

Mindfulness: A Powerful Tool

A key to inner peace is mindfulness. It's about being present, not judging the now. With this mindset, you let go of past and future worries, focusing on the present's peace and beauty.

Mindfulness can be as easy as breathing exercises, meditation, or mindful walking. With these, you connect deeper with yourself and the world, promoting inner calmness.

The Joy in Gratitude

Another ritual is gratitude. Each day, pause and appreciate what you're thankful for. This act can transform your worldview, bringing peace. It could be a kind act, a sunset, or loved ones' support. Recognizing these blessings helps find peace, even when times are tough.

Try a gratitude journal. Jot down what you appreciate regularly. This gentle practice reminds you of life's joy and abundance, helping cultivate inner peace.

How a Cheerful Mindset Helps

A cheerful mindset is key for inner peace. How? Stay positive and focus on now. This lets you tackle tough spots while staying peaceful.

Use uplifting thoughts and choose positive affirmations. Set aside self-doubt and embrace self-kindness and thankfulness. Celebrate wins, and forget about shortages. With a cheerful mindset, you can maintain inner calm.

It's a journey to find inner peace. It's hard work but worth it. Explore strategies that work for you. Remember, everyone's path can vary. Prioritize inner peace. Then, you can take on life's ups and downs with ease and stillness, leading to deep satisfaction and balance.

Reaching Out to Greater Consciousness

Set off on a rich journey of self-learning with the idea of greater consciousness. What's that? It's a heightened sense of awareness and a connection to the cosmos.

By diving into greater consciousness, you can uncover hidden talents and clear some of life's big questions. This spiritual enlightenment aids spiritual expansion and personal joy.

There are multiple paths to engage with your greater self and tap into cosmic wisdom. Why not try meditation? It's a strong way to calm the mind, find inner peace, and link the physical and spiritual spheres. Regular meditation lets you achieve a state of greater consciousness and pull useful advice and direction from within.

Expanding Awareness Through Mindfulness

Mindfulness is another practice that can aid in connecting with higher consciousness. By being fully present in the moment, you can develop a heightened sense of awareness and atonement to the divine presence. Mindfulness practices such as conscious breathing, body scans, and mindful movement can help you cultivate this level of consciousness in your daily life.

Additionally, exploring ancient wisdom traditions, such as yoga and contemplative practices, can provide pathways to higher consciousness. The integration of breath, movement, and intention in yoga can facilitate a deeper connection to the self and the universal energy. It can also support the expansion of consciousness and spiritual growth.

By embracing these practices and committing to your spiritual journey, you can forge a profound connection with higher consciousness. This connection can grant you invaluable insights, inner peace, and a sense of purpose that goes beyond the material realm. Open your heart and mind to the infinite possibilities that await as you embark on this transformative path.

Nurturing Your Spiritual Journey

Once you embark on your spiritual journey, it is essential to nurture and sustain it over time. Your spiritual journey is a lifelong process of growth, self-discovery, and transformation. To deepen your connection to spirituality and continue progressing, there are a few key elements to consider.

Taking Care of Yourself:

To foster your spiritual growth, self-care is key. Choose activities like meditating, writing, or outdoor time that speak to you. Do what refreshes your mind, body, and spirit. This helps you balance and feel good as you delve into spirituality.

Finding Your Tribe:

A supportive circle can boost your spiritual growth. Find those who align with your beliefs and passions. Do group stuff, go to spiritual meet-ups, or chat online with folks walking a similar path. It's a two-way street: exchanges of thoughts, learning and support help you gain insights and stay encouraged.

Never-ending Learning:

Always look for more knowledge and wisdom to broaden your spiritual outlook. Keep learning through reading, workshops, seminars, and diverse spiritual ideas. Stay open. Let new perspectives add to your spiritual beliefs and practices. A curious and open mind aids your spiritual growth.

To nurture your spiritual journey, you need commitment, introspection, and an unshakeable will for personal development. With self-care, a supportive tribe, and ongoing learning, you can attain a deep, rewarding spiritual bond that will guide your life.

Discovering the Spiritual

Diving into spiritual exploration, you'll embark on an adventure filled with discovery at forty. The potential rewards? Jaw-dropping insights and a fulfilled life. If you're curious about varied religions, eyeing self-improvement, or longing for a stronger bond with your higher self, spirituality can be your guide.

Such exploration can send inspiration, guidance, and handy tips your way. You'll probe the essence of your soul, face the uncharted bravely, and see the wealth spiritual rituals and beliefs give. It's more than outside routines. It lets you forge a bond with your inner wisdom, revealing your actual calling.

As you dive into this life change, note the wealth of resources to boost your spiritual growth. Old knowledge and new methods, an impressive range. Practices like meditation, mindfulness, and yoga can help forge a stronger spiritual tie. Connect with people of similar perceptions. Let mentors with experience guide and support you in your journey.

Going deeper into spiritual exploration requires readiness for a path filled with self-recognition, personal development, and awe-inspiring connection moments. Embrace this forty-year-old voyage. Allow it to steer you toward a life filled with purpose and spiritual consciousness.

Chapter 17

Visionary Goal Planning

Welcome to Chapter 17 on creating ambitious goals and creating a roadmap for the second half of life. In this chapter, we will explore the process of setting ambitious goals and crafting a strategic roadmap to guide you towards your vision.

Defining Ambitious Goals

Setting big goals is the first step towards creating a fulfilling and purpose-driven life in the second half. It's important to make sure these goals align with your desires.

Your vision is your hope, dream and aspirations. It'll help keep you motivated in tough times. So take time to think it through and envision what that would look like.

Alongside your vision, define the purpose that drives you. What meaningful impact do you want to make in the world? What legacy do you wish to leave behind? Understanding your purpose will fuel your motivation and infuse your goals with deeper meaning.

When defining these big goals think about what parts of your life are most important - career, relationships, health, personal growth or an interest. Reflect on what you want to achieve and how different areas align with each other.

First things first, break them down into smaller steps that can be completed along the way. Achieving small victories consistently will not only keep spirits high but also show progress.

Crafting your Roadmap

To reach any goal regardless of size having a plan is crucial for staying on track and achieving success. By breaking it down into manageable actions it'll relieve stress which derives from being overwhelmed by impossible tasks.

Start off by breaking down those big scary milestones into individual steps. This will allow for continual check ins throughout the journey rather than waiting till the end.

Find ways to measure progress such as checkpoints or markers along the way that'll provide a sense of accomplishment when reached.

Identify the Steps Involved

Very similar to breaking your overall goal into smaller pieces identify key steps necessary to reach each checkpoint. Each one should have their own clear objective otherwise things get blurred.

Once those steps are defined break them down even further into small tasks that can be assigned to a specific time and date. Doing so will build the roadmap you need to stay on track throughout the entire journey.

Establish Measurable Milestones

Next up is defining the milestones that signify progress and achievement. The great thing about these is that they're measurable allowing for improved progress tracking. If possible set specific targets or outcomes that can be measured along the way.

Consistently Review and Adjust

As you move along, it is crucial to continuously review and adjust your roadmap. Life has a way of throwing unexpected twists and turns and your roadmap should be able to twist with it. Allow changes in circumstances or priorities so that you can reach your destination smoothly.

Regularly assess yourself on your path to success. Make sure that you are still aligned with the goals and vision you had earlier. This is very important as it increases the chances of success while keeping you relevant too.

Building a roadmap isn't something you do once, rather it's an ongoing process. As time goes by, there will be new opportunities for insight that will require modifications to your plan. When this happens, don't panic! Embrace the process and remain open to making adjustments.

Evaluating Your Resources

In order to succeed in something, understanding available resources is key. Take some time off from actually doing things to assess your skills, network, support system etc.... Once you've gotten a good idea of them, start leveraging them on your journey.

Focus on Your Skills First

Start off by evaluating the skillset that you currently have available. Recognize areas where you excel in so that these skills can contribute towards your progress.

Once identified though don't stop there! Be open to developing new skills if they enhance what you already have. One thing people tend not to understand is that learning opportunities come from everywhere at any time! Embrace this growth mindset so that knowledge expands exponentially!

Building Out Your Network

Throughout life we're constantly building out our connections with others but how many do we truly pay attention too? Assess who within these professional connections can offer guidance when needed or even collaboration opportunities!

One thing is for certain however, no matter how much we try we cannot know everyone that exists in this world! So attend events outside of work or join organizations/online communities where like-minded people hangout instead. Building relationships with these individuals can offer a fresh perspective, open doors to new opportunities or even provide the support you need to stay motivated.

Leverage Your Support System

Having a good support system is key towards achieving ambitious goals. Assess the people in your life who genuinely believe in you and are willing to provide emotional support, encouragement or just hold you accountable.

Communicate your aspirations to this group of people, explaining how they can help your journey. Their ability to lend a helping hand at any time will be more than enough for when things get tough.

This covers everything from skills, network and even the people around you that will keep pushing you forward.

Overcoming Obstacles

Embarking on journeys like these is exhilarating but I won't lie… obstacles aren't far away. But despite what most think, they are not roadblocks! Instead think of them as growth opportunities if anything. There's nothing in this world you won't be able to pass once proper strategies, mindset and resilience kicks in! Just know that with every challenge comes an opportunity to learn! You just have to find it.

Resilience is key when facing obstacles head-on. It's the ability to bounce back from setbacks and adapt when unexpected roadblocks come into play. So, remember that whenever challenges come up…

They're temporary and can be navigated.

When faced with certain situations take a moment before acting and assess things properly first. Then by keeping focused on goals while maintaining a positive mindset creative solutions should come out faster than ever before!

An essential way to overcome obstacles is by breaking them into smaller pieces. Instead of getting overwhelmed by how large the problem is, focus on the current steps you need to take. This will let you make some progress and help build confidence.

Building a Support Network

Another key part to overcoming any obstacle is to surround yourself with people who believe in your vision. These people can guide, encourage and assist you when needed. They'll give different perspectives that might help solve your problem, and offer valuable insights that could make everything easier.

Moreover, it's essential to foster a mindset of continuous learning. Embrace the lessons learned from obstacles and use them as opportunities for personal and professional growth. Each challenge provides a chance to enhance your skills, broaden your knowledge, and become even more resilient in the face of future hurdles. Keep an open mind and seek opportunities to develop new skills and acquire additional knowledge that will serve you in conquering obstacles.

Remember, obstacles are just part of the journey towards your ambitious goals. Embrace them as opportunities for growth, and maintain your resilience, determined to overcome any challenge that comes your way. Keep pushing forward, and the rewards will be even more satisfying when you triumph over the obstacles that once stood in your path.

Embracing Personal Growth

Journeying into the second half of life presents a unique opportunity for personal growth and self-discovery. It's a time to explore new passions, uncover hidden talents, and redefine your sense of purpose. Embracing personal growth becomes essential as you work towards your ambitious goals, providing the foundation for continuous learning and development.

Self-discovery is a vital aspect of personal growth since it lets you understand yourself better; values strengths areas for improvement anything about yourself really or maybe not everything but close enough don't always need another sentence. Take time outta each day or week depending on how much time you have reflecting so you can gain insight into true desires.

Continuous learning is another key component of personal growth. It ensures that you stay adaptable and open to new ideas and possibilities. Seek out educational opportunities, whether it be through formal courses, workshops, or self-study. Expand your horizons by exploring different subjects and disciplines, and challenge yourself to step outside of your comfort zone.

As you embrace personal growth, remember that this journey is unique to you. Don't compare your progress to others or feel pressured to conform to societal expectations. Instead, focus on your own growth and celebrate small victories along the way.

Balancing Priorities

When pursuing ambitious goals, it becomes crucial to find a balance among multiple priorities. Effective time management techniques and strategies for maintaining a healthy work-life balance play a significant role in achieving this equilibrium.

Prioritizing tasks is the foundation of effective time management. By identifying and focusing on the most important activities, you can maximize your productivity and make progress towards your goals. It is essential to evaluate the urgency and importance of each task and allocate time accordingly

Creating a schedule and an organized list of things to do helps you stay on track. If you set realistic deadlines and break bigger tasks into small, manageable steps you're sure to make progress. And not only will you make progress but you can reduce the amount of stress that comes with it.

It's super important to find balance between work and personal life when trying to reach your goals. Otherwise there could be a risk of burning out way too early. Clearly defining what times are meant for work and what times are meant for personal needs is key to striking this balance.

And don't forget about self care! It's easy to get caught up in your busy life but taking time for yourself is very important. Spending quality time with loved ones or even just practicing mindfulness all contribute to success as well as overall happiness.

Reassessing and celebrating

You've reached some milestones already but have you stopped to look back at them? Celebrating these milestones serve as motivation and reinforcement for yourself. They give you a sense of accomplishment that keeps pushing forward.

With every milestone comes rewards as well. You should set some type of reward system up so that when achieving something big or small, they're celebrated in some way shape or form. These rewards can really be anything from eating at your favorite restaurant after completing a project or maybe just taking a moment for relaxation!

Celebrate these milestones with others too! Friends, family, co workers or people who understand your goals all appreciate when their achievements are recognized by someone else.

Evaluating your progress is crucial to accomplishing these goals you have once set. Monitoring your development, self-reflection, and making the necessary adjustments along the way will help ensure success.

Monitoring your progress helps measure how far you've come and allows you to notice weak points in your journey. Keep track of specifics milestones and accomplish one after another. You should find a way that works best for you personally. Whether it's through journaling, using tracking apps, or visually seeing a chart that shows progress so far.

Self-reflection provides an understanding of what strengths were used during certain tasks and identifying weaknesses that need improvements. Understanding yourself more will help make better decisions by knowing what does and doesn't work in certain situations.

Roadmaps always change as time goes on because goals and circumstances may evolve over time. Knowing this, expect to adjust accordingly when the time comes for necessary changes. Always stay flexible in achieving things in different ways if needed be. By doing so, lessons will continuously be learned with every adjustment made that'll bring you closer to achieving ultimate aspirations.

To conclude all this information into simple categories: Tracking progress, self-reflection, and adjusting are key components of any evaluation made towards ones progression.

Chapter 18

Building Your
Personal Brand

Welcome to Chapter 18: Building Your Personal Brand. In the digital age, a strong personal brand is key to success. Whether you're an entrepreneur, professional looking to take the next step, or striving to stand out in a competitive job market, it can be what makes all the difference.

In this chapter we'll delve into the importance of building a personal brand. We'll provide strategies that will boost your online presence and strengthen your networking skills. Here's what we'll go over:

Discovering and defining your unique value proposition.

Showcasing expertise through various channels.

Networking both on and offline.

Adapting your personal brand across different industries and professions.

And more!

Through these valuable insights and practical tips you'll learn how to measure the success of your personal brand in today's fast paced landscape! Let's start building for lasting success.

Defining Personal Branding

To professionals aiming to make themselves known in today's marketplace, having a personal brand has become crucial. But what exactly is it? A personal brand is made up of combinations of skills, experiences, and qualities that define who you are and how others perceive you. It's something that lets people know why they should trust you as an expert in whatever field you're in.

Now communicating just skills isn't enough when branding yourself personally. It takes intentionally shaping how you want people to see you by proactively managing your professional reputation. With a good one opportunity start coming towards you instead of being chased after.

The first steps of strategically creating this image are positioning yourself as a thought leader or influencer so that creating connections becomes easier.

So whether it be entrepreneurs, freelancers or working professionals:

YOU NEED TO BUILD YOUR BRAND AND START NURTURING IT!

Identifying Your Unique Value Proposition

Knowing what sets you apart from competition is extremely important when building a strong personal brand. This proposition defines two things:

1.- What you offer your audience or industry.

2.- How you're different from the competition.

Now how do you go about identifying it? Reflecting on your skills, experiences, and passions is a great way. What makes you stand out? What are your key strengths and areas of expertise? Think about what you excel at and what separates you from others in the field.

Whether it's through co-workers, mentors, or clients, another helpful way to get feedback is by asking them what they value about your work. You can also ask how they perceive your brand. These insights can be valuable and provide deeper understanding of your strengths.

Once you know about your unique value, make sure to weave it into personal branding efforts. Just as we talked about earlier with being genuine and relatable. And any chance where you need to write something that promotes yourself in some way is a good chance for this. Resume? Check! Online profiles? Check!

Remember, always think back on what you want people to feel when they hear your name or see anything from you. That will give the proper direction in everything you do.

Showing Your Expertise

Being an expert is only half the battle if no one knows about it. Once you've got your unique value proposition figured out, it's time to let others know too.

One of the strongest ways is showcasing expertise through different channels like:

Blogs: Start one yourself or contribute as a guest writer if that isn't feasible.

Social media: Share industry related things and answer questions from followers when you can.

Online portfolios: Build up a portfolio with past projects and achievements.

By consistently creating high quality stuff across all these channels, you'll gain credibility and start attracting people who are genuinely interested in what you have to say.

Building Trust with Your Story

The story of your personal brand has lot more power than many seem to realize. The right story will help create an emotional connection with others that makes them believe in what your brand stands for.

A few things to think about when crafting that story:

Know who's listening: Understand who exactly will be hearing this story so it can resonate stronger with them

Be real: Only share experiences that actually happened so there's authenticity behind everything

Stick out from others: Figure out why someone should use/buy from/subscribe to you. And emphasize it in your story.

Make people feel something: The best way to connect with someone is by making them feel some type of emotion. So use storytelling techniques that can make this happen.

Short and Sweet

Tell your story and be memorable. Make it easy to read, but have impact. Use vivid imagery, metaphors or anecdotes to make an impression.

It might take you a while and some effort to craft a compelling personal brand story. But if you do it right, your brand could attract loyal followers, opportunities and success.

Online Presence

In today's world having a strong online presence is key for your personal brand. It allows people to see your skills, expertise and unique value proposition on a wide scale. In this section we will look at strategies that can help optimize your online presence as well as create lasting impressions.

1. Get a better website:

Your personal website is like an online portfolio. Make sure it reflects who you are. People may not know what you look like in person so make sure the site showcases achievements as well as provides valuable content visitors want to see. Optimize everything so search engines can find keywords too.

2.Use social media platforms:

Social media gives you access to people in your industry as well as others that can benefit from what you provide knowledge-wise. Choose platforms where potential customers are active then start creating engaging stuff.

3.Clean up your act:

Monitor yourself on the internet regularly by searching yourself up on the web when you're free (or pay someone to do it). Responding professionally is important because sometimes people can be harsh in comments left behind when they're anonymous or with false names.Building a positive online presence comes from sharing valuable insights with others as well as collaborating with other professionals in the same field

Build Your Network

When you're building a personal brand, networking is essential. Connecting with others and building relationships can open doors to professional growth and new opportunities.

But when it comes to networking, there's a fine line between being strategic and just collecting contacts. Start by identifying key people or groups in your industry who you want to connect with. This could include potential mentors, industry leaders, or colleagues who share your interests.

Expand Online

LinkedIn and other social media platforms are ideal for expanding your network online. Create strong profiles that reflect the work you've done and the skills you bring to the table. Then engage with others by commenting on their posts, joining relevant groups, asking smart questions, and sharing valuable content.

Get Out There

While most of us have gotten used to connecting with professionals virtually over the past year, there's no replacement for in-person networking events. If you're attending an industry conference or hosting a meetup of local professionals soon, be prepared with business cards and a clear elevator pitch.

And remember: Networking isn't about what someone else can do for you - it's about forming meaningful connections that'll mutually benefit both parties. Approach every conversation as a chance to learn more about someone instead of immediately asking for favors or introductions.

If meeting professionals in person is too intimidating or not an option right now due to COVID-19 protocols, consider seeking workplace discovery sessions at different companies so that you can learn from their experiences without having any pressure on yourself.

Join online communities or forums that are in your field and engage with people there. This way you can form connections while also learning from others. This will make it easier to build a network for yourself.

Don't underestimate the power of social media either. Platforms like Twitter and Instagram can be a gold mine for networking opportunities. Commenting on other people's posts or sharing useful content can help you get noticed by the right people.

To wrap it all up, we need to realize how important effective networking is if we want to succeed with personal branding. By meeting new people, making meaningful relationships, and using online tools at our disposal, we open more doors and improve our chances of hitting that dream job.

Leverage Personal Branding for Career Growth

Your personal brand heavily influences your career growth. It's all about standing out in today's competitive market.

Building one starts by understanding what makes you special compared to everyone else in the industry. Once you understand this, effectively communicating it to potential employers becomes much easier. To get even deeper into it, showcasing your expertise and creating a compelling story is key.

If done right, this powerful narrative will resonate deeply with anyone who sees it.

The next step is leveraging your online presence which is probably the most important part of this process. A personal website lets visitors see what skills you have and what work experience you have under your belt before they ever talk to you directly.

Social media on the other hand opens up so many doors because everyone uses at least one platform now days.

Networking should never be underrated either as building connections both on and offline can be a massive step forward for career growth too.

Lastly, don't stay static with this process. Keep refining everything as often as possible or when trends start pointing toward new directions in order to stay relevant.

Mastering Versatility

When you're able to adapt your personal brand to different industries, you'll be a force to reckon with. You have the power to show off your skills, expertise, and achievements in ways that will draw people in. If you can highlight experiences that are transferable from one industry to another, it won't matter where you go or what a professional setting looks like - you'll still be of value.

The Power of Case Studies

We all know that credibility and authority are things others look for when working with someone new. One effective way to gain just those two things is by showcasing case studies relevant to an industry. Examples of how your expertise has made a positive impact in such settings will go a long way. Being able to apply skills across different contexts shows great versatility.

Cross-industry Networking

Building connections with people is always important. But it becomes even more crucial when trying to build a personal brand across various industries. By attending events specific to each industry, joining professional associations, and connecting with influencers and experts in them, you'll create valuable partnerships and connections everywhere.

Continuous Learning & Adaptation

Being open-minded enough to learn new things every single day is how you stay ahead of everyone around you. And it's this same skill that'll allow you to build a personal brand across multiple industries too. No matter what changes occur in an industry - trends, technologies or best practices - staying updated on them all is essential for success.

In the next section we'll discuss why measuring success is so vital and how data can help refine branding strategies as well as uncover new ones.

Understanding the effectiveness of your personal brand strategies is essential for recognizing the impact of your initiatives and making knowledgeable adjustments to refine and amplify your approach. By concentrating on critical metrics, you're equipped to uncover insights about how well your personal brand connects with your audience and pinpoint areas for enhancement.

A key metric to monitor is your digital footprint and audience interaction. Pay attention to the traffic your personal website garners, the growth in your social media followers, and the engagement levels (such as likes, comments, shares) your posts attract. These indicators are valuable for assessing the exposure and influence of your personal brand.

The expansion of your professional network is another vital aspect to track. Given the significant role networking plays in personal branding, observing both the quantity and quality of your new connections is important. Strive to broaden your network within your field and cultivate relationships with key influencers to augment your visibility and opportunities.

Moreover, the effect of your personal branding on career advancement should not be overlooked. Document any new career prospects, including job propositions, speaking engagements, or partnerships, that emerge thanks to your personal branding efforts. These instances are tangible proof of your personal brand's value and recognition.

Consistently review and interpret these metrics to confirm your personal brand aligns with your objectives and resonates with your intended audience. Utilize data to inform your strategy adjustments, ensuring continuous development of a potent and impactful personal brand.

Continuous Personal Brand Refinement

Developing a personal brand is a continuous endeavor, necessitating regular review and adaptation to maintain relevance in a competitive environment. This section delivers insights on evaluating the efficiency of your personal brand and implementing necessary changes to remain pertinent.

Initially, dedicate time to introspect about your current personal brand and its influence on your professional image. Assess whether your online persona and networking activities reflect your aspirations accurately. Question if you are effectively conveying your unique value and utilizing appropriate platforms to highlight your skills.

Further, scrutinize the feedback and engagement from your target demographic. Focus on their perception of your personal brand and seek areas for refinement. This may involve tweaking your brand narrative, altering your communication strategy, or exploring fresh networking avenues.

As you accumulate feedback, be prepared to adapt your personal brand strategy. Embrace emerging technologies and trends to bolster your online visibility and attract a broader audience. Continually aim to widen your network and interact with professionals who share your interests, encouraging significant connections and collaborative ventures.

Chapter 19:

Volunteering and
Giving Back

Welcome to Chapter 19, where we explore the joys of altruism and the importance of contributing to society. In this chapter, we delve into the world of volunteering and how it can bring fulfillment to both individuals and the communities they serve. Through impactful acts of kindness, we can make a positive difference in the world and experience a deep sense of purpose.

Understanding Altruism

In today's society, the concept of altruism plays a vital role in fostering a sense of empathy and creating a stronger community. Altruism, the selfless concern for the well-being of others, is a powerful force that drives individuals to contribute positively to society.

At its core, altruism involves acts of kindness and compassion without any expectation of personal gain. Whether it's volunteering time and skills, donating to charitable causes, or offering support to those in need, altruistic acts have the power to transform lives and make a significant impact.

What motivates individuals to engage in altruistic acts? It can vary from person to person. Some are driven by a strong sense of empathy, desiring to alleviate the suffering of others. For others, it stems from a deep-rooted belief in the importance of collective well-being and the desire to create a more harmonious society.

Altruism not only benefits the recipients of these acts but also brings immense satisfaction and fulfillment to the individuals involved. Studies have shown that engaging in altruistic activities can lead to improved mental well-being, increased social connections, and a greater sense of purpose in life.

The intricate connection between altruism and the greater good is undeniable. By embracing altruism, we cultivate a society that values empathy, compassion, and unity. Through acts of kindness, both big and small, we have the power to create a positive ripple effect that extends beyond ourselves.

The Benefits of Contributing to Society

When we choose to contribute to society, we not only make a positive impact on the communities we serve, but we also experience numerous personal benefits. Giving back is a transformative experience that can lead to personal growth, fulfillment, and a stronger social fabric.

One of the key benefits of contributing to society is the opportunity for personal growth. By engaging in altruistic activities, individuals have the chance to develop new skills, gain valuable experiences, and broaden their perspectives. Whether it's working with a non-profit organization, participating in community projects, or volunteering in education and healthcare, each experience offers a chance for self-improvement and learning.

Moreover, contributing to society provides a sense of fulfillment and purpose. Helping others and making a difference in someone's life can bring immeasurable joy and satisfaction. Research has shown that acts of altruism release endorphins in the brain, creating a "helper's high" that boosts overall well-being and happiness.

Furthermore, giving back creates a stronger social fabric within communities. When individuals contribute their time, skills, or resources to support others, they foster a sense of unity and connection. Communities thrive when people come together to address common challenges and work towards shared goals.

Contributing to society also has far-reaching effects. It can inspire others to get involved, creating a ripple effect of positive change. When people witness acts of kindness and witness the impact it has on individuals and communities, they too are motivated to contribute in their own unique way. By starting small and inspiring others, we can collectively create a society that values and prioritizes the well-being of all its members.

In conclusion, the benefits of contributing to society are multi-faceted. From personal growth and fulfillment to creating a stronger social fabric and inspiring others, giving back has a transformative power that goes beyond the immediate impact. As we explore the joys of altruism in this chapter, we encourage you to embark on your own journey of contributing to society and experience the incredible benefits it brings.

Finding Fulfilment Through Volunteering

Volunteering offers a path to personal fulfilment and a sense of purpose like no other. It is a transformative journey that allows individuals to connect with their inner selves, make a positive impact, and contribute to the betterment of society.

Countless individuals have discovered profound happiness and satisfaction through their volunteer efforts. This comes as no surprise, as numerous studies have shown that giving back and helping others leads to increased well-being and a sense of fulfillment.

One such individual is Jane Thompson, a dedicated volunteer at the local animal shelter. For Jane, spending her weekends caring for abandoned and mistreated animals has not only provided her with a deep sense of fulfillment but has also ignited a passion she never knew she had.

Through her compassionate actions, Jane has made a palpable difference in the lives of these defenseless creatures, witnessing remarkable transformations and heartwarming moments. The gratitude in their eyes and the joy they bring to her life have become the driving forces behind Jane's relentless commitment to volunteering.

Similarly, William Adams, a retiree with a wide array of skills, found his purpose through volunteer work at a community center. By sharing his knowledge and expertise with disadvantaged youth, William has not only contributed to their personal growth but has also experienced immense fulfillment himself.

Volunteering allows individuals like Jane and William to discover new strengths and talents, strengthen their connections with others, and gain a sense of accomplishment that cannot be replicated elsewhere. It fosters personal growth and provides a profound understanding of the power of compassion and selflessness.

As you embark on your own volunteering journey, remember that fulfillment lies not only in the impact you create but also in the personal growth you experience along the way. Whether you choose to mentor, serve at a food bank, or contribute towards environmental conservation, the rewards you reap will undoubtedly be immeasurable.

Choosing the Right Volunteering Opportunity

When it comes to volunteering, finding the right opportunity can make all the difference in your experience. It's important to choose an opportunity that aligns with your interests, skills, and values, allowing you to make a meaningful impact in areas that resonate with you.

Start by reflecting on what causes or issues are close to your heart. Are you passionate about environmental conservation, animal welfare, or education? Identifying your areas of interest will help narrow down your search for volunteering opportunities.

Consider your skills and expertise as well. What talents or abilities can you bring to the table? Whether it's graphic design, teaching, or event planning, your skills can be a valuable asset to organizations in need.

Furthermore, think about your values and what you want to contribute to society. Do you believe in equality, community development, or healthcare accessibility? Understanding your values will enable you to find organizations or projects that align with your principles.

Research different volunteer organizations or initiatives that focus on your chosen cause. Look for reputable organizations with a track record of making a positive impact. Check their mission, values, and the specific projects they offer.

Reach out to the organizations you're interested in to learn more about their volunteering opportunities. Inquire about the time commitment, required skills, and the impact you can expect to make through your volunteer work.

Remember, volunteering is not only about giving back but also about personal growth and fulfillment. By choosing the right volunteering opportunity, you can make a difference while gaining valuable experiences and creating lasting connections with like-minded individuals.

Making a Lasting Impact

When it comes to altruism and contributing to society, making a lasting impact is key. It's not just about the immediate help and support you provide; it's about creating sustainable solutions and empowering communities for long-term change.

One of the most effective ways to make a lasting impact is by focusing on sustainable solutions. This means identifying and implementing strategies that address the root causes of the issues you're passionate about. By working towards systemic change, you can create a ripple effect that benefits not just individuals, but entire communities.

Community empowerment is another essential aspect of making a lasting impact. By involving local communities in the decision-making process and ensuring their voices are heard, you can empower them to take ownership of their own development. This approach fosters a sense of pride, ownership, and responsibility, resulting in more impactful and sustainable outcomes.

Collaboration is also crucial for making a lasting impact. By partnering with like-minded organizations, individuals, and businesses, you can leverage resources and expertise to multiply your efforts. Together, you can create a more significant and more meaningful impact on the issues you care about.

Bringing it all together

By combining sustainable solutions, community empowerment, and collaboration, you have the power to make a lasting impact with your altruistic efforts. Remember, it's not just about the immediate impact you make, but also about the lasting change you create in the lives of others and the communities you serve.

Overcoming Challenges in Volunteering

Volunteering is a rewarding experience that allows us to contribute to society and make a positive impact. However, it is not without its challenges. From time constraints to personal obstacles, there are various factors that can hinder our altruistic endeavors. But fear not, for there are practical tips to help you overcome these challenges and stay focused on your mission.

1. Time Management: Balancing your personal and professional commitments with volunteering can be demanding. Prioritize your activities, establish a schedule, and allocate dedicated time for volunteering. Remember, even small contributions can make a big difference.

2. Skill Match: Finding the right volunteering opportunity that aligns with your skills and interests can be a challenge. Research organizations and projects that resonate with you, and don't be afraid to reach out for guidance. Remember, your unique talents can bring immense value to the cause you choose to support.

3. Emotional Resilience: Volunteering can expose us to heartbreaking situations and emotional challenges. It is essential to take care of your mental well-being and seek support from fellow volunteers or professionals if needed. Remember, self-care is crucial to sustaining your altruistic efforts.

4. Sustainability: Creating lasting change requires focusing on sustainable solutions. It can be disheartening when progress seems slow or obstacles arise, but persevere and remember that every step counts. Collaborate with like-minded individuals and organizations to maximize your impact.

5. Burnout Prevention: Overextending yourself can lead to burnout, diminishing your ability to contribute effectively. Pace yourself, set realistic goals, and prioritize self-care. Take breaks when needed, and remember that your long-term dedication is essential for creating lasting change.

By acknowledging and addressing these challenges, you can navigate the volunteer journey more effectively and stay committed to making a positive difference in the lives of others. Remember, your altruism and dedication are the driving forces behind building a more compassionate and inclusive society.

Celebrating Volunteer Achievements

Within every community, there are exceptional individuals who embody the true spirit of altruism, making significant impacts through their selfless acts. In this section, we shine a spotlight on these remarkable volunteers, celebrating their achievements and the positive change they have brought to society.

Inspiring Stories of Altruism

Meet Sally, a dedicated volunteer who has dedicated countless hours to improving educational opportunities for underprivileged children. Through her tireless efforts, she has created mentoring programs, organized fundraising events, and provided support to students in need. Sally's commitment to contributing to society has made a lasting impact on the lives of numerous young individuals.

Another inspiring volunteer is James, a passionate environmentalist who has spearheaded numerous conservation projects within his community. From organizing clean-up initiatives to raising awareness about sustainable practices, James has played a vital role in protecting the environment and inspiring others to do the same.

Recognizing Volunteer Excellence

It is essential to recognize and honor the exceptional achievements of volunteers who have gone above and beyond in their service to society. Each year, the Altruism in Action Awards celebrates these outstanding individuals, highlighting their selflessness, dedication, and remarkable accomplishments.

Through their volunteer efforts, these remarkable individuals have demonstrated the power of altruism and its ability to create positive change. Their stories serve as an inspiration to others, encouraging them to get involved and make a difference, no matter how big or small.

Join us as we celebrate these volunteer achievements and discover how they can inspire you to contribute to society in your own unique way.

Paying It Forward: Inspiring Others to Volunteer

Altruism and contributing to society are powerful acts that can create a lasting impact on individuals and communities. By engaging in volunteering, we not only make a positive difference ourselves but also have the opportunity to inspire and encourage others to join this meaningful journey. Here, we explore effective strategies for spreading the message of altruism and inspiring a ripple effect of positive change.

One of the most powerful ways to inspire others to volunteer is by leading through example. When we embody the values of altruism and actively contribute to society, we become living proof of the fulfillment and joy that volunteering can bring. Sharing our personal experiences and the impact it has had on our lives can touch the hearts of others and ignite their desire to get involved.

Another strategy is to create awareness about the benefits of volunteering and the importance of contributing to society. By leveraging various communication channels, such as social media, blogs, and community events, we can highlight the transformative power of altruistic acts. Sharing success stories and showcasing the positive outcomes that volunteering brings can motivate others to take that first step and embark on their own altruistic journey.

Lastly, it is essential to provide support and resources for individuals who are interested in volunteering. This can be done through organizing workshops, webinars, and networking events that offer guidance on finding suitable volunteering opportunities, developing necessary skills, and overcoming challenges. By providing a supportive environment, we empower aspiring volunteers to make a meaningful impact and create sustainable change within their communities.

Chapter 20

Realigning with
Your Passions

Welcome to the twentieth chapter of our transformative journey toward rediscovering and weaving your passions into the fabric of your everyday life. This chapter aims to underscore the significance of aligning your life with your passions and offers practical advice for integrating them into your routines seamlessly.

Life is far too valuable to be lived without purpose or enthusiasm. Rekindling your passions not only brings a newfound level of fulfillment and happiness into your activities but also allows you to cultivate a long-forgotten hobby, delve into new interests, or embark on a creative venture. Each step toward rediscovery draws you nearer to a life brimming with meaning.

We will walk you through identifying your passions, breaking down barriers to integration, establishing daily rituals, achieving balance, fostering passionate relationships, and cultivating self-compassion. Additionally, we'll discuss the transformative power of embracing change and outline strategies to maintain a passion-filled lifestyle. Our goal is to empower you to embed your passions deeply into your daily existence.

Prepare to embark on this exhilarating journey of rediscovery and integration. Let's explore the immense potential of aligning your passions with every facet of your daily life!

Understanding the Power of Passions

Before integrating our passions into our daily routines, recognizing their potential impact on our well-being is essential. Rediscovering your passions can infuse your life with immense joy and purpose, rejuvenating your identity and sparking a renewed enthusiasm for each day.

Engaging in activities that resonate deeply with our passions taps into a wellspring of intrinsic motivation and satisfaction. Whether it's painting, making music, or engaging in a sport, these activities fulfill a sense of purpose and achievement. They offer a medium for expressing our creativity, challenging our limits, and experiencing profound contentment.

Furthermore, reconnecting with our passions positively influences our mental, emotional, and physical health. Participating in passion-driven activities triggers endorphins, enhancing our mood, reducing stress, and bolstering our mental health.

Passions also forge connections with individuals who share our interests and values, enriching our social lives and fostering a sense of community. Moreover, integrating passions into our daily lives promotes personal growth and development, encouraging us to expand our horizons and refine our skills.

In the following segments, we will provide strategies for identifying your passions and rekindling your deepest interests. Understanding passions' power allows us to take deliberate steps toward making them a core part of our lives, paving the way for a more fulfilling and purpose-driven existence.

Identifying Your Passions

This section offers strategies and techniques to help you uncover and reconnect with your core interests. Identifying your passions is a crucial step in making them a central part of your daily life, enhancing your joy and satisfaction.

Begin by reflecting on activities and hobbies that evoke the most joy and fulfilment. What topics or subjects energize and excite you? Jotting down your thoughts can provide clarity.

Venture beyond your comfort zone to explore new hobbies or activities. Experimenting can reveal previously undiscovered passions. Enroll in a class, join a community, or pursue experiences that spark your curiosity.

Pay attention to activities where you lose track of time or achieve a flow state. These moments often signify a deeper passion connected to your true self. Focus on what brings genuine enthusiasm and fulfilment.

Remember, discovering your passions is an ongoing journey. It's perfectly normal for your interests to evolve or for new passions to emerge. Give yourself the freedom to explore and accept the changing nature of your passions as you weave them into your daily life.

Overcoming Barriers to Integration

Integrating our passions into daily routines can be challenging due to external commitments and time constraints. Life's busyness often sidelines our sources of joy and fulfillment. However, with practical strategies, you can navigate these obstacles and carve out space for your passions.

Prioritizing your passions is crucial. Reflect on what genuinely matters to you and how you can allocate time and resources toward those pursuits. This might mean adjusting your schedule or consciously choosing to make room for your passions.

Setting Boundaries

Establishing boundaries is vital for integrating your passions into your daily life. Clearly communicate your needs and limits to your family, colleagues, or friends. Setting boundaries helps protect your time and energy, allowing you to engage fully in your passions without guilt or overwhelm.

Delegating and Outsourcing

Consider delegating or outsourcing tasks that consume significant time but don't align with your passions. This could mean hiring help for household chores, seeking assistance with specific responsibilities, or collaborating with others who share your interests. By freeing yourself from non-passion-related tasks, you open up more space and energy to focus on what truly brings you fulfillment.

Finding Supportive Communities

Immersing yourself in communities of like-minded individuals can offer tremendous support. Look for groups, both online and offline, where you can connect with people who share your passions. These communities can provide encouragement, insight, and inspiration, as well as opportunities for collaboration.

As you work toward integrating your passions into your daily life, remember the importance of commitment and perseverance. Rome wasn't built in a day, and neither is the process of making your passions a routine part of your existence. Be patient with yourself and celebrate small victories along the way. With dedication and clear intentions, you'll find that incorporating your passions into your daily routine becomes second nature.

Creating a Daily Ritual

The journey to integrate your passions into your daily life begins with establishing a daily ritual. This section will guide you in making your passions an indispensable part of your daily routine.

First, dedicate specific times each day to your passions. Allocating a distinct time slot allows you to immerse yourself fully in activities that bring you joy and fulfillment. Whether it's engaging in photography, writing, or exploring nature, this dedicated time nurtures your passions consistently.

Setting goals and intentions is another crucial step. Define what you wish to achieve or experience in your areas of interest, providing a clear direction for your passion endeavors. Whether it's mastering a new guitar chord each day or writing a page of your novel, these small goals keep you focused and motivated.

Furthermore, align your intentions with your passions. Reflect daily on why your passions are important to you. Connecting with the deeper meaning behind your pursuits, whether for personal growth, creativity, or making a positive impact, cultivates a purposeful mindset that fuels your passion journey.

By crafting a daily ritual that includes dedicated time, goals, and intentions, you prioritize your passions, ensuring they become a vital component of your daily life. Through consistency and commitment, your passions will naturally intertwine with your daily activities, bringing you greater fulfillment and joy.

Finding Balance in Life and Work

Achieving a balance between work and personal pursuits is crucial when integrating your passions into your daily life. With strategic planning, it's possible to harmonize your commitments and make room for what brings you joy and fulfillment.

Effective time management is key to balancing your passions with other responsibilities. By organizing your activities and crafting a schedule that dedicates time to your interests, you ensure your passions aren't overshadowed by work and daily obligations.

Establishing work-life boundaries is essential. Create clear distinctions between work and personal time, safeguarding your personal hours from work intrusions. Designate specific times or days solely for indulging in your passions, free from distractions.

Being mindful of your energy levels is also critical. Recognize when you're most energized and focused, and allocate these peak times to your passion projects for maximum productivity.

Communicate your needs and boundaries to those around you, be it colleagues, family, or friends. By expressing the importance of your passions and your need for dedicated time, you cultivate a supportive environment that facilitates the integration of your passions into your daily life.

Finding balance is an ongoing process that may require adjustments. Remain flexible and open to changing your approach as necessary. By prioritizing your passions and embedding them into your daily routine, you enhance your well-being and overall satisfaction.

Cultivating Passionate Relationships

Fostering relationships with individuals who share your interests and support your passion journey can be incredibly enriching. Passionate relationships offer a sense of community and provide a platform for expressing your interests and ideas freely.

Being surrounded by passionate individuals encourages exploration, challenges you to broaden your horizons, and offers fresh perspectives on your passions. They can introduce you to new experiences, inspire you to push your limits, and provide valuable insights that propel you forward.

Moreover, passionate relationships serve as a source of motivation and accountability. Sharing your goals and achievements with others creates a supportive network that keeps you focused and motivated, especially during challenging times.

Whether through joining communities, attending relevant events, or connecting with like-minded individuals online, there are numerous ways to cultivate passionate relationships. Seek out those who uplift and inspire you and offer the same support and encouragement in return.

Integrating passions into your daily life is a collective journey. By surrounding yourself with passionate individuals, you create a vibrant support system that celebrates your milestones, offers guidance, and fuels your continued growth and exploration.

Nurturing Self-Compassion

The journey toward integrating your passions into daily life is a deeply personal and transformative experience. Along the way, it's vital to practice self-compassion and embrace the inevitable imperfections that arise. Understand that this exploration is unique to you, and stumbling is part of the process.

Adapting to your passions may involve trial and error, requiring patience and kindness toward yourself. Recognize that progress is gradual, and setbacks are natural. Approach yourself with the same compassion and respect you would offer a close friend.

Self-compassion emphasizes acceptance over perfection, valuing your efforts and prioritizing your well-being. During this transformative journey, let self-compassion be your beacon, guiding you through challenges and celebrating your achievements, no matter how small.

The Power of Self-Reflection

Regular self-reflection is a potent tool for fostering self-compassion. Take time to assess your progress in integrating your passions into your life. Reflect on the strides you've made and the positive impact your passions have on your well-being.

Carve out moments for journaling or meditation, connecting with your inner thoughts and feelings. This practice allows you to acknowledge your dedication and growth, reinforcing your commitment to embracing your passions.

Cultivating self-compassion is an ongoing practice. As you navigate the enriching path of integrating your passions into your daily life, remain patient and understanding with yourself, cherishing each step of this fulfilling journey.

Embracing Change and Growth

Aligning with your passions invites change and growth into your life, offering a path to greater fulfillment and purpose. The process of rediscovering and integrating your passions is merely the beginning of this transformative journey.

Welcoming change requires letting go of old habits and routines that no longer serve you. Be open to new opportunities and experiences that resonate with your passions. Embracing change can lead to unexpected and rewarding paths.

The journey of integrating passions into your daily life is rich with personal development. Immersing yourself in your passions enables you to acquire new skills, expand your knowledge, and overcome challenges, fostering resilience and personal growth.

Change and growth are integral to the process of rediscovering and integrating passions. Welcome their transformative effects and seize the opportunity to craft a more fulfilling and purposeful life. By embracing change and growth, you cultivate joy, satisfaction, and alignment with your true self.

Sustaining Your Passionate Lifestyle

Making your passions a core part of your daily life enriches every moment with joy and fulfillment. However, maintaining this passionate lifestyle demands dedication and conscious effort. Here are strategies to keep your passions vibrant and central to your everyday life.

Prioritize self-care as the foundation for sustaining energy and enthusiasm for your passions. Engage in activities that nourish your mind and body, whether through exercise, meditation, or enjoying hobbies that relax and invigorate you.

Commitment is key to a passionate lifestyle. Set attainable goals and structure your schedule to allocate regular time to your passions. Treat this time as sacred, ensuring it remains a fixed part of your daily routine. Consistent engagement deepens your connection with your passions, fostering growth and fulfillment.

Building a supportive community is invaluable. Share your passion journey with like-minded individuals or seek mentorship from those you admire. A supportive network enhances motivation, offering encouragement and inspiration to navigate any challenges that arise.

Integrating passions into your daily life is not just about personal fulfillment; it's a journey that enhances your overall well-being, enriches your social connections, and fosters personal growth. By embracing these strategies, you ensure that your passions remain a vibrant and enduring part of your life, illuminating your path to a joyful and purpose-driven existence.

Chapter 21

Self-Promotion
Without the Guilt

Welcome to Chapter 21 of our book, where we dive into the fascinating world of self-promotion. In this chapter, we'll explore effective strategies for showcasing your achievements confidently and without feeling guilty. Whether you're an aspiring professional looking to stand out in a competitive marketplace or a seasoned expert seeking career growth, these self-promotion techniques can elevate your professional trajectory.

Understanding the Importance of Self-Promotion

Before we delve into the strategies and techniques of effective self-promotion, it's crucial to understand why self-promotion matters and the positive impact it can have on your professional growth and opportunities.

Self-promotion is not about being boastful or arrogant-it is an essential part of showcasing your achievements, skills, and expertise to the world. By confidently highlighting your accomplishments, you can attract new opportunities, gain recognition within your industry, and advance your career.

When you showcase your achievements, you differentiate yourself from others in the competitive job market and effectively communicate your value to potential employers or clients. It allows you to demonstrate your capabilities, build trust, and establish yourself as an authority in your field.

Moreover, self-promotion helps you generate awareness of your personal brand and establish a strong professional reputation. By strategically promoting your achievements, you can increase your visibility both online and offline, attracting relevant opportunities that align with your career goals.

A strong self-promotion strategy allows you to take control of your narrative, shaping how others perceive your expertise and accomplishments. It enables you to proactively shape your career path and open doors to new and exciting possibilities.

In the following sections, we will explore practical strategies, tips , and techniques that will empower you to showcase your achievements with confidence , authenticity , quality , strength , quantity , power , impact .

Overcoming Barriers to Self-Promotion

Self-promotion can be challenging for many individuals due to several barriers that hinder their confidence . This makes them unwillingnessed . And no one wants to sees that - they want someone confident. to showcase their achievements. The two most common barriers that often arise are imposter syndrome and the fear of being perceived as arrogant . In this section, we will explore these barriers in detail and provide valuable strategies to help you overcome them.

Building a Personal Brand for Effective Self-Promotion

A strong personal brand is a powerful tool that can significantly elevate your self-promotion efforts . It allows you to showcase your achievements, highlight your unique strengths , and align with your professional goals. Building a personal brand is an intentional and strategic process that requires careful consideration of your values , expertise , and target audience .

When crafting your personal brand, it is important to define what sets you apart from others in your field. Identify the specific skills , experiences , or qualities that make you unique and build your personal brand around them. This will help you establish a clear identity and differentiate yourself in a competitive marketplace.

Your personal brand should also be authentic and aligned with your values. People are more likely to connect with and trust someone who is genuine and true to themselves. Reflect on your core values and ensure that they are incorporated into your personal brand. This will not only attract like-minded individuals but also help you build strong relationships based on shared values .

Once your personal brand is defined, the next step is to promote it. Use different platforms and channels to show off what you've done and make people aware of your brand. Develop a professional website or online portfolio that displays your achievements and expertise in the form of blogs or articles. It would also be smart to let potential employers or clients reach out to you through this platform as well.

Don't forget about social media! They can amplify your personal brand like no other. Building a strong online presence will help with visibility and opportunities for self-promotion.

Keep in mind that building a personal brand isn't something you just do once, it's an ongoing process throughout your career. You need to reevaluate your brand as you grow and evolve in order to stay true, be consistent, and adapt to align with new goals.

Creating A Self-Promotion Strategy

A successful strategy depends on how effectively it can showcase chosen achievements to the target audience. The right strategy could change how you're perceived completely while bringing more opportunities for success.

Here are some steps you should follow when developing a self-promotion strategy:

Set Clear Goals: Start figuring out what exactly you want to achieve from self-promotion. Do you want people to see certain skills? Are there any specific accomplishments?

Know Your Target Audience: Who do you want seeing these promotions? Understand their preferences, needs, and challenges so that the strategy can be tailored towards them.

Define Your Unique Value Proposition: Ask yourself what sets me apart from others? Once figured out highlight those strengths and accomplishments!

Evaluate Different Channels: There are multiple ways someone can promote themselves. Make sure traditional methods such as networking events have been explored along with digital platforms like social media.

Create Engaging Content: This one is pretty simple; create content that shows off achievements and expertise!

Establish Consistency: If nothing else making sure everything has a consistent look will go a long way when trying to build a brand.

Track and Analyze Results: Regularly analyze the progress of the campaign. If you notice something isn't working, change it up, and always make notes on what's working.

Crafting Self-Promotion Materials

Of course, making sure all self-promotion materials catch the eye is important. Without that, no one will even give them a second look.

Resumes and cover letters are usually the first things someone sees when looking to hire someone. Make sure to customize both so that they show off your skills and achievements accurately. It's also very important to align these with the specific requirements of the job you want.

Furthermore, an online portfolio can act as a strong self-promotion tool to present your work samples and projects. Organize your portfolio in a visually appealing and user-friendly manner. Include high-quality images, detailed descriptions, and tangible outcomes to effectively demonstrate your expertise.

Social media profiles also play a significant role in self-promotion. Optimize your profiles by describing your accomplishments, skills, and professional goals. Share industry-related content, thought leadership articles, and updates on your achievements to engage with your audience and establish yourself as an expert in your field.

Remember to maintain consistency across all your self-promotion materials. Your personal brand should shine through each element, reflecting your unique skills, values, and passions.

Key takeaways:

Customize resume and cover letter to showcase relevant experiences and achievements.

Create online portfolio that presents high-quality work samples and demonstrates expertise.

Optimize social media profiles to reflect professional achievements and engage with audience.

Maintain consistency across all self-promotion materials to reinforce personal brand.

Leveraging Networking and Relationship Building

Networking and building relationships are key components of successful self-promotion. By strategically leveraging networking opportunities you can not only expand professional network but also effectively showcase achievements. Here are some strategies to help make most of networking:

1. Attend industry events & conferences

Take advantage of industry events & conferences to connect with professionals in field. Engage in meaningful conversations exchange ideas share accomplishments. These events provide valuable opportunities build relationships create lasting connections.

2 Join professional organizations & communities

Become member of professional organizations & communities related to industry Actively participate in discussions attend meetings & events contribute expertise These platforms offer supportive environment for networking allow showcase achievements targeted audience

3 Utilize social media platforms

Social media platforms like LinkedIn provide vast network of professionals from various industries Build engaging profile share relevant content actively engage with others network By consistently showcasing achievements expertise attract attention potential collaborators clients employers

4 Offer genuine support & value

Networking not just about self-promotion Show genuine interest in others offer support provide value whenever possible By being valuable resource establishing mutually beneficial relationships enhance professional reputation open doors new opportunities

When networking remember to be authentic approachable & respectful Building strong relationships takes time effort can lead long-term self-promotion success

Navigating Social Media for Self-Promotion

Social media platforms have revolutionized the way we communicate and connect with others. They also provide an incredible opportunity for self-promotion and showcasing your achievements to a wide audience. When utilized effectively, social media can be a powerful tool in your self-promotion strategy. To navigate social media for self-promotion, it's crucial to develop a thoughtful approach. Start by identifying the platforms that align with your professional goals and target audience. For example, LinkedIn is ideal for networking and showcasing your professional achievements while Instagram and YouTube are great for creative industries and visual storytelling

After selecting the right platforms, create a consistent and compelling presence. Leverage stunning visuals and gripping captions to showcase your accomplishments and expertise. Use hashtags related to your industry to increase your visibility and attract professionals with similar interests as well as potential customers.

Engaging with your audience is vital in establishing a strong online presence. Responding to comments and messages, along with actively participating in relevant discussions and communities, demonstrates your expertise and builds credibility within the industry.

Don't shy away from using social media features such as live videos, stories, and polls. These will help you go above and beyond in engaging viewers. It's important that people remember you.

Striking a balance between self-promotion and providing value to your audience is very important. Avoid solely talking about yourself; share content that others can find useful or enjoy, like industry trends or insightful resources. This way you position yourself as an authority figure whom they can rely on for information all while attracting a loyal following.

Lastly, regularly analyze metrics to assess whether or not you're making progress toward maximizing impact. There are several factors worth paying attention too but some of the most important ones include engagement rates, reach, and audience demographics.

It's important to keep in mind that social media is just a tool which needs to be used strategically alongside self-promotion efforts. With this strategy you'll be able effectively showcase achievements; engage audiences; build a strong online presence; open new opportunities.

Keeping it Real: Balancing Authenticity & Humility

You need authentic connections in order for this approach to work properly! When promoting themselves people often end up going against their own values-don't do this! The goal is leaving long-lasting impacts on others by showcasing accomplishments true-to-self!

Luckily there's another essential ingredient known as humility-it prevents individuals from coming off arrogant when sharing achievements. People love success stories but what they don't like is when somethings being shoved down their throat.

So how can you strike this balance? Well for starters, self-promotion is not about bragging or validation. It's all about showcasing unique contributions, skills, and expertise. When it comes to promoting accomplishments focus on the value provided instead of just boasting achievements.

Listening actively and empathetically is a great way to build connections with others. Why? When you show interest in what people have to say they're more likely to view you as an ally rather than a competitor.

Lastly, promoting the success of others can help create a supportive environment. Success isn't simply a zero-sum game; lifting others up will always go hand-in-hand with personal growth. By doing so you demonstrate humility and build a positive reputation around yourself.

The Bottom Line

At the end of the day self-promotion isn't all that egotistical when done right. With the proper balance between authenticity and humility individuals are able to inspire those around them while creating long-lasting impacts within their own endeavors.

Self-promotion is not a one-time thing. It's a journey that requires consistent effort, and the ability to adapt. If you continue to promote yourself properly, then the rewards will be bountiful.

To build self-promotion success effectively, it's essential to develop strategies that continuously showcase your achievements throughout your career journey. By doing this you're constantly on people's minds.

One good strategy is to update your personal brand regularly. As you grow more experienced and hit new milestones make sure you update the things that matter most. Your resume, portfolio, and online profiles are key places where people can see what's new with you.

Another important aspect of sustaining self-promotion success is staying up-to-date with industry trends. The landscape as we know it changes every day so it's important for us to change with it if we want to stay relevant. New opportunities arise from this kind of willingness too which could really take our careers to new heights.

Finally, don't underestimate the power of networking and building relationships. Expanding our professional network can lead us into many open doors and opportunities in the future. Attending events within our industry and connecting with professionals are two great ways to start expanding our circle of connections.

Chapter 22

Resilience in
the Face of Ageism

Welcome to Chapter 22, in which we'll cover ageism and workplace discrimination. In this chapter, we'll explore strategies to address these challenges and embrace the value of experience. Ageism is a significant issue that can limit opportunities and advancement for people in their careers. By recognizing the signs of age discrimination - and using your knowledge to your advantage - you can navigate these obstacles and achieve lasting success.

The Reality of Ageism in the Workplace

Ageism is a common problem that affects both individuals and organizations within the workforce. Despite legal protections, age discrimination continues to be an issue that impacts careers at every stage. Understanding the reality of ageism is crucial for combating workplace discrimination and fostering an inclusive environment.

Recognizing Signs of Age Discrimination

Ageist behavior isn't always easy to identify - it's often subtle and covert. To combat it, employees must learn how to recognize signs that suggest someone may be experiencing bias because of their age. This knowledge will enable you to take proactive steps toward addressing ageism in your workplace.

Biased Language

People who discriminate based on age typically use biased language. Keep an ear out for comments or jokes made about older employees' capabilities in comparison with younger workers'. The use of disrespectful terms can create a hostile work environment.

Exclusion from Opportunities

If you notice patterns of being skipped over for promotions, more difficult assignments or training opportunities, then it's likely that such decisions are being influenced by your age instead of your merit as an employee. Being excluded from things necessary for professional growth can hinder career progression for mature workers.

Unfair Performance Evaluations

Age discrimination can manifest as unfair performance evaluations. Managers might give higher ratings to younger workers who didn't perform as well as older ones did. Unjust appraisals like these undermine confidence in seniors' abilities while hindering career progression.

Stereotyping Based on Age

Ageist stereotypes leave no room for nuanced understanding of older employees. For example, assuming an older person is less productive, unable to use modern technology or resistant to changes solely because of their age is unfair and detrimental to career progression. Challenging these assumptions is crucial for fighting back against age discrimination.

By learning how to identify the signs of age discrimination, you can actively foster a workplace that values experience and treats employees fairly regardless of their age.

Confronting Ageist Stereotypes

Ageism and workplace discrimination significantly harm progress in careers for older workers, but it doesn't have to be this way. We'll explain common ageist stereotypes that persist in professional settings and how you can challenge them. It's important to confront these stereotypes head-on so as not to pass them on.

Leveraging the Value of Experience

Experience is valuable - there's no doubt about it. It sets people apart by allowing them to contribute insights, problem-solving skills and a deeper understanding of industry intricacies that others might lack. By showing your employer what you bring with experience, you present yourself as an invaluable asset.

One way to effectively showcase your experience is by highlighting specific accomplishments from past roles. Providing concrete evidence backs your claim that you're capable of doing the job at hand well. Additionally, consider sharing relevant case studies or success stories related to the position for which you're applying - this helps employers visualize how they would benefit from having your experience on board too.

Additionally, take every chance you get to mentor and guide colleagues. Especially those who are in their earlier careers. By sharing your knowledge and offering guidance, you don't only help others grow but also reinforce your expertise. This mentoring process can foster a sense of intergenerational collaboration which breaks down barriers and overcomes workplace discrimination.

Remember, valuable experience comes from continuous learning and growth. Stay up-to-date with industry trends, attend workshops and conferences, and earn more certifications or training if possible. Keeping up with the industry shows your adaptability and willingness to stay current which helps counter age-related biases.

Lastly, consider joining industry associations or professional networks to continue expanding your outreach and visibility. Engaging with like-minded professionals gives you opportunities for collaboration, knowledge sharing, and access to potential career advancements.

All in all, experience is extremely valuable in the workplace. By effectively showcasing your expertise through mentorship programs or just by staying current on industry trends will help position yourself as an asset. You will be able to overcome workplace discrimination while thriving in your career.

Building resilience when faced by ageism

Ageism is a challenge experienced throughout many careers.It's crucial that we use the right mindset to overcome these challenges while maintaining a positive outlook on life.

One of the first steps in building resilience is acknowledging that age does not define worth nor abilities! Embrace all your experience and knowledge it brings true value!

Seek support from close friends or mentors whenever you face these challenges! Having a strong network can provide guidance whenever needed! And they can also help navigate any other problems caused by age discrimination!

Maintaining a Positive Mindset

A positive mindset is probably the best tool you have when combatting ageism! Focus all energy on strengths rather than dwelling on weaknesses! Thinking this way won't allow negativity into your mind! Practicing self-care is essential when looking for resilience! Take care of both physical/mental well-being by doing activities that make you happy and relaxed. This routine will strengthen your ability to get past setbacks and persevere through all challenges!

Overcoming Age-Related Challenges

Resilience is all about adapting and overcoming obstacles! When it comes to age-related challenges, defying stereotypes is the best way to overcome them! Showcase your skills, expertise, and adaptability! Let everyone know how good you are at what you do!

Keep developing your skills and stay up-to-date with everything happening in your industry. Learning opportunities can come from everywhere such as formal education or even online resources! By staying informed and knowledgeable you demonstrate growth which helps improve on weaknesses.

Don't ever forget that ageism should not exist anywhere but since it does we also have a responsibility in stopping it. By empowering yourself, becoming more resilient and showing others that being against age-discrimination is the way to go; we move forward into a more inclusive workplace.

Strengthening Professional Networks

Building strong professional networks contributes greatly when battling ageism and workplace discrimination. Networking doesn't only help you find new opportunities but also provides a platform for countering age-related issues in the workplace. Having connections gives you access to more valuable resources which makes tackling these problems easier.

Embracing Lifelong Learning

Embracing a lifelong pursuit of learning and development is key to maintaining your worth in the workplace as you navigate ageism. Recognizing the value of experience, it's important to actively search for resources and opportunities that can help you enhance skills and demonstrate adaptability.

Constant learning is what ensures you remain up-to-date with industry advancements and trends, which can help to counter workplace discrimination based on age. By staying current, employees at all stages proactively challenge stereotypes and showcase the fact that they can contribute meaningfully to an organization's success.

The good news is that there are many resources available to support professional development. Online courses, webinars, workshops - these convenient vehicles will allow you to expand your knowledge base while also acquiring new skills. Additionally, professional associations and networking groups offer invaluable opportunities for collaboration with peers while encouraging continuous learning.

Beyond formal education

But embracing lifelong learning goes beyond signing up for an online course or attending a lecture. Instead it involves seeking out challenges so that individuals can tackle them head on within a workspace environment. This means employees must take on projects they've never encountered before while actively engaging in problem-solving. Simply put - by demonstrating willingness to learn and adapt, workers are showcasing resilience while reinforcing the value of experience.

Investing in Self-Improvement

Investing time into personal growth isn't just about combating ageism but also about combatting workplace discrimination as a whole. That being said though, taking ownership over personal professional growth is a proactive step towards fighting both issues by allowing continued skill development and acquired knowledge.

Allocate time specifically for developing knowledge surrounding new topics or skills while setting goals along the way. Following this commitment will not only ensure career growth but also give confidence boosts since success will be evident regardless of age.

It's easy to forget but it's worth reminding: The value of experience cannot be taught or learned from any educational program or class.Regardless if that person has been working only for a short period of time or long, experience is as valuable as it gets. By embracing lifelong learning and development you are defying ageist stereotypes and positioning yourself as one of the most valuable contributors in the workplace.

Negotiating for Fair Treatment

Developing effective negotiation strategies is crucial for anyone looking to combat ageism and workplace discrimination. By advocating for fair treatment, employees can navigate age-related biases and create a more inclusive work environment while putting themselves in position for higher paying job titles or opportunities to grow.

In salary negotiations

Keep these tips in mind once you find yourself in salary negotiations:

Research your worth: Before entering into any discussion, arm yourself with information. You are your best advocate on something like this so putting time into finding out what salaries look like across different organizations in your specific field will be key.

Emphasize value, not years: Age doesn't equate to value - that's important to keep in mind. When negotiating, come prepared with examples of how you've brought value to the company over the course of your tenure there so far. This will give you an opportunity to highlight skills outside what would typically be seen from someone within your age bracket.

Promotions and growth opportunities

Fighting against biases becomes even more difficult when moving up the ladder within an organization so it's important to keep this front of mind during any promotions or growth opportunities discussions:

Play offense, not defense: Your previous success doesn't guarantee future success but it does confirm that you're capable of it. During these discussions be sure to have a deep understanding of the background surrounding responsibilities that come along with positions above yours while highlighting how your experience gives you an edge over other candidates who may be younger but less experienced than you.

Employer responsibility

Workplace discrimination is never limited solely to employees because employers play a big role too. Here's some insight on how companies should approach fostering a more inclusive work environment through addressing ageism:

Awareness and understanding

Creating an inclusive workplace environment starts with promoting awareness. Employers should educate their workforce about the negative effects of ageism while emphasizing how important it is that all employees, regardless of age, are treated with respect and fairness.

Diversity in hiring practices

Workforce diversity brings varied perspectives, creativity, and innovation so it's a win for everyone involved. Employers who actively seek out employees of different ages break down biases related to people's age which then fosters a more inclusive work environment.

Training programs

Offering training programs on unconscious bias can help reduce age discrimination. Employees should be given the chance to learn about issues related to age as well as the impact that comes along with any stereotypes related to it.

In doing this, companies will create a workspace where all employees at every stage can thrive and find the most success possible.

In addition, we can fight ageism by implementing policies and practices that encourage intergenerational collaboration. For example, mentorship programs and team-building initiatives can bridge the gap between the generations of employees. With these programs, older employees can mentor younger ones while also providing guidance and support.

We can also empower the next generation through knowledge sharing opportunities. By creating channels for open communication in which older employees can share their ideas and expertise with newcomers, we foster an environment that fosters growth in more ways than one.

The ability to embrace diverse perspectives is essential for empowering the latest generation of workers. When a workplace fosters a culture of inclusivity regardless of age, all generations feel included and valued.

Resilience Comes From Within

As we come to the end of this chapter on resilience when it comes to workplace discrimination due to ageism, let's look back at some important points made. Ageism is still a problem in many businesses today. It limits advancement opportunities based on an individual's age instead of valuing their experience.

To fight against ageism, one must first embrace their own resilience. And then they have to use that resilience to acknowledge their abundance of experience making them valuable for any role or project thrown their way.

Another way to combat discrimination is by extending your professional network as far as it will go. That way you have access to resources that could help you make headway even when you're faced with obstacles because of your age.

Lastly (and most obviously), never stop learning! You should always be open-minded when presented with opportunities that will expand your skills or teach you something new about your field. Doing so shows employers and coworkers alike that no matter how old you are, no barrier will stop you from bringing value to a project or company as a whole

Chapter 23

A Lifestyle of Curiosity

This time, we're diving into the transformative role curiosity plays in driving perpetual self-enhancement. Far from being merely a fleeting interest, curiosity acts as a relentless drive for knowledge, serving as a key engine for personal advancement and satisfaction. In this piece, we'll unpack the significance of maintaining curiosity, its advantages, and the positive impact it can wield across various life facets.

At its core, curiosity is the spark that propels us into exploration and discovery. It awakens a sense of wonder, prompting us to question, seek out new experiences, and welcome learning moments. This continuous quest for knowledge opens up fresh viewpoints, ideas, and possibilities, fueling ongoing personal evolution.

We'll delve into the neuroscience behind curiosity, its nurturing in young minds, its connection to creativity, its influence on interpersonal relationships and self-development, and tackle the obstacles to staying curious. Additionally, we'll offer actionable advice on fostering a curiosity-rich lifestyle in our everyday routines. As we venture into a future where curiosity leads, we unlock a realm of boundless potential and infinite opportunities for both personal and professional progression.

Curiosity: A Portal to Personal Expansion

Curiosity stands as more than a mere characteristic; it's a bridge to personal expansion and fulfillment. By welcoming curiosity, we open ourselves to a universe of possibilities, setting the stage for broadening our horizons, uncovering new ventures, and embarking on a self-exploration voyage.

A prime benefit of curiosity lies in its profound effect on personal development. The drive to gain knowledge, explore diverse perspectives, and question our preconceptions fuels our intellectual and emotional growth, steering us toward a richer self-awareness and purpose.

Welcoming New Ventures

Curiosity empowers us to greet new opportunities with enthusiasm. It pushes us beyond our comfort zones, enabling personal and professional growth. This active pursuit of new knowledge and experiences unlocks our potential, leading to deeper life satisfaction.

Moreover, curiosity bolsters our problem-solving skills and nurtures innovative thinking. When faced with challenges, a curious mindset encourages us to examine numerous solutions, think inventively, and develop unique problem-solving strategies. This curiosity-driven exploration of the unknown propels innovation and guides us to greater achievements.

Broadening Perspectives

Curiosity acts as a driving force in broadening our perspectives. It compels us to move past familiar territories, embracing diverse viewpoints and ideas. By seeking out new experiences and interacting with different cultures, we enhance our understanding of the world and appreciate its vast diversity more deeply.

Fostering curiosity transforms us into perpetual learners, always in pursuit of knowledge and self-enhancement. It feeds our desire for knowledge, urging us to explore new subjects, engage with various disciplines, and continually stretch our intellectual limits. This ongoing growth enriches both our personal and professional lives, contributing to a fulfilling existence.

In sum, curiosity offers a multitude of benefits, from personal development to broadening our outlook on life. By keeping curiosity alive, we can tap into our fullest potential, seize new opportunities, and enjoy the journey of discovery and self-realization.

The Brain Science Behind Curiosity

Curiosity, a fundamental human trait, has captivated thinkers and researchers for ages. Recent advances in neuroscience have illuminated how curiosity operates within our brains, influencing cognitive functions. Grasping the brain science of curiosity yields insights into enhancing brain performance and fostering lifelong curiosity.

Neuroscience research reveals that curiosity triggers the brain's reward pathways, leading to dopamine release, associated with pleasure and motivation. This process generates excitement and eagerness to explore and learn. Engaging our curiosity, our brain undertakes complex cognitive tasks such as attention, memory, and problem-solving, bolstering overall brain function.

Prefrontal Cortex's Role

The prefrontal cortex, crucial for executive functions like planning and decision-making, is significantly engaged in curious individuals, indicating an enhanced level of cognitive involvement and information processing.

This brain region also assesses the relevance of information. When faced with something new or unexpected, it helps us gauge the importance of the information and decide if it warrants further exploration. Curiosity activates the prefrontal cortex to evaluate new stimuli, prioritizing and focusing our attention on intriguing aspects.

Boosting Cognitive Skills

Curiosity significantly impacts cognitive abilities and overall brain health. Engaging in curiosity-driven learning promotes synaptic plasticity, essential for memory, skill acquisition, and adaptation. Additionally, curiosity fosters a growth mindset, the belief that intelligence and abilities can evolve through effort and learning, enhancing cognitive flexibility and resilience.

Incorporating curiosity into daily life benefits brain health and cognitive functionality over time. By remaining curious and pursuing activities that challenge our thinking, we can continuously expand our knowledge, sharpen cognitive skills, and embrace the world's wonders.

Fostering Curiosity in Young Minds

Children's innate curiosity drives their natural desire to explore and understand their environment. As guardians, educators, and mentors, it's vital to nurture this curiosity, laying the foundation for a lifelong love of learning. By creating the right environment and employing specific strategies, we can encourage curiosity in children across various contexts, including home, school, and the community.

Encouraging Open-Ended Questions

Promoting curiosity in children involves stimulating open-ended questioning. By posing thought-provoking questions and letting children discover their own answers, we spark their curiosity and foster critical thinking, expanding their knowledge and cultivating a curiosity-led learning approach.

Creating a Learning-Enriched Environment

A crucial step in nurturing curiosity is establishing a learning-enriched environment. Surrounding children with books, puzzles, and educational toys opens up independent exploration and discovery avenues. Hands-on activities and experiential learning further stimulate their curiosity by engaging all senses.

Supporting children's curiosity with a positive and encouraging attitude is essential. Celebrating their inquiries and encouraging pursuit of interests makes children feel valued and confident, fueling their passion for learning. Active listening and engaging in meaningful discussions deepen their curiosity, promoting exploration and connection.

Collaborative Learning and Embracing Mistakes

Collaborative learning significantly contributes to nurturing curiosity. By fostering environments where children can collaborate, share ideas, and learn from one another, we stimulate their curiosity and encourage exploration of different viewpoints. This collaboration enhances curiosity in problem-solving and fosters curiosity-driven learning.

Additionally, creating a culture where mistakes are viewed as growth opportunities is crucial. Encouraging children to face challenges and learn from their errors helps them develop a growth mindset and fuels their curiosity to discover new paths and solutions.

Instilling a Lifelong Learning Passion

Nurturing children's curiosity is about more than early development; it's about instilling a lifelong learning passion. By providing a strong foundation in curiosity-led learning, we set them on a path of continuous growth and self-discovery. Curiosity enables children to become lifelong learners, adaptable, innovative, and always eager to explore new ideas.

The impact of curiosity on educational development is profound. By fostering a curiosity-driven mindset in children, we empower them to be active learners, curious about the world, eager for knowledge, and engaged in the learning process.

Curiosity and Creativity: Unlocking Innovation

Embracing curiosity is the gateway to unleashing creative potential. When we allow curiosity to guide us, we access a wellspring of inspiration and innovation. Curiosity fuels our imagination, encouraging us to think beyond conventional boundaries and devise original ideas and solutions.

Cultivating curiosity taps into our innate sense of wonder and exploration, leading us to approach challenges with an open mind, ready to explore new perspectives and possibilities. This curiosity-driven mindset stimulates creativity, urging us to transcend traditional thinking and venture into unexplored domains.

So, how do we foster curiosity to boost our creative capabilities? Here are several strategies:

Venture into the Unknown

Challenge yourself to venture beyond your comfort zone, exploring new subjects or disciplines. Engaging with the unfamiliar sparks curiosity and invites fresh ideas.

Embrace Inquiry

Persist in questioning. Curiosity thrives on challenging established norms and seeking deeper insights. Questioning opens up new viewpoints and can ignite inventive ideas.

Seek Diverse Inspirations

Expose yourself to a wide array of inspirational sources, such as literature, art, nature, or conversations with diverse individuals. Interacting with varied stimuli ignites curiosity and opens new creative pathways.

Promote Playfulness

Reconnect with your inner child and encourage playfulness. Curiosity and creativity are closely linked to a playful mindset. Free yourself from the fear of mistakes and allow room for experimentation and enjoyment.

By nurturing curiosity and blending it with creativity, you embark on a path filled with endless inspiration and innovation. Curiosity serves as a catalyst, pushing us beyond our limits and inspiring the creation of truly remarkable things. Let curiosity lead the way and unlock your vast creative potential.

Navigating Curiosity Obstacles

Curiosity is a formidable force driving personal advancement and evolution. Nevertheless, several common obstacles can impede our ability to remain curious. To fully unleash curiosity's potential, identifying and navigating these barriers is crucial.

A primary obstacle to curiosity is a fixed mindset, the belief that our intelligence and capabilities are static and unchangeable. This perspective can spawn a fear of failure and a hesitance to explore new concepts or take risks. By adopting a growth mindset-the conviction that our abilities can grow through dedication and effort-we can break through this barrier and fully embrace curiosity.

Embracing a Growth Mindset

A growth mindset enables us to view challenges as learning and growth opportunities. It teaches us to view failures as necessary steps toward success. By embracing a growth mindset, we cultivate resilience and perseverance, allowing us to overcome obstacles and maintain curiosity.

Another hurdle to curiosity is the fear of the unknown. Venturing beyond our comfort zones can be daunting, as it involves exploring unfamiliar ground. However, by shifting our perspective to view the unknown as a growth and discovery opportunity, we can surmount this obstacle and wholeheartedly embrace curiosity.

Venturing into the Unknown

Embracing the unknown demands a readiness to take risks and explore uncharted territories. It involves relinquishing the need for certainty and welcoming the excitement and possibilities that accompany venturing into the unknown. By fostering curiosity and venturing into new realms, we broaden our horizons and cultivate a mindset of continuous learning and development.

Moreover, perfectionism can also obstruct curiosity. The pursuit of perfection often leads to a fear of making mistakes or taking risks. By releasing the quest for perfection and adopting a growth mindset, we can navigate this barrier and approach new ideas and experiences with curiosity and openness.

In summary, by recognizing and navigating barriers such as a fixed mindset, fear of the unknown, and perfectionism, we can unlock curiosity's power and foster a mindset of ongoing learning and development. Embracing a growth mindset enables us to view challenges as opportunities, embrace the unknown, and let go of perfectionism. With a curiosity-driven mindset, the possibilities for personal growth and fulfillment are boundless.

Curiosity in the Professional Sphere

Curiosity plays a crucial role in professional development and sparks innovation within the workplace. When team members are encouraged to cultivate curiosity, it paves the way for fresh ideas, new perspectives, and boundless possibilities. Promoting a curiosity-rich culture leads to enhanced productivity, creativity, and employee satisfaction.

Curiosity ignites a desire for exploration and growth, motivating individuals to pose questions, challenge established norms, and seek inventive solutions. By nurturing an environment that values curiosity, organizations can unlock their workforce's potential and drive continuous improvement.

Professional growth is intricately linked with curiosity. By keeping curiosity alive, team members are driven to acquire new knowledge, develop new skills, and stay abreast of industry trends. This mindset of perpetual learning enables individuals to adapt to changing scenarios and contribute significantly to their organizations' success.

Innovation flourishes in a curiosity-fueled environment. Encouraging employees to explore new possibilities and think outside conventional boundaries leads to groundbreaking ideas and solutions. Curiosity kindles the creative spark that fuels innovation, allowing companies to remain competitive and evolve in an ever-changing business landscape.

When curiosity is valued and encouraged in the workplace, it fosters a culture of open-mindedness, collaboration, and idea sharing. Employees feel empowered to express their thoughts and take calculated risks, resulting in a more engaged and motivated workforce. By valuing curiosity, organizations can fully tap into their employees' potential and cultivate a culture of growth and innovation.

Curiosity and Interpersonal Connections

Curiosity extends beyond personal growth and development, playing a pivotal role in our relationships and interactions with others. By integrating curiosity into our communications, we deepen our understanding of others, foster empathy, and strengthen our connections.

Curiosity opens the doorway to authentic connections. By actively seeking to learn more about those around us, we pave the way for meaningful conversations and a deeper appreciation of their experiences and viewpoints. It encourages us to pose questions, listen attentively, and engage in a manner that demonstrates genuine interest.

When we're curious about others, it signals our readiness to understand and empathize with their thoughts, feelings, and experiences. This curiosity enables us to view the world through new lenses, promoting empathy and bridging the gap between individuals.

Additionally, curiosity in relationships encourages growth and evolution. It inspires us to explore new facets of ourselves and our partners, continuously learning and evolving together. It creates a safe and open space for courageous conversations, where trust and vulnerability can thrive.

By valuing curiosity in our relationships, we foster an environment that prioritizes connection and understanding. We cultivate an atmosphere where both parties feel seen, heard, and valued, enhancing the quality of our connections and strengthening our bonds.

Curiosity as a Catalyst for Personal Evolution

Curiosity is a potent driver of personal evolution and introspection. When we welcome curiosity, it unveils a realm of opportunities for self-improvement, knowledge expansion, and heightened self-awareness. Curiosity serves as a catalyst, propelling us toward new experiences and deeper insights.

By indulging our curiosity, questioning, and exploring, we embark on a self-discovery journey and continuous learning. Curiosity motivates us to venture beyond our comfort zones and seek fresh perspectives, pushing the limits of our perceived capabilities.

Adopting a curious approach to life opens us to new ideas and growth opportunities. It challenges our assumptions, broadens our horizons, and deepens our understanding of the world. Curiosity drives our desire to learn, pushing us to acquire new knowledge and develop new competencies.

Self-reflection is crucial for personal growth, and curiosity plays a key role in this process. By posing meaningful questions and seeking honest answers, we gain insights into our strengths, weaknesses, and aspirations. Curiosity encourages introspection, aiding us in identifying areas for enhancement and facilitating personal development.

Curiosity and self-reflection create a feedback loop of growth and self-awareness. The more curious we are, the more we learn about ourselves, and the more we reflect on that knowledge, the better equipped we become to navigate life's challenges and pursue our objectives.

Chapter 24

Work-Life
Integration Techniques

In this chapter, we will discuss various strategies and techniques to help you seamlessly integrate your work with your personal life. We will also talk about the importance of embracing your personal interests and passions because they play a big role in making you happy.

Stick with us as we uncover the benefits of blending work with life, provide guidance on figuring out what your personal interests are, explore ways to bring these with you to work and offer practical solutions for overcoming challenges. We will also touch on how remote work environments affect work-life balance and the role organizations have in supporting their employees' well-being.

So if you're ready to learn how to have fun while working, let's get right into it!

Understanding Work-Life Integration

Work-life integration is all about finding harmony between our responsibilities at home and at our jobs. It prioritizes finding joy in everything we do so that no matter where we are or what we're doing, we're always fulfilled.

Work-life integration helps us be better people overall by understanding that work isn't just a way to make money but an opportunity for growth as well. The more interested you are in something, the less it feels like a chore which means you'll enjoy everything more!

By doing things this way, people can excel at their jobs while still having time outside of them. This method allows for flexibility because people aren't locked into only one thing but can do multiple throughout their day which is proven to relieve stress.

Throughout this chapter, we'll go through all the benefits of living like this along with tips on how to identify personal interests and even steps on how to merge them with your job. We'll also cover some challenges that come up when trying to achieve this lifestyle along with solving them. Lastly, there's a section specifically made for people who currently or are looking forward to working remotely.

So join us as we dive straight into all the treasures inside integrating activities from home and at work!

Examples of successful work-life integration litter the world around us, showing how well it works for people and organizations. Molly Thompson, a marketing whizz, snaps product photos in her free time. She then takes those photos and slaps them on social media platforms for her company. This lets her do what she loves while adding value to her role at work.

Beyond that, integrating personal hobbies into your work day helps you be more productive. When people can find joy in their job and love what they're doing, they'll have the motivation to keep going. It's not just about the "keep going" part either-someone who loves what they do will produce better quality stuff.

When a workplace is good enough to let its employees bring their own lives into work with them, everyone benefits. Companies that are actually worth working for allow employees to even take time off if they need it-no questions asked.

By doing this, companies improve retention rates by holding onto talent with a passion for their craft. They also make themselves incredibly attractive to top-tier talent who are looking for jobs, all so they can foster a positive work environment.

The bottom line here is that work-life integration has been proven over and over again as something amazing. It boosts productivity, makes people happy with their jobs, helps them maintain good mental health and much more.

Finding Personal Interests

A big step towards achieving work-life integration is finding out what you enjoy outside of your career. As nice as it sounds to bring every aspect of life together with your job-it won't happen unless you've got interests.

These hobbies will provide balance in your daily routine-if you don't have a balancing act of activities then everything becomes as dull as dishwater. A healthy mix between things we love and things we have to do is one way to tackle adult monotony.

But how do we go about finding our interests? Here are four tips:

Try new stuff: You'll never know if you like something until you try it. Spend some time exploring new hobbies and activities that pique your curiosity.

Think back to your youth: Your younger self may have had a passion for something-maybe you still do. It might be a small thing, but there's a chance that reconnecting with an old colorful part of your life can bring out newfound enthusiasm.

Consider beliefs and values: Take a moment to reflect on what you hold dear. What are the things in life that mean the most to you? Are there any causes or activities that align with these values?

Pay attention to what gets us going: When working or doing anything for that matter, we feel energized by certain tasks or projects. Pay close attention to this as it will give deeper insight into personal interests.

Finding personal interests isn't like downloading a game on your phone. It's more like playing Pokémon Go blindfolded-it takes time and patience but when you finally find something good, it'll all be worth it.

Integrating Hobbies at Work

Another big step towards work-life integration is melding our hobbies with our job responsibilities. This creates an environment where both professional and personal spheres fuel each other-allowing them to grow together.

We need balance between our passions and careers in order to keep ourselves happy.

Integrating personal interests with your career can be done in a few ways. First, see how your hobbies and passions can apply to your job. There's always a way to use creative skills or problem-solving abilities. Seek out opportunities where you can contribute those things while working towards your goals.

Another thing is creating a supportive work environment. Try to collaborate with people who have similar interests as you do or join groups that focus on things that you're passionate about. This way it'll make it easier for you to combine personal interests into the workplace

Using Personal Interests for Professional Development

Integrating personal interests isn't just fun and fulfilling, but it's good for professional growth too. These interests can help improve skills, expand knowledge, and bring fresh new perspectives to the table. It leads to higher job satisfaction and opens up new doors in your career.

Besides professional benefits, integrating personal aspects of life into work also helps balance things out. When you engage in things you love it brings happiness throughout your day which reduces stress levels and improves well-being overall.

To sum it all up, having an interest in what do at work will get rid of the feeling that the two don't go together. By aligning passions with careers and creating an encouraging work environment we can strike balance in our lives.

Handling Challenges in Work-Life Integration

Work-life integration will always have its challenges but once we implement these strategies they become easier to overcome:

Time Management

The first challenge is managing time effectively. Balancing both areas of life at once seems impossible but with tasks prioritized and a realistic schedule set, there's no limit to what can be achieved.

Setting Boundaries

Setting boundaries is another one since technology has blurred them between work and personal time. To face this issue head-on clear boundaries need to be laid down by defining specific hours for rest/work etc.. It's okay if there are instances where these boundaries are crossed but as long as everyone respects each other's space it's fine.

Seeking Support

The last challenge is asking for help which can be tough. It feels like we're admitting defeat when in reality all we want is to maintain a normal life while avoiding burnout. There's nothing wrong with sharing your concerns with loved and trusted ones, having a strong support system will help provide advice, encouragement, and assistance when needed.

By tackling obstacles like managing time, establishing boundaries, and seeking support, the hurdles of work-life integration can be jumped over. In this next section we'll discuss how setting priorities and creating boundaries are key in achieving a harmonious work-life integration.

Setting Priorities and Creating Boundaries

A successful work-life integration is the result of setting priorities and creating boundaries. By effectively managing your time and spreading it across different aspects of your life, you can achieve a great balance that brings fulfillment.

Getting everyone on board is crucial in setting priorities. Communicate your needs and expectations to co-workers, family members, friends-everyone. Make sure they understand when you're available and committed to something.

Taking Care of Yourself

When working towards an integrated lifestyle, putting yourself first is important. Take some time off to recharge your battery and strengthen your mental well-being. Do activities that bring joy into your life like exercising or meditating.

And remember! Setting boundaries isn't just about when you're at work or not. Make sure you allocate quality time for yourself, relationships, hobbies - everything important to you really - outside of work hours. That way all areas of your life will feel fulfilled.

Dividing Time between Work and Life

Finding balance between these two requires smart time management: prioritizing tasks while setting realistic deadlines ensures efficient work while saving room for personal errands.

Try following the technique called "time-blocking" where you label specific slots during the day as times for certain things: personal tasks or rest for example. This way you know there's dedicated time throughout the day for everything reducing the chances of imbalance.

Lastly! It's important to always keep in mind that integrating life with work is both dynamic and ongoing; adjustments along the way shouldn't be excluded nor judged but embraced because as things evolve so do needs and aspirations. And by finding the right balance a fulfilling integration can be achieved successfully

Build a Daily Routine

Create a daily routine that serves as a strong foundation for work-life balance. This should include dedicated time for work, personal activities, and self-care.

Predictable schedules are essential for productivity and can help you maintain a sense of balance and structure in your life.

Establish Physical and Mental Boundaries:

By designating a specific area in your home as your workspace, you're creating physical boundaries between your work and personal life. Additionally, rules to minimize distractions are necessary to ensure uninterrupted work time.

Take Regular Breaks:

Breaks help maintain focus and prevent burnout. Throughout your workday incorporate short breaks to recharge yourself and engage in activities you love doing.

Being mindful of the challenges and opportunities that remote work presents is key in taking proactive steps to achieve successful work-life integration. With the right strategies and mindset, remote workers will find success on both fronts, professionally and personally.

Cultivating Supportive Work Environments

Organizations play an integral role in achieving successful work-life integrations. They must create supportive environments where individuals have the resources they need to effectively juggle their responsibilities at home while also being productive at work. In this section we'll cover some of the strategies companies can adopt to promote this:

Company Policies and Initiatives

Creating company policies that prioritize good balance between your professional life with everything else is crucial. Policies can be things like flexible working hours, remote options or paid time off when handling personal commitments. By having policy's employees will feel more comfortable using them knowing their employer values their well being inside/outside of work.

Flexible Work Arrangements

Offering flexibility arrangements is another way organizations can support integration. Managers must understand/accommodate different employee needs so they can foster an environment where people value personal responsibilities outside of their job scope.

Work Culture & Communication

Having an open line of communication within company walls plays a crucial role in promoting the integration we need. A healthy work-life balance mindset is needed from the top down. Managers should be supportive of employees prioritizing self-care and respecting their personal boundaries.

Once we have successful integration, we gain more productive employees, happier employees and higher retention rates. It creates a win-win situation for both parties involved.

Sustaining Work-Life Integration in the Long Run

After you've successfully implemented all of these strategies into your life, it's just as important to maintain them. Evaluating whether your work-life integration is still meeting your needs on a consistent basis will ensure continued success.

Being adaptable is a must when it comes to sustaining work and life integration. Keep in mind that things can change over time, so you'll need to be flexible and open to changing your strategies at times. Always be mindful of any changes happening within your personal or professional life that may cause a shift.

Regularly evaluating your work-life integration strategies ensures that they stay effective as time progresses. Take note of what works best for you and what doesn't. Doing this will allow you to keep up a successful work-life integration at all times.

Remember, there's no one-step solution to work-life integration. It takes constant reflection, adaptation, and evaluation to make it work in the end. By doing this consistently, you'll find yourself with a well-balanced lifestyle tailored exactly towards your needs.

Reaching Work-Life Integration: Final Thoughts

To sum it all up, reaching a successful work-life integration requires making an effort to balance personal interests with professional obligations. In this chapter we've gone over the whole concept and its impact in today's workplace.

We covered the many benefits of proper integration including increased productivity, improved mental health, and enhanced job satisfaction. Real-life examples have shown us how well combining both worlds can go for our overall happiness.

Finding meaning in both aspects of our lives is possible by identifying what genuinely makes us happy then using them as part of our daily routines. Setting priorities and creating boundaries along with a good support system are key factors when it comes to maintaining a healthy work-life balance

Chapter 25

Travel and
Global Mindset

Travel is a powerful teacher in and of itself. The lessons we gain from it are not entirely about the bucket list destinations we visit, they're more about what we learn on our journey to self-discovery and self-improvement. Personal growth happens when you leave your comfort zone and engage with things outside of your routine.

The opportunity to learn is one of the most valuable aspects of travel. When you interact with people who come from different backgrounds, you gain empathy and understanding through their perspective on life. Now, that's some personal growth right there! Hardships will happen during trips, but they foster resilience and an adaptive spirit in us.

New cultures present new ways of living life as well. By exploring these while abroad, you'll quickly develop a global mindset that will open doors to countless opportunities for personal growth.

Learning New Skills

You can also acquire skills that aren't typically available in your day-to-day life by traveling. For example, you may take part in cooking classes where traditional dishes are taught or even pick up another language along the way. Maybe photography is something you've always wanted to get into? Foreign lands provide an astounding aesthetic worth capturing.

Stepping Out Of Your Comfort Zone

It's no secret stepping out of what's familiar makes us feel uneasy… but so does growth. Embrace this feeling! It will be challenging at first, but over time your confidence will grow significantly along with many other aspects of yourself as long as you keep challenging it.

Exploring New Cultures

Traveling is an insurmountable way to learn from other people and the ways of their lives. This can lead to you cultivate understanding and empathy with others. And the more we appreciate how different communities face challenges, find joy, and hold resiliency, the more we will appreciate the shared human experiences that unite us.

With this new found empathy you can create meaningful connections with people who are completely different from you. Travel helps you build a global mindset through experiencing new places, embracing cultural immersion, and seeking understanding and empathy.

Solo Travel: A Journey of Self-Reflection

Solo travel isn't just an adventure but also a time for personal development. When you go on your own journey it gives you freedom to reflect on yourself and become independent. It's your time to break free from your comfort zone and discover what makes up you.

When you're traveling alone there is nothing for anyone else's agenda or preferences. You have the freedom to do whatever you want, wherever you want it – making your own decisions while relying only on yourself. It's such a strong sense of self-reliance that it'll forever change how independent you are.

Exploring new destinations by yourself forces fear out of your mind by throwing hurdles at you head-on. Whether they be navigating unfamiliar streets, talking in languages not granted by birth right or making new friends - solo travel pushes growth on every inch of your body.

Alone time is essential when growing as a person especially in an environment far far away from home. But having those moments allow us to connect with ourselves about life, our goals/aspirations - all without any distractions that keep us occupied back at home.

By dropping yourself into different cultures while interacting with people who were raised in them – solo travel will make sure empathy, understanding as well as respect for others grow within us all. We all know traveling broadens our worldview but it also teaches us not to judge a book by it's cover. And finally, solo travel will nurture your self-reliance and ability to adapt in any environment.

So whether you're exploring the luscious landscapes of New Zealand or hopping through Tokyo, Japan - solo travel offers us all an opportunity for self-discovery, personal development as well as independence.

Developing Intercultural Competence with Travel

As our world becomes more interconnected so does our need to better understand each other. And this expanding necessity is why developing intercultural competence is essential today. But thankfully traveling around the globe gives us all the tools we need to navigate and appreciate diverse cultures.

Cultural immersion lies at the core of intercultural competence development. When you take the time to get involved in different environments, you gain firsthand experience and understanding of various cultures. Whether it's exploring ancient temples in India, eating traditional cuisine in Italy, or taking part in ceremonies in Japan, every encounter has something valuable to offer you. This allows for insights that wouldn't be possible without being there.

Another key component of developing intercultural competence is interacting with people from diverse backgrounds. Engaging in conversations, sharing stories, and forming connections with individuals from all walks of life allow you to learn from their experiences. Not only do these interactions foster empathy and cultural sensitivity - they also strengthen your open-mindedness by challenging your assumptions. Allowing for a much easier time bridging any cultural gaps that may arise.

Traveling also gives alternative perspectives on important issues such as social, political, and environmental challenges. Having differing viewpoints helps develop a deeper understanding of global problems and the interconnectedness we all share. With this information on hand it's much easier to meaningfully contribute towards fixing these issues.

Lastly, developing intercultural competence through travel equips you vital skills needed for moving through multicultural environments confidently. Being able to adapt to new situations and effectively communicate across language barriers are just two examples of many that have great value in today's highly connected world.

By immersing yourself in foreign cultures head first and making countless connections along the way, travel becomes a truly transforming tool for personal growth and global understanding.

Starting today will be best for personal growth along with a greater global outlook.

Overcoming Challenges: Building Resilience and Adaptability

Like many other things we undertake during our lives traveling tests us constantly on our abilities to overcome unforeseen challenges, but what does it help build? Resilience and adaptability! When navigating unfamiliar territories we often find ourselves face-to-face with unexpected situations which we then need to find a way through. As soon as we're pushed out of our comfort zones and into the unknown, it becomes necessary to tap into our inner strength and get creative with our solutions.

Overcoming language barriers, adapting to new customs, and dealing with delays may all be frustrating at first. But in the end, each challenge teaches us valuable life lessons. By doing so we develop resilience which is essentially the ability to bounce back from setbacks confidently. It helps us adapt much faster while becoming more flexible mentally.

Skills learned during travel go far beyond just that however. Having the two skills mentioned above can have a positive impact on many other areas in life. This includes both personal and professional challenges that we would face on any given day.

Think of traveling as another chance at facing adversity but coming out stronger than before. Leaving our comfort zones encourages growth while equipping us tools necessary for this journey called life.

Expanding Your Comfort Zone: Embracing the Unknown

Few things push us to the edges of our comfort zones quite like personal development. Usually, it's the unfamiliarity and uncertainty that turn people away. But by embracing change, you'll open doors to many incredible experiences. And with time, these will help you grow as a person.

Visiting new places where everything feels unfamiliar can be a tough experience for most people. The language is different, the food is foreign to your taste buds, and not even your daily routine is the same. You're thrown into an environment where there's no choice but to adapt and learn how to navigate through.

This forces you to grow mentally in ways you wouldn't imagine. Your ability to handle problems gets tested every day. You have no choice but to trust your gut when making decisions with little information provided. This self reliance builds up confidence over time.

All these changes are just on the surface level. Do something good enough times and it becomes second nature after all! The stuff that's deeper within us are our character traits - what make us who we are at our core.

After traveling long enough and embracing its unknowns, we learn to appreciate different perspectives more easily. To become adaptable when faced with a situation we've never been in before. Even when we see someone whose life couldn't be more different than ours, we find common ground rather than focusing on our differences.

The next time you get a chance to travel somewhere new don't run away from it out of fear of stepping out of your comfort zone . Dive right in! Test yourself physically and mentally! Give it 100% effort! By doing so you'll go through plenty of hardships but come out stronger than ever before!

Building Connections Across the Globe

Not only does traveling show us more parts of this world, it also introduces us to other humans along the way too . By traveling far beyond any normal range that one would usually stick within , you give yourself access to more than just the things you can see and touch.

There'll be times where you find yourself needing help or advice. These are the moments where having a global network comes in handy! It's not for fun, although it does have its perks. Most of the time traveling involves spending money too!

When visiting unfamiliar places, we naturally come across all sorts of people . People who dress different. People who speak in languages that we don't understand . Even people who may not share the same values as us . But what do we do when all these differences are thrown onto us at once ? We seek out common ground instead!

This alone has a positive impact on our personal development because it forces us to adopt new perspectives. To think about life through someone else's point of view . And by doing so, we're giving ourselves an endless supply of knowledge, insights, and experiences that no book could ever provide.

The relationships built through traveling with others can also turn into great opportunities for both personal and professional growth. Imagine moving to a completely different country only knowing one person there! That'd be tough right? Now imagine if you had multiple connections there instead… I'm sure it'd be much easier!

Not only would you have someone to help you adapt to your new surroundings , but they could also introduce you to their friends who work in a field that interests you ! See how powerful this is? By making friends everywhere you go it essentially acts as a cheat code for success !

Even though being part of something like this sounds amazing , don't forget that forming them is just as hard as maintaining them . While abroad use your intuition! You'll know whether or not somebody is worth having around after spending a few minutes with them.

Travel gives us an ability to build connections all over the world and develop a global network. From there, we're able to cultivate personal growth, gain a broader perspective, and create a global mindset. So let's take advantage of this power of travel to not only explore the world but build long lasting connections as well.

Travel as Education: Lifelong Learning on the Road

It's no secret that traveling helps develop your personality while you grow as a person. But even though you're just visiting places and experiencing different cultures around the world; you can still see it as educational . It offers plenty of opportunities for learning and acquiring new knowledge, skills, and insights.

Once you start on this journey, multiple doors will open up that'll help you in ways you didn't think possible. You could be exploring historical sites one day while trying local food the next; maybe even engaging in meaningful conversations with locals after that. Both interactions will continue expanding your mind and understanding of things around you.

One of the best things about education through travel is being exposed to different perspectives and ideas. Immersing yourself in new cultures puts an appreciation for diversity deep into your core; helping develop an inclusive mindset that challenges preconceptions and biases.

Furthermore, going from place to place provides chances to learn practical skills too. For example navigating through unknown transportation systems or adapting to customs from other countries - every challenge comes with its benefits that eventually lead to better problem-solving abilities.

Cultural Immersion: Learning Beyond the Classroom

Being submerged in another culture helps gain knowledge like never before. Traveling grants access to routines, daily life practices, cultural activities and more. By partaking in these events or simply observing them unfold; gaining genuine understanding becomes easy.

Talking with people from backgrounds unlike yours opens up a whole new world for exchange - where views broaden and challenges test limits for growth. These moments foster personal growth by promoting understanding, tolerance, and appreciation for diverse cultures and viewpoints.

Continuous Learning: A Lifelong Journey

One of the most remarkable aspects of travel as education is that it's a journey that never ends. Each destination visited holds an opportunity for learning and discovery. For example, whether it's a historical landmark, a local museum, or just a good old marketplace; each new experience enriches your knowledge and broadens your understanding of the world.

Moreover, travel also gives you the chance to learn about yourself. Stepping out of your comfort zone and encountering new situations leads to self-discovery, personal reflection, and improved self-awareness. By doing so through traveling, you develop a deeper understanding of values, strengths, and areas for personal growth.

Traveling as education is something that'll improve your life forever as it nurtures personal development. Whether you decide to embark on this journey with friends or by yourself; what matters is that you're growing all around while improving how you see things in general.

Sustainable Travel: Fostering a Global Consciousness

It's one thing traveling without thinking about anything else other than having fun. But when it comes to sustainability we must consider our impact on not only the environment but also the communities we visit.

By making conscious choices and being mindful of our actions, we can make a difference. Choosing eco-friendly accommodations, supporting local businesses, and minimizing waste are just some ways to practice sustainable travel.

Sustainable travel not only benefits the environment but also contributes to personal growth. It allows us to connect with nature, experience diverse cultures, and gain a global perspective.

Embracing sustainable travel can be life-changing. It encourages us to become responsible consumers, promotes responsible tourism and preserves the treasured beauty of our planet for future generations.

Travel as a Journey in Personal Transformation

Get inspired by these real-life stories that highlight profound growth, self-discovery and a broader world view achieved through immersive travel experiences. Each story showcases the transformative impact that travel can have on an individual's life.

Meet Sarah who embarked on her solo backpacking trip across Europe. Through navigating new territories and embracing the unknown she gained confidence and independence that carried over into her everyday life. Stepping out of her comfort zone fostered personal growth.

Join David as he ventured into Southeast Asia to volunteer in remote villages. Through his cultural immersion he developed deep empathy and understanding for other ways of living. His newfound passion for making an impact led him into pursuing further education.

Walk alongside Emma as she explored the diverse landscapes of South America. By overcoming language barriers, adapting quickly to new environments & customs she honed her resilience and adaptability skills. Her journey shaped her professional goals in international relations.

These stories are mere glimpses into how transformative travel can be. Whether it be embarking on your own solo adventure or fully immersing yourself in another culture - there is no ceiling to personal growth from traveling.

Reflections: A Once In A Lifetime Journey

As we close this door on personal development through travel it is important to reflect back on how profound exploring the world can be for our lives. Travel is more than just visiting new places; it changes everything about us.

By immersing ourselves in other cultures, we also gain a deeper understanding of who we are. While the process of doing so can be uncomfortable at times, it is always necessary. We must challenge our beliefs & values.

Chapter 26

A Guide to
Midlife Reinvention

Self-reflection will be a big part of this process. It's vital in uncovering your true passions and finding out what path is best for you. Setting goals and creating a plan to achieve them will ensure you stay on track and make any significant changes that are necessary.

You're going to need resilience too. Everyone faces challenges, there's no way around it. So we'll discuss how to be resilient while sharing inspiring stories from people who have overcome obstacles during their reinvention journeys. Since we're already discussing careers, we'll focus on making changes and personal growth as well.

Overcoming the doubts that come with change will also be covered. Alongside ways on how you can build confidence throughout the process. While following along with this journey it's important for you to surround yourself with like-minded individuals who want you to succeed as well.

Finally, we'll guide down the path of sustaining success which is very much different from achieving it initially.

If all of this sounds good then let's dive into Chapter 26

Embracing Change: The Key to Reinvention

Reinventing yourself isn't easy, especially when it comes to embracing change. Our brains are wired for routine so breaking free from comfort zones is gonna take some time but at the end of it all it's definitely worth it.

It's no question fear and resistance hold us back but once we embrace these new perspectives they won't bother us anymore. There's a lot more potential than what lies in our comfort zones.

Getting over fear is definitely easier said than done though so there needs to be a mindset shift here. Let go of old beliefs and allow other perspectives in your life because at this moment those might just be holding you back.

With change also comes adaptability. There's going to be failures but rather than dwelling on them learn from them so next time you know exactly how things should go.

Whenever embarking on something new a lot of times we aren't going to know what's coming. It's important for you to be willing to learn and grow from experiences and approach everything with an open mind.

Thinking about possible positive outcomes is going to help a bunch too. If you close your eyes and clearly visualize the person you want to become, creating that vision is only a few steps away.

You're also going to need some support along the way. Surround yourself with individuals who have successfully reinvented themselves as well. Build relationships with those who've already been here because they know exactly how it feels.

Remember this isn't something that happens overnight, if it did then there wouldn't be much fulfillment in it. But by embracing change in every aspect of your life, opportunities will continue presenting themselves.

Icons of Reinvention: Inspiring Success Stories

Reinventing yourself in midlife can seem like an impossible task but these success stories prove that statement completely wrong. From everyday people all the way up to millionaires, these icons have shown us how we can completely reshape our lives at any age. One example is Oprah Winfrey who started out with a rough upbringing but became a media mogul and philanthropist later on. She had to work hard to transform herself and all the struggles she faced into growth opportunities for success.

Another famous figure is Colonel Sanders, the KFC founder. Although he faced roadblock after roadblock, including business failures and personal problems. He didn't let age or adversity define him. He reinvented himself in his sixties instead, creating the iconic KFC brand.

These stories of success should inspire us and help us find our own path to our true passions.

They don't mean it's too late for you either. Whether you're trying to change careers, grow personally, or just looking for something new, these people's stories show that if we try hard enough, we can do anything.

Self-Reflection: Discovering Your Inner Desires

Reflecting on ourselves is a necessary step when trying to change how we are as people. It allows individuals to go deep within themself so they can uncover what actually makes them happy or passionate in life.

During this journey of self-reinvention it is crucial that we take time out of our day so that we can really think about things like values strengths and aspirations. Doing this will align your actions with your authentic self which means more purposeful living and fulfillment in life.

We can reflect on ourselves using various methods such as writing in a journal meditating or talking with others who know us best like friends or mentors. Activities like this will allow us to gain clarity on what matters most in life.

Once we have discovered our inner thoughts and desires we can start making choices based off them. It could be changing careers starting a passion project prioritizing personal growth whatever really makes you happy as long as it helps you live your best life possible

Setting Goals: Charting Your Course for Change

When you want to make changes its important that you set goals. By doing this it will help you make an effective map in order to achieve your desired outcome and make sure you stay on track.

Here are a few tips that can help with setting goals:

1. Define your vision:

Start by thinking about the ideal future for yourself. What do you want to achieve through this journey of reinvention? Be specific and think about how certain areas of your life need significant changes.

2. Prioritize:

Think about what goals should be number 1 based off their impact on the overall journey. Then consider long-term benefits and just make sure they align with your values and passions.

3. Break it down:

Large tasks can look scary especially if they seem impossible so divide them into smaller milestones that way you can get small wins along the way while staying motivated.

4. Be specific:

1. Make your goals SMART:

Specific, Measurable, Achievable, Relevant, Time-Bound

i. Clearly define what you want to accomplish

ii. Be realistic with the targets you set for yourself

iii. And make deadlines – they'll help keep you accountable.

5. Create an action plan:

Outline the specific steps and actions that will lead you to your goal. Break everything down into smaller tasks and be as detailed as possible. Set a timeline and schedule to ensure consistent progress throughout.

6. Stay focused and flexible:

Keep in mind where you want to end up but also be open to adjusting plans when necessary – life happens!

With the right goals set in place and an action plan ready, taking control of your own journey will feel empowering. You'll confidently navigate through whatever obstacles come your way knowing exactly how far you've come already.

Resilience: Overcoming Challenges Along the Way

In our journeys of reinventing ourselves, resilience plays a big part.

The ability to face challenges head-on is what keeps us moving forward no matter what those challenges are. In this section we'll explore more about resilience itself along with real-life stories that showcased remarkable strength and determination in times of great despair.

Lessons from Real-Life Resilience

Meet Sarah who underwent a complete transformation after being fired from her job which was quite discouraging at first but she didn't give up on herself.. Instead, Sarah used that opportunity as fuel for growth and embraced new opportunities whenever they came knocking on her door.. Her unwavering determination eventually paid off because not only did she find success again but she also found fulfillment in her work like never before..

Another inspiring story is that of Mark who felt like every step he took towards becoming an entrepreneur there was another hurdle waiting for him halfway there.. From having his financial sources cut off to having fierce competition all around him - Mark's resilience was tested everyday.. For some, these challenges would've been enough to make them quit but not Mark.. He had a clear vision of what he wanted and every challenge that came his way was just another opportunity to learn from.. And now, standing tall is his business thriving in its glory.

Strategies for Resilience

Resilience is like a muscle you develop over time so here are a few strategies that'll help you build it:

1. Develop a Growth Mindset: Embrace challenges as opportunities for growth and view setbacks as temporary obstacles that can be overcome.

2. Practice Self-Care: Prioritize self-care activities such as exercise, meditation, and relaxation techniques to build emotional and mental strength.

3. Seek Support: Surround yourself with a network of supportive individuals who uplift and encourage you during challenging times.

4. Learn from Setbacks: Embrace failures as valuable learning experiences and use them to fuel personal and professional growth.

Remembering that resilience doesn't necessarily mean avoiding challenges altogether is crucial.. It's more about developing the inner strength to face anything life throws at you.. By adopting this mindset along with using the strategies above - nothing will be able to stop your rise!

Rebranding your career takes a lot of planning and getting out of your comfort zone. We have experts that help with this and give you steps to make things easier. If you're considering changing fields or just exploring other opportunities in the same industry, the information we provide will be valuable on your journey.

We made a series of articles where people talk about their success stories to inspire others. They all transitioned into new careers without any hiccups. It shows how transforming can lead to better things if you're willing to take that step.

You'll see how others transitioned into another field within this chapter. From creating their own businesses to taking on different industries, they've all found success on their path.

Growing Spiritually: Changing the Way You Think

When you think about it, personal growth is what leads someone to change themselves no matter what aspect it is. The mind, body, and spirit are all part of this journey, but focusing on one at a time can lead individuals down a prosperous path.

One way for some personal growth is learning something new every day. Reading books and attending workshops can help you change the way you think which could open up new doors for ideas. Things like embracing challenges, overcoming limiting beliefs, and building a mindset that says change is good can help when wanting something fresh.

The body also plays a role in this process too as strange as it sounds. Making sure not only what you eat but that self-care plays an important role will also have effects both physically and mentally. When working out regularly energy levels go up along with improving overall health leading to less stress and more confidence.

Lastly there's spiritual growth which goes by connecting with yourself spiritually through meditation or finding purpose in things around us. By nourishing the spirit individuals gain clarity and peace allowing them to align actions with who they really are.

Many amazing stories came from people going through personal growth during their reinvention process These stories demonstrate the power of transforming the mind, body, and spirit. From CEOs who prioritize mindfulness to athletes who harness their mental strength, these success stories serve as beacons of hope and inspiration for those seeking their own personal transformation.

The road to personal growth is endless but it's what sets people up for success when rebranding themselves. By bringing strategies into practice anyone can unlock potential and create a new life.

Having someone to support you can make all the difference. People who have experienced success and are in a similar boat as you can help keep you motivated and focused.

Build relationships with people who are going through something similar. You'll have experiences to share, ideas to exchange, and support to offer. Together, these things create a sense of belonging and can help each other get through difficult times.

Building a network that supports you can be done in various ways:

- Attending workshops
- Going to seminars

- Industry-specific conferences

The internet is great too! You can join forums or social media groups where like-minded people from around the world hang out.

Here's an example: Jane Adams was fed up with her previous job and decided she wanted a change. She joined local professional networks, attended industry events, and surrounded herself with people who knew how it felt. With their insight, advice, and encouragement she was able to achieve everything she wanted.

Building this type of network is crucial if you want to reinvent yourself. It's not just about getting emotional support but also being open for new opportunities and collaborations. So go ahead and connect with people who've experienced what you did or even better, lots of them.

Overcoming Doubts

Embarking on a journey of transformation comes with its own doubts and insecurities. It's natural to ask whether or not we're capable of making big changes in our lives. But by building confidence we're able to overcome these doubts and embrace the power of transforming ourselves.

A strategy for building confidence is acknowledging your limiting beliefs then challenging them head-on. Try identifying negative thoughts that weigh heavily on your mind then flipping them into positive thoughts.

Rack your brain for any past accomplishments or skills you've learned over time then remind yourself about them. By doing this, creating self-assurance becomes easier which will push us further along our journey.

Visualization Exercise:

Try starting each day imagining yourself successfully pushing through the changes you want to make. Picture all of the positive things that come with your transformation. The satisfaction, fulfillment, and happiness will follow. When visualizing your future self, it'll be easier to gain confidence which then leads to motivation.

Another strategy is putting yourself in situations where you'll have no choice but to take risks. Every time you push yourself out of your comfort zone and try something new, it'll build up your confidence little by little. Then as you go on and become more comfortable with change, start increasing the difficulty of every challenge.

You're not alone:

Always remember that you don't have to do this alone! Surround yourself with friends and family or even mentors who are rooting for your success. Share your goals with them, let them know what worries you, and ask for their guidance. With this support system in place there's nothing holding us back from our reinvention journey!

Throughout your reinvention process, it's important to be kind to yourself and practice self-compassion. Acknowledge that setbacks and challenges are a natural part of the journey, and don't let them undermine your confidence. Celebrate your progress, no matter how small, and remain resilient in the face of obstacles.

By implementing these strategies and exercises, you can build the confidence needed to overcome doubts and fears during the reinvention process. Embrace the power of personal transformation and unlock the limitless possibilities that await you.

Sustaining Success: Thriving in Your Reinvented Life

Reinventing yourself and making significant changes in life is an incredible achievement, but the journey doesn't end there. Sustaining success and thriving in your reinvented life requires dedication, perseverance, and the right mindset. In this final section, we will explore strategies and habits that will help you maintain progress and continue to flourish in your new life.

One of the key aspects of sustaining success is learning from success stories of individuals who have gone through similar transformations. Hearing about their experiences, challenges, and triumphs can provide you with valuable insights and inspiration. These success stories show that it is possible to overcome obstacles and create a fulfilling life, giving you the motivation to keep pushing forward.

Another essential strategy for sustaining success is continuously evaluating and adjusting your goals. As you navigate your reinvented life, it's important to reassess your aspirations and make necessary changes to stay aligned with your evolving desires. This flexibility will enable you to adapt to new opportunities and challenges, ensuring that you continue to grow and thrive in your journey of reinvention.

Lastly, building a supportive network is crucial for sustaining success. Surrounding yourself with like-minded individuals who understand your goals can provide the encouragement and accountability needed for growth. Establishing meaningful connections with others who share similar experiences provides additional motivation against any hurdles that come your way.

Chapter 27

Overcoming Midlife
Limiting Beliefs

Welcome to Chapter 27: Overcoming Midlife Limiting Beliefs. During midlife, it's common to feel held back from growing and embracing new opportunities due to beliefs we hold within ourselves. However, there's good news – We have the ability to challenge these limits and make a life for ourselves full of possibilities.

In this chapter, we will go over strategies and mindset shifts that will help you overcome these beliefs often encountered in this stage of life. By understanding and confronting these limiting beliefs head-on, you can unleash your true potential and reach an infinite midlife.

Are you ready to explore yourself in ways you never could before? Let's jump into it and find the tools needed to create the life you want while overcoming midlife limiting beliefs.

Understanding Limiting Beliefs in Midlife

Before we can learn how to overcome them, it's crucial that we understand what limiting beliefs are. These are thoughts and attitudes that prevent us from reaching our goals. They usually come about from previous events, conditioning by society or even negative self-perception.

During mid-life is when these thoughts become very obvious. It'll almost seem like they take over our entire brain. Our abilities suddenly see doubt in themselves while feeling stuck on the current situation at hand or doubting if we're able to make changes at all. This ends up creating a wall against personal growth which then smothers our dreams as well as aspirations.

Here are some common mid-life thoughts holding people back:

The belief that starting something new is too late

Feeling too old to learn or adapt

Thinking only younger generations can obtain success or happiness

Believing others' needs must be fulfilled before your own

Deciding taking risks is dangerous or irresponsible

It all starts with becoming aware of when they appear so they can be understood and worked through properly. When they do show up, it'll usually manifest as negative self-talk, self-doubt or even a fear of stepping out of our comfort zones. Once a thought is noticed, it can then be challenged by asking yourself if it's true or false.

Understanding these beliefs in mid-life requires thought and the ability to question ourselves. By examining why we believe these things and how true they actually are will help get rid of them so new narratives can be created in their place to support growth and potential.

Identifying Limiting Beliefs

Now that you have an understanding of what limiting beliefs are and where they come from, it's time to identify the specific ones that affect you specifically. In this stage, being self-aware is crucial as well as the capability to dive deep into your thoughts and emotions.

Start off with seeing which areas of your life feel stuck or unfulfilled. Then make sure to ask yourself why you believe you're either incapable or unable to reach certain goals or chase specific dreams. Finally, see what fears, doubts or negative thoughts hold you back from doing anything about it.

Uncovering them even more

Journaling is incredibly powerful when trying to uncover these beliefs. Take some time every day to write down how you're feeling, what's going through your mind at the moment and any observations you'd like to take note of. Paying close attention for patterns or recurring themes could bring light on something that needs addressing.

After journaling comes techniques that'll help further uncover them so they can then be challenged:

The most common questions people ask themselves after reading this chapter:

Visualization: Sit down and visualize obtaining your goals. As you do take note of any negative thoughts that come up. These thoughts will help you identify your limiting beliefs.

Self-reflection: Every now and then, sit down quietly by yourself and ask yourself why you believe what you believe. Stay honest with yourself and don't be afraid to open up.

External feedback: Speak with friends, family members or mentors who can provide an unbiased opinion on the things that they see you doing wrong.

Therapy or coaching: Consider seeking professional aid from a therapist, counselor or coach who specializes in limiting beliefs. They will be able to help guide you through the process of identifying and overcoming these beliefs.

Most importantly, is to remember that this process doesn't happen overnight. It requires a lot of patience love for oneself and a commitment towards personal growth. As you go through this journey always celebrate each step forward!

Examining the Impact

To put it simply, limiting beliefs really mess up our mindset as well as our overall well-being. When we hold onto certain beliefs that restrict our potential we become limited in what we can achieve in life. These beliefs act like road blockers preventing us from being open to new opportunities and taking risks.

Imagine having a belief that tells you that "you aren't good enough" or "success is only for others". This way of thinking shapes the way we see ourselves making us doubt even our own abilities at times. The impact of these self-limiting beliefs isn't just restricted to career choices or personal growth but also affects things like relationships, happiness as well as overall satisfaction with life itself. When we start believing these things about ourselves it becomes easier for us to think negatively. The more negative thoughts we have the more actions will reflect them which means... absolutely nothing gets done.

Physical health is also affected by limiting beliefs not just mental health alone! Stress anxiety depression are all examples of how these restrictive ways of thinking lead to poor health.

However, by examining the impact of limiting beliefs you can start freeing yourself from their grasp. It all starts with realizing how much they negatively affect us once we have a good understanding. Only then will we be able to take the necessary steps in order to challenge and over come these self-limiting beliefs!

Throughout this chapter we will explore effective strategies and mindset shifts that will help you overcome the struggles of self-limiting beliefs. By breaking free from these chains you will be able to reach your full potential which will allow you to create a life filled with true fulfillment.

The Power of Mindset Shifts

Overcoming limiting beliefs is more than just positive thinking. It's about changing your mindset as a whole. The way we think shapes our reality for better or worse. By doing so we are opening ourselves up towards new possibilities and opportunities.

Mindset shifts involve challenging our thoughts as well as our current beliefs that hold us back. Replacing them with ones that empower, ones that build us up.

One powerful strategy for changing our mindset is through self-reflection and self-awareness. Identifying what exactly it is that holds us back allows us to consciously choose whether or not we want those beliefs taking space in our minds!

Another tactic we can do is to surround ourselves with positive influences. By reading inspiring books, listening to uplifting podcasts, or learning from people who have pushed through similar obstacles, we can start changing our mindset into a limitless and powerful one.

Changing our beliefs also requires a growth mindset. This means that we need to accept the idea that our intelligence and abilities can be improved by putting in effort and hard work. If you believe that there are limits to personal development, you'll never grow.

It's important for us to remember that shifting belief systems take time and effort. It won't be easy replacing deep-rooted beliefs, but with determination and dedication, it's possible. Start challenging yourself and removing the negative thoughts so that you can achieve success and fulfillment.

Challenging your limits

Breaking barriers goes beyond what you think is possible for yourself - now it's time to step out of your comfort zone. In doing this, countless opportunities for growth will come your way.

At first, venturing outside of your comfort zone may seem scary or uncomfortable which is completely normal. By taking risks and embracing the unfamiliarity of things is where real self-improvement starts to happen. Remember: You're capable of more than you think.

To get started on breaking past those walls you built up inside your head:

Identify areas in life where limitations are holding you back

Is it in relationships? Your career? Or perhaps even personal development?

Start small and set goals since every little push towards growth matters

Eventually expand those boundaries as going too fast could lead to unwanted outcomes

However, don't confuse pushing limits with complete recklessness either; everything should be calculated properly before making moves

It all comes down to preparing mentally, learning the needed tools, then taking the plunge into discomfort (baby steps matter!)

Each time stepping out of your comfort zone strengthens resilience while building confidence at the same time. The more you challenge yourself today, the more you'll be able to take on in the future. Lastly, learn from mistakes made and celebrate every single win - big or small.

Always remember: Discovering what else you're capable of only happens once you confront fears and overcome perceived limits.

Another strategy is to surround yourself with a supportive network of individuals who uplift and inspire you. Seek out mentors, friends, or a coach who can provide guidance and encouragement along the way. Sharing your journey with like-minded individuals can give you the motivation and accountability you need to keep pushing forward.

Additionally, cultivating a growth mindset can enhance both resilience and persistence. A growth mindset is the belief that our abilities and intelligence can be developed through dedication and effort. By adopting a growth mindset, we open ourselves up to new possibilities and are more willing to persevere through challenges.

Remember, overcoming limiting beliefs is not a linear process. You may encounter obstacles and setbacks along the way, but with resilience and persistence, you have the power to persist and continue on your path to personal growth.

Transforming Self-Talk and Inner Dialogue

The way you speak to yourself has a powerful impact on your mindset and ability to overcome limiting beliefs. Negative self-talk can reinforce those beliefs, keeping you stuck in a cycle of self-doubt and limitation. However, by transforming your self-talk and cultivating a supportive inner dialogue, you can empower yourself to break free from these constraints and embrace a more positive and fulfilling life.

One technique for transforming self-talk is through the use of positive affirmations. Affirmations are positive statements that you repeat to yourself, reinforcing new and empowering beliefs. By consciously choosing affirmations that challenge and replace your limiting beliefs, you can gradually reshape your inner dialogue and create a more supportive and encouraging self-talk.

Start by identifying the specific limiting beliefs that you want to address. Then, create affirmations that directly oppose those beliefs and reflect the reality you want to experience. For example, if you struggle with self-doubt about your abilities, affirmations such as "I am capable and competent" or "I have the skills to succeed" can help reprogram your self-talk boost yor confidence.

Consistency is key when using affirmations. It's important to repeat them regularly, ideally daily, to reinforce the new beliefs and replace the old, limiting ones. Whether you say them aloud or silently to yourself, make sure to infuse your affirmations with conviction and belief. Visualize yourself embodying the qualities and experiences you desire as you repeat your affirmations.

In addition to positive affirmations, any activity or practice that promotes self-compassion and self-care can contribute to transforming self-talk and inner dialogue. This may include journaling, meditation, or seeking support from a therapist or coach who can help you navigate and reframe your thoughts and beliefs.

Remember, transforming self-talk takes time and practice. Be patient with yourself as you replace old patterns with new, empowering ones. Over time, you'll notice a shift in your inner dialogue, as well as the way you perceive yourself and the world around you. By embracing positive self-talk and cultivating a supportive inner dialogue, you can break free from limiting beliefs and unlock your true potential in midlife.

Seeking Support and Accountability

Sometimes, overcoming limiting beliefs requires external support and accountability. It can be challenging to navigate this journey alone, which is why seeking guidance from coaches, mentors, or support groups can be immensely beneficial.

Getting support from a pro coach has been proven to help people in countless ways. They can give you valuable insights, tools, and techniques to challenge your limiting beliefs. By doing so, you'll be able to overcome them. Life coaches are great at helping you notice patterns of behaviour, beliefs, and behaviours that might be holding you back. With their guidance, you can create a more powerful mindset.

Accountability is also crucial when trying to shake off limiting beliefs. If there is no one there reminding us about our actions or progress we'll never stay focused on making positive changes. Accountability gives us the structure needed to improve ourselves.

Finding someone who is on the same journey as you could accelerate the speed of growth tremendously. Knowing that others have faced and overcame similar challenges can make it easier for someone to push through hardship.

Keep in mind that even though asking for help may feel like a sign of weakness it's really not. People who ask for support typically end up reaching their goal faster than if they didn't get help from others.

Embrace Limitlessness

There's a lot of potential that comes with old age and its very important we take advantage of it too. Once we unlock our fullest potential nothing will be able to stop us from living the life we want.

You might currently think that what I just said doesn't apply to you because If I told myself this I wouldn't believe me either but It's true! Every single person has potential locked away deep inside themselves which once harnessed could change their lives forever.

In this chapter we went over many mindset shifts and strategies needed to change these limiting beliefs into limitless ones. While doing this You'll find yourself challenging your self-imposed limits much more often which Is great because in order for us to grow we need to step out of our comfort zones every now and then.

Most importantly we need to start believing in ourselves again. This alone has the power to completely change our lives. If we replace all the negativity that goes on inside of our heads with empowering affirmations we can reshape our beliefs and unlock unimaginable potential.

Just know that this is not a journey you have to go through alone. Seeking support, guidance, and accountability from coaches, mentors, or support groups will make everything much easier. Let's unlock the greatness in us and embrace a limitless midlife.

Chapter 28

Health Screenings
and Prevention

Welcome to Chapter 28 on health. In this segment, we want to highlight and stress the importance of making adequate time for health screenings and prevention strategies. Prioritizing these two things will guarantee optimal well-being. By doing so you can ensure that whatever resources you need are available and also unlock the secret to living a longer life.

Taking an active approach when it comes to your health means that you stay ahead of any potential health issues and protect your overall well-being. Checking for diseases in their earliest stages is vital in maintaining good health because it allows for timely intervention and effective treatment.

Although peace of mind is a major benefit, it makes up only one part of all the benefits that come from professional health checks. It lets us make informed decisions about our body and helps us develop preventive measures like vaccinations, lifestyle modifications, and regular exercise which all help in reducing your risk of developing certain conditions.

Additionally, integrating a well-balanced diet filled with nutritious foods into your life can promote overall well-being while at the same time lowering the risk of chronic diseases.

Different types of illnesses have different types of check-up methods so it's important to be aware when choosing which test to take. This chapter will go over screenings for common conditions such as cancer, heart disease, diabetes as well as genetic testing which allows us to identify potential risks within our own bloodline.

Having access to medical resources is extremely crucial because having accurate results will dictate if we're taking proper care or not. We'll guide you on finding reputable healthcare providers here as well as clinics and hospitals that specialize in preventive healthcare.

To further improve this practice we will explore integrative medicine - a combination between conventional medical practices with alternative therapies - this new approach has gained popularity due to how beneficial it's been in preventing illnesses.

We can't always rely on professionals though which is why we will provide resources in order for people to broaden their knowledge on what they should be doing to stay healthy and what they should avoid.

Lastly, we'll make sure that long-term preventive habits are always present. Making it easier for people to incorporate these habits into their daily life and maintain them over time will ensure good health and well-being.

So, let's embark on this journey together and discover the power of health screenings and prevention - the best medicine for a vibrant and fulfilling life.

Understanding the Importance of Health Checks

Regular health checks are a cornerstone of preventive healthcare. These routine screenings are essential for early detection of potential health issues and play a vital role in promoting disease prevention and overall well-being.

By undergoing regular health checks, you can take proactive measures to identify any underlying health concerns before they develop into more serious conditions. This early detection allows for timely interventions and can greatly improve treatment outcomes.

Health checks encompass a variety of screenings, including but not limited to blood tests, physical examinations, and imaging studies. These tests can help identify risk factors, monitor existing conditions, and detect signs of potential health problems.

The Key Benefits of Health Checks

Regular health checks are important not only for disease prevention but also to give a good overview of how healthy you actually are. They let doctors measure useful information like your blood pressure, cholesterol levels and the general functionality of your organs giving you an idea about how healthy you really are. This is also a chance for healthcare professionals to help offer personalized guidance on maintaining a healthy lifestyle.

Diseases can be prevented if they're caught early enough so doing health check ups is super important. Things like cancer, heart disease and diabetes can all be dealt with more effectively when caught in their early stages which these checks can help detect. By analyzing these early warning signs doctors can recommend treatment before things get worse.

Health screenings also make it easier for people to take charge of their own health because they actively see what's going on inside their bodies and understand what risks they're taking by doing or not doing certain things that may affect their health long term.

Remember, prevention is the best medicine by far.

By prioritizing regular health checks, you are investing in your long-term well-being and taking proactive steps towards a healthier future.

Without a well-balanced diet, your body won't stand a chance. The food you eat is what provides your body with all the essentials it needs to stay healthy. Nutrients, vitamins and minerals are just a few of these things. Without them, your immune system will weaken and you'll get sick easily.

This doesn't mean all you have to do is eat healthy and nothing bad will happen to you. But by making conscious choices about food, you can definitely lower the risk of many diseases and keep your weight on the right track.

Certain nutrients have proven time and time again that they're super helpful in preventing disease. Antioxidants are found in colorful fruits and vegetables – they fight free radicals which cause chronic diseases like cancer, heart disease and more. Then there's omega-3 fatty acids found in fatty fish that has been linked to reduced inflammation.

Nutrition's Effect on Disease Prevention

A good diet can really make all the difference when it comes to disease prevention as research has shown us:

Diets rich in fruits and veggies can reduce the chances of developing certain types of cancer.

Too much salt or sugar leads to high blood pressure and diabetes so avoid processed foods as much possible.

Heart disease and stroke are less likely if whole grains are part of your daily diet.

Weighing too much is never good for anyone – even children. Maintaining a healthy weight prevents obesity-related conditions such as joint problems or type 2 diabetes.

Tips for A Healthy Diet

If you want preventive healthcare to work for you then having a well-rounded balanced diet is where its at:

Try eating fruits with different colors so that way you get all sorts of nutrients from each one.

Grains should always be whole instead of refined – quinoa would be one such example.

Lean proteins are great! Poultry, tofu, legumes and fish should be enjoyed often!

Red meat isn't bad for ya but eating too much of it is. Same goes for high-fat dairy products and processed foods.

Salt can ruin your blood pressure and sugar your blood sugar levels, so avoid anything that comes in a package if you can.

You gotta stay hydrated! Drink enough water throughout the day.

By following these tips, you'll be able to make better choices when it comes to food. You definitely don't want disease coming after you because of something that could've been prevented from a simple diet change!

Screenings for Common Health Conditions

There are certain medical checks that should be done regularly. These checks need to happen so that way they can detect common conditions early on which will then help keep them under control. Medical screenings are essential in maintaining a healthy body – they're what lets us know ahead of time how our bodies react to certain things, the possible risks and what steps we should take next.

Cancer screenings include mammograms (breast cancer), pap smears (cervical cancer) or colonoscopies (colon cancer). All 3 tests detect early signs of cancer which allow people to get treatment as soon as possible.

Heart disease is one thing everyone fears but not many people actually think about doing anything about it until its too late. It's very easy to find out how healthy your heart is just by checking cholesterol and blood pressure levels every once in a while.

There's 2 types of diabetes: type 1 and type 2. Both develop from different causes however both can develop complications over time if not kept under control. Being tested for diabetes is easy – all doctors do is check your blood sugar levels with a small prick on your finger!

Other conditions such as osteoporosis, glaucoma or sexually transmitted infections are also important. That being said, health checks shouldn't only be done when you're feeling bad – they need to happen even when you're at peak health!

Genetic testing is changing the game in preventive medicine. By analyzing an individual's DNA, a genetic screening can reveal health risks and lead to personalized prevention strategies.

Of course, regular check-ups are crucial. But with genetic testing, healthcare providers can identify subtly hidden susceptibilities for certain diseases or conditions.

Ultimately, this means people can gain a better understanding of their body as a whole. And through that understanding, they gain the ability to come up with plans tailored to their own needs.

For example, if someone is at high risk of cardiovascular disease because of genetics- measures can be put in place early on to reduce the possibility. This could include lifestyle changes or even medication.

Genetic testing can also help doctors determine how someone will respond to certain medications. This information allows them to prescribe drugs based on an individual's unique makeup - thus avoiding negative side effects.

While all this sounds great - it's important that we use caution when implementing these techniques. Genetic tests should always be done under the guidance of a professional and interpreted by certified labs

With proper implementation though, there's no doubt genetic testing has made its way into our lives and homes - ultimately leading us down the path of healthier lifestyles overall.

Accessing Quality Medical Resources

When it comes to your health you don't want anything short of the best medical resources available. So it's critical you don't cut corners here either.

Start by researching and gathering information about various healthcare facilities in your area. Look for facilities that have a strong reputation for providing high-quality healthcare services.

Online reviews can be helpful but take those with a grain of salt. Friends and family are always reliable sources too so make sure you get their input as well.

It's also worth checking if they accept your insurance or offer affordable payment options. There's no point going somewhere super fancy if you'll break the bank doing so - especially for something preventable like regular check ups or screenings.

Integrative Medicine for Prevention

Integrative medicine is the best of both worlds. It combines conventional medical practices with alternative therapies to promote prevention and overall wellness. So integrating it into your own lifestyle can be really beneficial.

Integrative medicine acknowledges how complicated health can be. It's a mix of many things including physical, mental, and emotional aspects of well-being. But by implementing things like acupuncture, herbal solutions, yoga, mindfulness practices it takes a holistic approach to preventative care.

One of the main benefits integrative medicine has is the way it focuses on personalized treatment plans. Health checks and screenings are used to figure out potential risks for someone's health. Then using that information they create a unique plan for every individual. This ensures that diseases will be avoided and overall health will be maintained to the highest degree possible.

Empowering patients with knowledge is another thing integrative medicine focuses on heavily. By educating them on specific symptoms they're able to make informed decisions about their own health. This includes implementing preventative measures and making lifestyle changes too.

The Role of Complementary Therapies

Complementary therapies are one part of integrative medicine. They help complement conventional medical treatments while promoting general well-being. These types of therapy are often used to alleviate symptoms, manage stress, and support natural healing processes in our bodies.

When prevention comes into play complementary therapies can help address imbalances and promote general wellness as well. For example acupuncture could be used to help manage chronic pain which reduces reliance on medication.

By curling these types of treatments into preventive healthcare people can access more options for treatment and achieve holistic approaches easier.

We've reached a new era in preventative healthcare thanks to integrative medicine. It recognizes how important personal care is empowering patients so they can take proactive steps to ensure their own health is safeguarded. By taking advantage of both conventional treatments along with alternative therapies there's now an inclusive approach that promotes prevention and overall wellness.

Prevention Knowledge Because Knowledge is Power

There's no doubt about it education empowers us all especially when it comes to our health so being aware of prevention strategies isn't just helpful its critical at times. With this knowledge we can take control of our well-being and make informed decisions.

Regular health checks are the building blocks for preventative medicine. Letting professionals detect potential issues early enough to intervene quickly. Whether that means routine screenings for blood pressure, cholesterol levels or specific testing for conditions such as cancer or diabetes. These things form a foundation for proactive health care.

Prevention strategies go beyond just these checks though. Knowing which minimal lifestyle changes will lead to good health is also critical. Eating a balanced diet, keeping your weight in check, exercising regularly, and practicing stress management techniques are just some things that help. Vaccinations are important too.

These aren't the only modifications you should be aware of either specific screenings for common health conditions play a huge role too. Regular screenings for things like heart disease and diabetes can assist with catching potential problems early so you can have the best chance at surviving them.

Also knowing what your genetics look like helps out as well. By understanding certain risks you'll be able to change aspects of your life that could lead you down a path towards them.

To make sure you're getting the best for your health, research the healthcare providers, clinics, and hospitals that are accessible to you. Keep in mind things like how reputable they are, their medical services' quality, and their expertise.

To ensure that you make well-informed decisions about your health and can then work with your provider, it's important to look for reliable resources. With these resources you'll be able to expand your knowledge on preventing diseases and screenings. By staying updated on recommendations as well as trends in health, you can work towards having a healthy life.

Sustaining habits is crucial in order to see results from preventive measures and keep protecting yourself from any threats. One way of doing this is by making them part of your daily routine so that they become second nature. You could set reminders for checkups or medication intakes. And follow advice on lifestyle modifications.

Having people around also helps when it comes to maintaining habits. Let family or friends know about your goals and ask them for support if needed. Joining community groups or finding others with similar goals will help too.

Chapter 29

Legacy and Impact Thinking

Legacy is a powerful concept that we'll explore throughout this chapter. Your actions can have lasting effects, and your choices will shape your journey and the future.

Understanding Legacy and Its Significance

Legacy isn't just about our personal achievements. It encompasses the impact we leave behind that affects others and the world as a whole. You can only appreciate how important legacy is when you understand that every action you take leaves an indelible mark.

When boiled down, legacy refers to who we are at our core. All of it: our principles, values, choices, and actions. The way people remember us is an embodiment of our legacy - it's what influences generations after generations.

Going Beyond Personal Achievements

Yes, what we accomplish in life reflects part of our legacy. But don't be flattered by those things alone; they're not enough to make a lasting difference for everyone else around you.

True testament to your character are the lives you help change for the better. How much good did you do? When it comes to creating a better world, providing mentorship or being charitable will always play a more important role than individual success.

To create something extraordinary with your actions though. To shape the world around you into something much more meaningful and profound requires one thing - understanding legacy itself.

Defining Impactful Actions

So then what does it mean to create impactful actions?

For starters, it means using them to make positive differences in individuals' lives as well as society's. Changing history requires actions that go beyond simple accomplishments; they must act as catalysts for change and leave their mark on time itself.

There are many ways to bring about these changes too: kindness that touches hearts, advocating for causes dear to us or even leading projects aimed at improving everyday life - all of these yield positive results by inspiring others which leads them towards change too.

What's more is impactful actions aren't always grandiose gestures or massive projects. Sometimes, the smallest acts of kindness or empathy are what resonate the most with individuals and communities.

It's important to note that personal achievements don't define legacy either - it's all about how we impact others and the world. Through empathy, compassion, and careful decision-making, you can shape a legacy that extends far beyond your own life. You'll be setting up an influential path for those who come after you too.

Uncovering the Power of Purpose

Your actions will always be more significant when they're guided by purpose. This is a key part of leaving a mark and creating a legacy that lasts forever.

Having a clear sense of purpose drives us to take impactful actions. Benefiting not just ourselves, but also the world around us. It gives meaning and direction to our endeavors. Guiding us towards choices that can shape our legacy.

By understanding the power of purpose, we can tap into our true potential. And make a difference that resonates far beyond our individual achievements. When our actions are driven by a sense of purpose, they become fueled with passion and intention. Making them more impactful and meaningful.

When we align our actions with a purpose larger than ourselves, we become part of something greater. Our contributions extend beyond our immediate sphere of influence. Creating a ripple effect that touches the lives of others and inspires them to carry forward our legacy.

Whether it's dedicating ourselves to a cause we believe in, pursuing a career that aligns with our values, or simply making choices that have a positive impact on those around us. Purpose empowers us to leave a mark that withstands the test of time.

The Ripple Effect of Impactful Actions

When we take impactful actions, we have the power to leave a mark that extends far beyond our immediate sphere of influence. This is known as the ripple effect.

The concept suggests that even small actions can create change on an enormous scale. Just like dropping pebbles into water causes ripples to spread outward. Our impactful actions can have far-reaching consequences for people in need.

Imagine everyone striving to make positive change at once! The world would be so much better off! Each person's individual changes contribute to creating collective progress as human beings.

Leaving A Mark Through Leadership

Leadership is all about creating lasting legacies through action. Effective leaders inspire others, drive change, and leave their marks for generations down the line!

True leadership goes beyond merely leading teams or organizations. It involves guiding and empowering others! Encouraging them along their own unique journeys towards meaningful goals! By leading with purpose and passion, leaders can inspire their teams to make a positive difference and leave their mark on the world.

Leadership isn't just about achieving success. It's about using that success to uplift others! By helping those who follow them learn how to utilize their own strengths and talents. They can create a ripple effect of positive change. And this will extend far beyond their own sphere of influence.

So long as they continue to speak with conviction, act consistently, and take inspiring actions... Leaders will always be able to cultivate a culture of impact and legacy. Helping those around them develop values like integrity, empathy, innovation etc... Which in turn motivate meaningful actions that leave lasting marks on the organizations they lead!

Leadership exists outside of the realms of traditional authority. It can be found in many places, whether it's leading a community initiative or spearheading a social cause. Or even inspiring change within your own family. Every single person has the potential to become a leader and with that, they're able to make an impact.

When we embrace leadership as a whole and use it for positive change, we contribute to something greater than ourselves. By empowering others and leaving them inspired, we create an effect that'll shape the future.

Welcoming Change for Lasting Impact

If you want to leave behind a lasting impact on this world you need to be willing to accept one thing: change. This world is constantly evolving and in order to create something that will last forever, it's important for us to adapt our actions based on what's happening around us.

By embracing these changes we're able to stay ahead of what's coming next. Exploring new opportunities and finding innovative ways to create change is possible only if we accept change when it comes knocking at our doors.

Change isn't always easy but if you look at it from another perspective you'll realize that growth is only possible through change. And by accepting this fact, we set ourselves up for success every time life throws us a curveball.

Lastly, by embracing change you're allowing yourself and your actions to evolve alongside the people you wish to inspire. By staying aware of these changing dynamics and challenges faced by society today - We can leverage our actions once more in order to address pressing issues that have been affecting generations before us.

Adopting an Impactful Mindset

To truly leave behind a mark that won't be forgotten - An impactful mindset must be obtained first. This mindset consists of understanding just how powerful our actions are when used correctly. And with this understanding harnessed inside all of us... We can unlock our full potential in making meaningful changes throughout time.

Developing an impactful mindset is something that takes time but it all starts with realizing that the actions we take today will shape the future. Even the smallest decision holds power in creating a better world. By having this engraved in our minds, we begin to look at every action as an opportunity to make a difference.

A method of cultivating such a mindset would be to set clear intentions for each and every one of your actions. This way, we know that everything you do is meant to benefit others and create a positive impact on those around us.

Another key aspect of an impactful mindset is having a growth mindset. When we have this, we realize that our potential isn't fixed and can be developed over time. If we adopt this mentality, we're more likely to approach obstacles and setbacks with resilience and the desire to learn and grow. By embracing a growth mindset, we're able to engage in continuous self-improvement which makes us more effective when trying to make change happen.

In addition, cultivating an impactful mindset requires empathy for others' needs and aspirations. When you put yourself in someone else's shoes, it'll be easier to see how your actions can provide value. This way of thinking allows you to come up with solutions that actually address real-world challenges.

Ultimately, an impactful mindset is about being proactive and realizing that our actions do make a difference. By adopting this mentality, you'll constantly be looking for opportunities big or small for positive change.

Nurturing Relationships for a Lasting Legacy

If you want your accomplishments to live on after you're gone, then nurturing relationships is essential. The impact of our actions has the power to create lasting connections that carry on long after we take our last breath.

When building these bonds with like-minded individuals or communities, collaboration becomes possible. By pooling together resources from multiple sources puts us in a position where giants problems can now be solved by everyone contributing their own strengths.

On top of collaboration being possible there are many other benefits too such as inspiration, guidance, and encouragement from others. All three of these fuel each individual's drive for positive action.

Something important worth mentioning when talking about relationships is innovation and relevance being difficult without them too. In today's world things change at the blink of an eye so it's crucially important that we stay connected with people who are going through the same exact thing as us.

Why? Because they help us adapt better than anyone else could ever hope for! They also help us see things from a different perspective which is needed when trying to change something for the better.

Cultivating Meaningful Connections

Building genuine connections all start with active listening and caring for others. If we don't then it's impossible to understand their needs and aspirations.

Networking events, conferences, online platforms all provide us with valuable opportunities to connect with people who have the same exact passion as us. For this reason, you should never approach these interactions with a closed mindset. Think about how much value you can actually pull from an authentic relationship compared to just a business card.

Lastly, building relationships requires ongoing effort and investment. As humans, we were designed to be part of communities so naturally if we want them around for the long run we have to put in work!

By nurturing relationships, we create a ripple effect that extends beyond our immediate circle of influence. As our connections grow stronger and more expansive, the impact of our collective actions multiplies, creating a positive wave of change.

When we collaborate and support each other, we inspire those around us to do the same. Our efforts become contagious, encouraging others to take impactful actions and leave their mark as well. This ripple effect has the potential to spread far and wide, shaping the legacy of countless individuals and communities who, in turn, inspire future generations.

In conclusion, nurturing relationships is an essential element in creating a lasting legacy. By building meaningful connections, fostering collaboration, and embracing the power of collective action, we amplify the impact of our actions, leaving a mark that endures for years to come.

The Journey Continues: Sustaining Your Legacy

Creating a legacy is not a one-time endeavor; it is an ongoing journey that requires dedication and effort. To sustain your legacy and ensure that your impactful actions continue to leave a mark, it is essential to employ effective strategies for continual growth and adaptation.

One key strategy for sustaining your legacy is to embrace a growth mindset. By continuously seeking new knowledge, honing your skills, and pushing the boundaries of what you can achieve, you can evolve with the changing times and make a lasting impact.

Adaptation is also crucial in sustaining your legacy. As the world around us evolves, it is essential to remain flexible and open to new ideas and opportunities. By embracing change and being willing to explore different avenues, you can ensure that your legacy remains relevant and impactful.

Lastly, building a network of like-minded individuals who share your passion and vision is vital for sustaining your legacy. By nurturing relationships and seeking collaborations ,you can amplify the impact of your actions and create a collective legacy that endures beyond your individual efforts.

Chapter 30

Dealing with
Change and Loss

One of the best ways to combat the stress of change is by building a strong support group. This network can provide you with the necessary guidance, encouragement, and understanding needed during those times of change. On top of that we will also discuss just how important it is to have a support system and help you come up with strategies for creating one.

With that being said, we will also take some time to discover coping strategies for managing change in a healthy way. These tips should be practical enough for anyone reading this to put into practice right now. They'll help you build up your ability to embrace changes, even if you're not sure what's coming next.

For our last topic we'll be discussing personal losses. Losing someone or experiencing an event that dramatically changes your life can be tough on anybody. To help people through these hard moments we'll offer insights on how they can navigate through grief and find meaning in those dark times.

That's not all though! We'll also explain how resilience helps us get through change and give out self-care practices to keep readers mentally fit during their own journey throughout life.

Understanding The Nature Of Change

Change is something that every single person goes through at almost any given point of their lives. Whether it's career transitions or adjusting relationships; it's always there somewhere. If somebody isn't prepared then they might find themselves struggling to adapt when things go bad.

This section will teach readers how to prepare themselves mentally before it happens as well as go through techniques to make them more open-minded about what's changing around them. But don't worry… we won't leave them hanging without support either!

For example - they'll learn what kind of coping strategies are needed when facing such changes like losing loved ones or having extreme events happen in their lives (unexpectedly). Alongside these most likely tragic events - there will be other techniques taught throughout this chapter too like building a support system, practicing self-care, and learning to embrace new opportunities.

One of the biggest lessons learned throughout this chapter is that change may be inevitable but with the right mindset and strategies any person can learn to cope and thrive even when times get rough.

Coping with change is tough. Accepting that life moves on and learning how to do the same is a hard process. It isn't something you can just shrug off without a second of thought, it takes time. And sometimes that's what gets us stuck in a rut that we don't want to climb out of. But! If you follow these tips and tricks for navigating through transitions, I promise you the process will be easier.

1. Embrace the Change: As much as it sucks to change, accepting it is healthy. This is where you'll start moving towards actually getting over whatever "it" is.

2. Stay Present: Take things one step at a time, and avoid dwelling on the past or future.

3. Find Support: Reach out to friends, family, or support groups.

4. Self-Care: Engage in activities that bring you joy, relaxation, and stress relief.

5. Positive Mindset: Try not to go down rabbit holes of negative thoughts when going through changes.

6. Set Realistic Goals: Celebrate wins along the way! Make sure they're reasonable too - baby steps are still steps!

7. Resilience: Practice mindfulness, develop problem-solving skills, and build strong friendships / relationships.

8.Seek Professional Help if Needed: If all else fails there are professionals who specialize in personal growth so don't hesitate to reach out.

Remember! Growth takes time itself so be patient with yourself because there are brighter days ahead - even if that means taking an extra day or two or three-hundred-thousand-million pesky years (metaphorically speaking of course).

Whether it's the death of a loved one or a major life change, experiencing personal losses can be incredibly difficult. The depth of grief and the emotions that come with loss can feel unbearable. But it's important to know you don't have to go through this alone.

When faced with personal losses, there are many different emotions you will experience. It's normal to feel sad, angry, confused and even guilty. These feelings can be overwhelming and confusing but allow yourself to grieve. Give yourself all the time you need to process your emotions and acknowledge what you've lost.

While grieving, it is necessary to seek support from friends and family members along with professionals. Surrounding yourself with individuals who understand what you are going through will bring comfort during such a challenging time in your life. Reach out to loved ones or consider speaking with a therapist who can guide you through this difficult time.

A helpful coping method for personal losses is finding meaning in them. While grief may feel like it will last forever, trying to find ways these losses give purpose and meaning will actually make you grow stronger in the long run. This could involve joining support groups, engaging in creative outlets or pursuing activities that make you happy.

Healing from personal losses takes an unimaginable amount of time which is unique for everyone on an individual level. Be patient with yourself as the process cannot be rushed. As we navigate our way through these rough emotions, eventually we'll start feeling hopeful again.

Coping with these issues takes time as well as being deeply personal so always take care of yourself first during times of sorrow. In order to keep your mental health at bay try practicing mindfulness or engaging in physical exercise.

Always remember that your personal losses do not define who you are as a person; they simply shape your story. In no time at all after some love from friends and family combined with your own resilience, you'll find strength once more allowing new chapters filled with hope and healing to be written.

That said, remember that it takes time and effort to build resilience and adapt to change. Be patient with yourself and allow for setbacks along the way. You may not always succeed, but success lies in trying even when it feels like you can't.

In the next section, we'll explore self-care practices for coping with these changes and maintaining your wellbeing during tough times. By prioritizing self-care, you can enhance your resilience and navigate through these storms of life with strength.

Self-Care Practices for Coping with Change

During difficult times, it's important to prioritize your mental wellbeing just as much as anything else. While it may seem hard at first, sticking to some self-care strategies will help you build resilience and adapt to your new circumstances. Here are a few things to consider:

1. Prioritize Your Basic Needs

Always do what's best for YOU first - don't let anyone tell you otherwise! Make sure that your basic needs are being met; getting enough sleep, eating nutritious meals, staying hydrated etc.

2. Practice Mindfulness and Relaxation Techniques

There are certain relaxation techniques that can help calm your mind which benefits you greatly when going through change. Techniques such as deep breathing exercises or meditation work great!

3. Engage in Physical Activity

Physical activity doesn't only benefit your physical health but also helps majorly with mental health too! It boosts endorphins (making you happier), improves mood, and reduces stress levels - who wouldn't want all this?

4. Seek Emotional Support

Never be afraid to reach out if you need someone to talk too! Talking about experiences/emotions provides support; a helping hand if you will (or need). It's also good for gaining perspective on things.

5. Engage in Activities That Bring You Joy

Engaging in activities that uplifts spirits is highly recommended during any period of change one goes through - believe us! Taking up hobbies/practice creative outlets bring lots of joy to everyday life.

6. Set Boundaries and Practice Self-Compassion

In times like these (and always) you need to learn how to set boundaries in order to stay sane. It's easy to get caught up in things that aren't benefitting you, learn how to say no when necessary, delegate tasks, and allow yourself breaks without feeling guilty - it's okay!

By incorporating these self-care practices into your routine, you can better cope with change, reduce stress, and maintain your mental and emotional well-being. Taking care of yourself is not selfish but necessary for navigating through life's transitions.

Times of Change Nurturing Relationships

Maintaining healthy relationships is tough enough as is let alone while going through a period of change! However building support & meaningful connections are crucial for navigating through difficult periods. Here are some tips:

Change is a part of life, and it's something that people react to differently based on their own personal experiences. It's important to be empathetic and understanding when it comes to others' emotions and experience with change. The best thing you can do is listen actively, validate their feelings, offer support without judgement or criticism. All of this will help you build stronger relationships with the people around you as well as create a safe space for open dialogue.

3. Set aside time for quality connections

It's easy to become overwhelmed in times of change and forget about spending time with loved ones. Make sure you make an effort to plan activities (whether virtual or in-person) that allow you to bond, relax, and enjoy each other's company.

4. Show active support

Showing your support by actively engaging in your loved ones' lives is the best way to show them that you care. Celebrate their successes, lend them an ear when they need someone to talk to, offer assistance when needed; all these actions re-enforce how much you care about them. By actively supporting one another, relationships are strengthened and a sense of mutual care and appreciation is created.

5. Be adaptable and flexible

Expectations must always be adjusted during large changes in our lives because change often requires us to adapt. Being flexible in your interactions builds strong relationships with the people around you because they know that no matter what happens, no matter how things may change between the two of you.. nothing changes between you two.

6. Seek professional help if needed

There's only so much we as individuals can handle on our own before seeking out some sort of professional help becomes necessary.. Don't hesitate if things ever get too overwhelming for everyone involved.

Remember that having a strong support system and taking care of your relationships is vital for the well-being not just for yourself but also those who surround you.. Strengthening bonds with others will allow you to face any challenge that comes your way.

Embrace the Unknown

What's certain is that change always brings about new opportunities for growth and personal development.. The hard part is embracing it. Change may be challenging, but it also gives us the chance to discover hidden talents, explore new places and take exciting risks.

Coping with change involves stepping outside of our comfort zones, embracing what we don't know and being open to whatever may come next. When we see it as a stage for personal transformation, our mindset shifts and we can approach change in a more optimistic and enthusiastic manner.

When faced with change.. assess the situation, evaluate every opportunity it might bring along with it, lean on your strengths, skills and interests. Embracing those opportunities requires a proactive attitude - so take that and make some calculated risks.

One way of embracing change is by seeking out new experiences and challenges.. Trying out different hobbies or careers is an option. By actively seeking new opportunities in life (no matter how small they might be), you expand your horizons which ultimately opens you up to a world full of possibilities.

Having people around who think like you do instead of those who tend to pull you back are also incredibly helpful while navigating through these changes in your life. They'll provide guidance as well as encourage you when things get tough.

Always keep this in mind:

Change is an invitation for growth and personal development; Embrace everything that comes your way no matter how difficult the situation may seem at first because once its over; once everything starts making sense again - You'll have evolved into an even better version of yourself than before.

It's common to feel overwhelmed when faced with change and personal losses. The internal conflicts we experience can create emotional turmoil that makes it hard to find peace.

The good part is that there are a few strategies you can use to help with this. One way of tackling these issues is through self-reflection. When you're faced with changes, take some time out of your day and think about what exactly is causing the conflicts inside of you. You may not even know what the root causes are at first, but the point is to just sit back, get some clarity on how you're feeling and allow yourself to grieve or process anything difficult that has happened. Trust us, it'll make your life much easier.

If self-reflection doesn't really help you out as much as it should, reach out for professional support. People like therapists and counselors have spent so long studying this exact thing for a reason! They'll guide you and provide a space where all of your emotions are safe and can be explored throughout any challenges you've been facing recently.

Oh and another underrated thing: journaling! It's honestly magical seeing all those words hit paper. Write down everything that comes to mind - no matter how negative it may be. By doing so, your perspective will start to shift towards something more positive.

Taking care of yourself is also crucial during these times. Going through change while experiencing loss takes a toll on both the body and mind, which is why prioritizing self-care should never come second. Try doing things like going on walks in nature or practicing mindfulness meditation - they'll help reduce stress!

Offering Support

At the end of the day we all need someone close to us who'll listen without judgement. If family isn't your go-to choice there's nothing wrong with reaching out to friends in order receive encouragement from them rather than advice.

Remember that there's no rush in resolving internal conflicts either. This stuff takes time - especially when going through difficult moments. We can't stress this enough: be kind to yourself. These moments are hard, but with some self-reflection, professional support and a strong support network, you'll be just fine.

We lose many of those most important to us as we age, but accepting that and understanding that loss is a part of life's great cycle is what allows us to carry on, our loss is not a personal externally inflicted tragedy it is the beginning of a new phase and like all new beginnings there will be problems along the way, but come to an understanding with your loss and how it can fuel a new part of your life through the inspiration of those that have gine before.

Chapter 31

Networking in Your Forties

As the professional landscape shifts, so does networking. In this stage of life, you'll lean on your connections to get ahead and propel yourself forward in ways that make sense for you individually. That's what we'll help you do here.

We're going to look at how networking has changed from when you first started out and why it's more important than ever now. We've also included some interesting statistics on age discrimination from an AARP survey so stay tuned!

But before we jump into that let's go through the chapter roadmap:

- Importance of Networking in Your Forties
- Utilizing Social Media
- LinkedIn Profile Optimization Tips
- Engaging with Others Effectively

So let's dive into the importance of building meaningful connections and how this can benefit you throughout your forties.

The Importance of Networking in Your Forties

In any stage of your career, but especially during this time period, it's all about who you know. That doesn't just mean meeting someone and telling them about yourself or asking if they have a job opening right now.

There's a lot more nuance to it than that. You want instead to make valuable relationships with other professionals while doing great work at your current position(s). This way if something were to happen where you're no longer employed there or looking for something new, they would be excited to advocate for you.

This is how leaders are made! It takes a village and by leveraging others expertise and audience size, opportunities will come knocking at the door.

Networking strategically opens up a whole new layer of resources & insights that aren't readily available through traditional channels. Plus it allows others to understand your unique value proposition positioning you as one desirable candidate for career advancement.

You could always just hope someone else sees how great of an employee/leader/etc..you are but odds are in such a clogged space, they won't find you. So actively seeking them out and communicating your worth will do wonders!

Using this tailored approach will ensure that the connections you make align well with your goals and interests. By understanding these things, you'll naturally start to gravitate towards the right individuals and opportunities.

Expanding Your Reach with Social Media

When it comes to networking in your forties, social media is going to be a godsend! There are over 3 billion people on social media so you're bound to meet someone who can propel you forward.

But let's dive into some of the more specific benefits…

- Amplify your visibility
- Connect with industry experts
- Stay up-to-date with trends & events
- Participate in online discussions
- Showcase your expertise

1. 2. Determine your target audience: Find out who you want to connect with that will help you achieve your career goals? Are you trying to expand your client base, find a mentor, or work with industry experts? If so, then tailor your networking efforts to reach this target audience.

2. Set measurable objectives: It's important to set clear and measurable objectives for your networking activities. For example, you might aim to attend a certain number of networking events each month, connect with a specific number of professionals on LinkedIn, or secure a certain number of industry-related opportunities through networking.

3. Prioritize quality over quantity: In your forties, it's crucial to focus on quality rather than trying to accumulate a large number of contacts. Build meaningful relationships with individuals who can add value in your professional journey.
4. Leverage social media: Social media platforms allow users the chance to connect with so many other people they wouldn't have been able to do otherwise. Establish an online presence by using platforms such as LinkedIn, Twitter, and Facebook. With these tools at hand you can connect with industry professionals and join relevant groups while also sharing what you know.
5. Seek out industry events: Find events specifically designed for those in the same field as yourself that can help meet the goals set in step two. At these meetings there is potential to meet like-minded individuals where insights about the industry are shared and valuable connections built

When assessing our networking goals we should be sure we're doing all we can to maximize our effectiveness because remember skillful networking comes down cultivating meaningful connections not collecting business cards

Building A Tailored Approach

In order for us to network successfully in our forties we'll need a tailored approach that helps us make connections that matter towards achieving our goals

One way we can achieve this is by leveraging social media when expanding our networking reach using platforms such as LinkedIn, Twitter, and Facebook allows users the ability

Effective Communication Techniques

In this section, we will explore communication techniques that can elevate your networking efforts and help you establish genuine relationships with your professional network.

Active Listening

Active listening is a vital skill that allows you to fully engage and understand what others are saying. When networking, it's important to listen attentively to the person you're conversing with. Show genuine interest by maintaining eye contact, nodding, and providing verbal cues to indicate that you're actively listening.

By practicing active listening, you demonstrate respect for the other person's thoughts and opinions. This not only enhances your networking interactions but also helps you build rapport and establish a solid foundation for future collaborations.

Asking Impactful Questions

Asking impactful questions during networking conversations can demonstrate your genuine interest and expertise. Craft questions that go beyond small talk and show a deeper understanding of the industry or profession you're networking within.

Consider asking questions that invite others to share their experiences, insights, or challenges. These types of questions facilitate meaningful discussions and allow you to establish yourself as a knowledgeable and valuable resource within your professional network.

Maintaining Genuine Connections

Building a strong professional network is not just about making initial connections; it's also about nurturing and maintaining those relationships over time. Ensure that your networking efforts are focused on building genuine connections rather than simply collecting contacts.

Follow up with individuals you meet by sending personalized messages or emails expressing your appreciation for their time and the insights they shared. Stay connected with your network through social media platforms like LinkedIn, Twitter, or Facebook, leveraging social media to interact, share relevant content, and stay up to date with their professional endeavors.

Remember: Networking is a two-way street! Be proactive in offering support, advice, or recommendations to your contacts when appropriate. By demonstrating your willingness to contribute and help others, you strengthen the bonds within your professional network.

Check out these additional resources:

The Art of Business Card Etiquette- Tips on how to utilize and manage business cards effectively in networking situations.

10 Networking Questions That Aren't "What Do You Do?"- Alternative questions you can ask to initiate more meaningful conversations.

How to Benefit from Small Talk at Work Events- Tips on making small talk less awkward and more valuable during professional events.

Twitter is all about the speed. It's a platform that thrives on quick networking. If you want to reap rewards from it, then do this:
1) Follow influencers, thought leaders, and organizations in your industry.
2) Take part in relevant Twitter chats and use hashtags to join conversations.
3) Share insightful content and news in your field to show that you're a professional who has something valuable to say.
4) Engage with other professionals - retweet their content, respond to their tweets, and have conversations with them!

Using Facebook Professionally

Typically viewed as the social platform for friends and family, Facebook can still be leveraged professionally. Here's how you do it:
1) Create or tweak your existing profile so it's suitable for professional use.
2) Join industry-related groups to meet people who're also interested in what you are.
3) Share achievements, articles, and insights about your industry to flex your expertise while engaging with your network.
4) Use Facebook Events to find conferences or networking events tailored for your line of business.

If used wisely, these platforms can help you extend how far you reach when networking. Once that happens, doors will open up, deals will flow in!

Navigating professional events

In this section, we will guide you through the art of navigating events to maximize your networking opportunities. Attending conferences, trade shows and seminars within your industry can provide invaluable chances to connect with like-minded professionals, potential clients and leaders. By following a tailored approach and leveraging social media, you can make the most out of these events and expand your professional connections.

Picking the right events

When picking an event to attend professionally it's important to consider what exactly you hope to gain from it? As well as considering who you want to target as an audience. Look for seminars or conferences that are relevant to your position or industry; doing so will make sure that everyone there has something in common with at least one thing about yourself. Researching these events beforehand is key so you know when they happen and when they don't.

Approaching new contacts

Making a conversation with someone new might make you anxious but having some strategies up your sleeve can help strike up conversations effortlessly. Start by introducing yourself confidently followed by expressing genuine interest in their professional background. Engage in meaningful conversations by using different techniques like active listening as well as asking open-ended questions.

Following Up Effectively

Networking is just another way of saying "maintain connections". After talking with someone at an event always try to follow up within 24-48 hours using a personalized email referencing previous talking points between yourselves. This will show them that whatever was discussed still resided in your thoughts long after the conversation had ended.

Mentoring and Being Mentored

Seeking out mentors or being one yourself isn't unheard of for people at any age but definitely vital once you hit forty as they offer valuable insights while also giving support as you navigate your career.

The Power of Mentoring

Having someone who's already achieved success in a field similar to yours provides many benefits which range from gaining knowledge on how they accomplished such feats all the way to learning from their mistakes.

Being a Mentee

Mentorships offer you an amazing chance to learn and grow within your career. Don't be afraid to approach potential mentors, as they could guide you towards new opportunities or help you navigate challenges and provide valuable industry insights.

Nurturing Mentorship Relationships

A mentorship relationship is something that requires effort from both parties involved if it's going to last. As the mentee, it's important to be proactive and willing to take on feedback as well as put any guidance given into action.

Update your mentor on your progress regularly. Make sure to inform them of any challenges you face as well. Engage with your mentor on social media, share resources, and build a connection outside of a face-to-face relationship.

Mentorship is reciprocal; when you grow in your career, consider offering mentorship to others to pay it forward.

Networking for Career Advancement

Networking is a valuable instrument for career advancement during the 40s. By strategically connecting with vital individuals, seeking out new opportunities, and positioning yourself for growth and development, you can take your professional journey to new heights.

A tailored approach to networking is vital in this stage of your career. Identify the individuals and networks that align with your goals and interests. Look for opportunities to leverage social media platforms such as LinkedIn, Twitter, and Facebook to expand your reach and connect with industry professionals.

When networking for career advancement, it's important to remember that it's not just about making connections but also nurturing them. Actively engage with your professional network by attending relevant events, participating in discussions, and offering support and guidance to others.

Seek out mentors who can provide invaluable insights and guidance to help you navigate your career path. At the same time, be willing to mentor others and share your expertise since these relationships can be mutually beneficial.

Connecting with Influential Individuals

To advance your career, it's necessary that you connect with influential individuals who can open doors for you. Attend industry conferences or workshops where these people may be present so that you have the ability to meet them in person. Use a tailored approach when approaching them so that they'll be more likely remember you after the event has passed.

While connecting with influential individuals ask genuine questions that show interest in their work. You should also find ways in which value may be added during conversation Whether through an email or handwritten note make sure to send a follow-up message after the event has ended.

Seeking Out New Opportunities

Networking can offer you a lot of opportunities to advance your career. Keep an eye out for job postings, projects, or collaborations that align with your goals. Leverage your professional network to get insider information and recommendations.

Additionally, actively position yourself as a thought leader in your industry. Share your expertise and insights through blog posts, social media updates, and speaking engagements. You should do this because not only will it enhance your visibility but also attract exciting opportunities from employers and partners.

Remember that expanding one's personal network is a continuous process. Stay proactive on who you connect with, update your network regularly so they don't forget about you, and seek new ways to grow professionally. By doing all these things you can speed up the progression of your career in your 40s.

Overcoming Networking Challenges

Networking at such an age comes with its own unique set of challenges that must be handled properly if success is desired. Nonetheless when using the right strategies along with a tailored approach these obstacles become easy to overcome.

Time Constraints

When networking in their forties most people tend to have limited time which makes sense considering most individuals at this point are working long days balancing family commitments and personal responsibilities.

To overcome this obstacle, prioritize networking in your schedule. Set aside time each week, or month, to attend events, reach out to contacts and engage in online exchanges through social media platforms.

Confidence Issues

Another obstacle stems from feeling confident while networking. Especially for those who may have taken a career break or changed industries. It's understandable to feel unsure or anxious when reaching out to new people or attending events.

To boost your confidence start by focusing on your strengths and achievements. Remind yourself of the value you bring to any table and remember all the knowledge and experience you've gained throughout your career. Actively listen during conversations so that you can build a connection with others.

Maintaining Work-Life Balance

Work-life balance becomes more important in your forties. And it becomes more difficult to maintain as well. Juggling professional commitments, personal obligations, and self-care might leave little time or energy for networking activities.

To overcome this issue take a strategic approach to networking. Make realistic goals and focus on quality over quantity. Prioritize opportunities that align with your interests and goals, don't feel like you need to attend every event just because someone invited you - but do remember that making connections is about building meaningful relationships rather than gaining contact information.

By addressing these common issues, enhancing your networking efforts will be easier than ever before! This will be vital when trying to expand your professional network through social media platforms so that you can gain optimal benefits from them!

Always be genuine. Show a sincere interest in their work, achievements, and challenges. By actively listening and asking meaningful questions, you can deepen your understanding of their professional journey and offer relevant support.

Your relationships are not just what you get from them though. What can you give back? Be proactive in helping others by sharing valuable resources, making introductions, or providing guidance when appropriate. By doing this you become a resource that people know they can rely on.

Maintaining long-term connections is vital for the continuous growth and success of your professional network. By staying in touch, offering support, and leveraging social media, you can nurture these relationships and reap the benefits of a strong and thriving network.

Putting Your Networking Skills into Action

Now that you have learned strategies and techniques for networking in your forties, it's time to put your skills into action. Creating an effective networking plan and executing it confidently can significantly enhance your professional opportunities and help you stay ahead in your career.

To begin, take a tailored approach to networking by identifying the right networks, events, and individuals to connect with. Set clear goals for your networking efforts and align them with your desired outcomes. By focusing on quality connections rather than quantity, you can establish meaningful relationships that yield long-term benefits.

Leveraging social media platforms is also crucial in today's digital age. Use platforms like LinkedIn, Twitter, and Facebook to connect with industry professionals, join relevant groups, and stay up to date with industry trends. By leveraging the power of social media, you can expand your reach and make valuable connections that can propel your career forward.

Remember communication is key! Ask questions! Engage! And be genuine!

Chapter 32

The Happiness that
is Simplification

Welcome to Chapter 32, where we delve into the transformative power of minimalism and simplicity. In a world filled with constant distractions and overwhelming choices, embracing a minimalist lifestyle can bring true satisfaction and joy. It's time to declutter, simplify, and focus on what truly matters.

The Essence of Minimalism.

Minimalism is more than just a design trend; it's a lifestyle that can bring clarity, peace, and contentment to our daily lives. At its core, minimalism is about decluttering, simplifying, and focusing on what truly matters. By embracing minimalism, we can free ourselves from the burden of excess and create space for the things that truly bring us joy, satisfaction, and fulfillment.

One of the key benefits of minimalism is the ability to declutter our physical spaces. By removing unnecessary possessions and simplifying our surroundings, we can create a sense of calm and tranquility in our homes. This not only reduces stress but also enhances our ability to focus and be present in the moment. A clutter-free environment can also have a positive impact on our mental well-being, allowing us to feel lighter and more at peace.

But minimalism extends beyond our physical spaces. It's about simplifying all aspects of our lives, from our schedules and commitments to our digital presence and consumption habits. By reducing distractions and prioritizing what truly matters, we can experience increased clarity, productivity, and overall satisfaction.

By embracing minimalism, we can shift our focus from the accumulation of things to the quality of our experiences. Rather than chasing after material possessions, we can choose to invest our time, energy, and resources into meaningful relationships personal growth ,and experiences that enrich our lives . Minimalism allows us to break free from the societal pressure to constantly strive for more instead find contentment in what we already have.

In the next sections, we will delve deeper into the practical aspects of minimalism, exploring how to simplify our living spaces ,streamline our wardrobes, cultivate inner peace ,and more. By uncovering the essence of minimalism, we can unlock the power of simplicity and pave the way for a more fulfilling and satisfying life.

Simplify Your Living Space.

Create an organized and clutter-free living space that promotes a sense of calm and tranquility. Embracing minimalism in your home can transform it into a sanctuary where you can truly relax and recharge. Here are some practical tips to help you declutter, organize, and create a minimalist home:

1. Start with Decluttering

Begin by removing items that no longer serve a purpose or bring you joy. Take a thorough inventory of your belongings and ask yourself if each item aligns with your values and enhances your life. Let go of the unnecessary   embrace a more intentional approach to material possessions .

2. Choose the Essentials

Focus on keeping only the essentials in each room. Minimalism is about having what you need and truly love rather than an abundance of unnecessary things . Select furniture and decor that are functional timeless ,and versatile .

3. Optimize Storage Solutions

Invest in smart storage solutions to keep your things organized and out of sight. Shelves, baskets, and bins can be used to store items neatly while maintaining a clean and clutter-free look. Adopting a "place for everything" approach will make it easier for you to maintain order and simplicity in your living space.

4. Embrace Minimalist Design Principles

A minimalist design can create a calming atmosphere in any home. A neutral color palette with clean lines makes the room feel open and serene. Keep decor simple by avoiding excessive ornaments and knick-knacks.

5. Clean and Maintain Regularly

Regular cleaning is key to maintaining the aesthetic of minimalism. Dedicate time each day to put things back where they belong so surfaces remain clutter-free. By adopting this routine, you'll be able to uphold the simplicity and order that you've created.

By simplifying your living space, you can create an environment that facilitates peace of mind and relaxation. Embrace the beauty of minimalism and discover the transformative power of simplicity in your home.

Streamline Your Wardrobe.

When it comes to embracing minimalism, simplicity is key, and this extends to your wardrobe as well. Building a minimalist wardrobe involves curating a collection of high-quality, versatile pieces that truly reflect your personal style. By streamlining your wardrobe, you can enjoy numerous benefits and find greater ease and satisfaction in getting dressed each day.

One of the advantages of having fewer clothes is the elimination of decision fatigue. With a carefully curated collection, you'll spend less time pondering what to wear and more time focusing on what truly matters in your day. Additionally, a minimalist wardrobe allows you to appreciate the value and versatility of each item, giving you a sense of satisfaction and reducing the urge for constant shopping.

To create a minimalist wardrobe, consider adopting the concept of a capsule wardrobe. A capsule wardrobe consists of a limited number of essential pieces that can be mixed and matched to create a variety of outfits. This approach encourages mindful purchasing and thoughtful curation of items that can be worn in different combinations and for various occasions.

When curating your minimalist wardrobe, prioritize quality over quantity. Invest in well-made, timeless pieces that are durable and can withstand the test of time. Opting for neutral colors and classic styles ensures that your wardrobe remains versatile and adaptable to changing trends.

Remember, minimalism is not about depriving yourself but rather about intentionally choosing items that hold value and bring joy to your life. By streamlining your wardrobe and embracing simplicity, you can not only declutter your physical space but also cultivate a sense of clarity and contentment in your everyday dressing.

Mindful Consumption.

When it comes to minimalism, embracing simplicity goes beyond just decluttering our physical spaces. Mindful consumption is an essential aspect of living a minimalist lifestyle. It involves being conscious of our buying habits, reducing waste, and making sustainable choices in all areas of our lives.

By adopting a mindful approach to consumption, we can reduce our environmental impact and find greater fulfillment in our everyday lives. Making intentional choices about what we bring into our homes and lives allows us to prioritize quality over quantity, making room for the things that truly matter.

One very important part of mindful consumption is conscious buying. It's the practice of being really thoughtful about what we buy and considering how those choices affect us in the long run. Do we even need it? Does it match up with our values, and does it hold real value for us? By asking ourselves these questions, we can steer away from impulse purchases that only last a little while and focus on acquiring things we actually need and love.

Another big part of mindful consumption is reducing waste. This means trying to cut down on cluttering our space with useless stuff, getting rid of or reusing thing when we don't want them anymore. If you're more circular minded, you'd know that this would help make the future more sustainable.

Making sustainable choices beyond our physical possessions is also extremely important. Choose to support eco-friendly brands, try not to use single-use plastics much, and focus on appliances that do not waste energy just to name a few.

Overall though, by practicing mindful consumption in general, we can actually reduce our impact on the environment quite a bit. Doing so also allows us to be more free and live without much worry.

Tips for Mindful Consumption

1. Before making a purchase, ask yourself if it aligns with your values and if it will truly add value to your life.
2. Avoid impulsive buying and take time to consider your choices.
3. Support eco-friendly brands that prioritize sustainability.
4. Reduce, reuse, and recycle to minimize waste.
5. Opt for energy-efficient appliances and reduce your energy consumption.

6.   Choose experiences over material possessions whenever possible.

Simplify Your Digital Life.

In today's digital age, it's easy to become overwhelmed by constant notifications, information overload, and the pressure to always be connected. But there's a way we can find balance again though by embracing minimalism and simplicity in your digital habits which helps reduce distractions, increase focus, and improve your overall well-being.

Declutter Your Digital Devices

Start by decluttering your digital devices. Just as physical clutter can create stress and overwhelm, a cluttered digital space can have the same effect. Delete unnecessary files, apps, and emails. Organize your digital files and folders in a logical and minimalist way too so you only keep what you need.

Manage Your Online Presence

Next, take a step back and evaluate your online presence. Are you spending too much time on social media or mindlessly scrolling through endless newsfeeds? Consider setting boundaries there to limit the time you spend on the app.

Practice Digital Minimalism

Just as it's important to be mindful of your physical consumption, it's essential to apply the same mindfulness to your digital consumption. Rather than mindlessly consuming endless content, be selective about what you consume online. Choose quality over quantity and prioritize content that aligns with your interests, values, and personal growth.

By simplifying your digital life, you can create a more intentional and fulfilling online experience. Embracing minimalism and simplicity in the digital realm allows you to focus on what truly matters, reduce distractions, and find a sense of balance in a digital-driven world.

Cultivating Inner Simplicity

While minimalism often focuses on decluttering and organizing our physical space, true simplicity extends beyond external possessions. It extends to our inner world where we can cultivate peace, clarity, and contentment.

Mindfulness practices play a vital role in the pursuit of simplicity. By practicing mindfulness we become more aware of our thoughts, emotions and desires. This increased awareness enables us to recognize and let go of unnecessary mental clutter so we can focus on what truly matters.

Self-reflection is another valuable tool for cultivating inner simplicity. Taking the time to evaluate our values, goals, and priorities helps us identify what brings us joy and fulfillment while letting go of what no longer serves us. It allows us to align our actions with our authentic selves and simplify our lives accordingly.

Personal growth is a continuous journey towards simplicity. By developing a growth mindset we embrace change and embrace the process of simplifying our thoughts, beliefs, and habits. We learn to let go of attachments and cultivate a sense of detachment from material possessions and external validation.

As we simplify our inner world we may discover newfound freedom joy satisfaction by embracing minimalism as a means to cultivate inner simplicity we unlock greater clarity mindfulness resilience in facing life's complexities

The Joy of Slowing Down

Embrace slow living And find true satisfaction in the present moment In our fast-paced society the art of slowing down is often overlooked yet minimalism and simplicity can be the keys to unlocking a more fulfilling and contented life.

By embracing minimalism you free yourself from constantly hustling and bustling letting go of unnecessary commitments and obligations. Simplifying your schedule allows for more time to focus on what truly brings you joy and satisfaction.

Mindfulness and relaxation techniques play a crucial role in slowing down and finding inner peace. Incorporating practices such as meditation deep breathing and gentle yoga can help you cultivate calmness presence.

While the world around us may encourage us to constantly strive for more minimalism reminds us to find contentment in the simple moments. By letting go of the need for constant busyness and achievement you can discover the joy of being fully present in each experience.

The art of doing less to achieve more is a core principle of minimalism. By focusing on what truly matters eliminating distractions prioritizing your time energy on activities relationships that bring you most satisfaction

So strip things down to its core. Slow down, be happy in this present moment, and find joy living your life simply.

Minimalist Parenting.

Uncover how minimalism will change the way you parent, offering a clutter-free and nurturing space for your kids. Minimal parenting means simplicity and peace with strong connections.

Let's be clear though, minimal parenting isn't about taking things away from your kids. It's about forming a bond with them through intention and thoughtfulness. By simplifying this lifestyle, you can focus on what really matters in their development.

Simplicity is all that minimalist parenting needs to operate. By clearing toys out of the house and only having meaningful items around - it'll spark creativity and resourcefulness in them.

This principle ties back to the saying "quality over quantity." Stick to well made toys that allow for open-ended play. Trust us they'll thank you when they're older!

When it comes to spending time together, make sure it's valuable! Stop packing their schedules full of activities so tight that there's no room left for rest or family bonding time.

Values such as mindfulness, responsibility, and gratitude are also taught by this style of parenting. Share the load- let them help with household chores and decisions- empower them!

Always remember that there isn't one right way to practice minimalist parenting. Do what works best for you and your family while sticking to the principles listed above!

The Joy of Less.

Minimalism is the freedom you're looking for. It's the chance to take back control of your finances and find a peace of mind that you never thought possible. And it all starts with finding joy in less.

Sustainability: Why We Need Minimalism.

It seems like every day more and more people are beginning to embrace minimalism. Far from just a personal choice, minimalism is our one-way ticket to a better world.

Minimalism isn't about reducing our physical footprint, it's about fostering a mindset that sees simplicity as superior - especially when it comes to things like consumerism and excess. Our overconsumption is doing serious damage to the environment, but by embracing minimalism we can make sure future generations don't have to suffer for our mistakes.

Instead of thinking about how much money or how many possessions we have, minimalists focus on the experiences they create and the quality of their lives. If everyone lived this way, sustainability would come naturally because less consumption means less waste.

With eco-friendly practices like reusing instead of throwing away or buying ethical products instead of those that damage the earth, we can live in harmony with nature rather than taking advantage. All it takes is adopting sustainability into our everyday routines and making it a habit!

By protecting and preserving Earth, we're creating a better world not just for ourselves but for future generations as well.

Chapter 33

Investing in Your
Passion Projects

Welcome to chapter 33. In this part of our book we are going to break down how you can potentially turn your hobbies into income. And we will also be delving into balancing your passion projects with life's obligations.

So if you're looking to let those creative juices flow and make some extra cash while at it, this chapter is for you.

Whether it's painting, photography or writing, a lot of people believe that these activities have the potential to generate income. Imagine being able to do what you love and getting paid for it? Sounds amazing right?

It's not always going to be sunshine and rainbows though, understanding how to juggle everyday responsibilities with things you love can be hard at times. Finding the time or money may seem impossible. But just know that we got your back.

We will cover various topics here that include:

Finding a hobby with enough demand in the market.

Building a profitable side business.

Creating an online presence.

Nurturing your hobbies and managing your time better.

Leveraging collaborations and networking opportunities.

Financial planning.

Diversifying income sources.

And effective marketing and branding techniques.

Our goal is simple... teach you everything we know about making money from things you enjoy doing!

Discover Your Moneymaker

Do you want to turn your hobby into something profitable? We'll show you how by researching market demand and finding ways to monetize your passions! That way not only will you have fun, but also create another revenue stream along the way.

Step number one is identifying what interests or skills do you already have. Think long and hard about activities that excite you and areas where you already excel. If it's photography, writing or cooking... these should become foundations for potential new incomes.

After those are discovered, start researching where there is demand in those markets. Look for niche markets or specific areas within your hobby that have high demand but low competition. Finding your unique selling proposition and standing out in a crowded marketplace is key.

Lastly, the power of online platforms cannot be understated. Websites like Etsy or eBay can provide a platform to sell all your goodies!

Now, remember: finding a lucrative hobby isn't just about making money. It's about enjoying your passions and doing what you love while also having the potential to make a living from them. That being said, let's dive right into the possibilities and maximize your income with hobbies.

Developing a Side Business for Profit

Are you ready to turn your hobby into a side business? Here are the essential steps you need to follow if you want to turn that passion of yours into a potential income source. Whether it's crafting, photography, writing or any other hobby, we'll guide you through everything you need to know when trying to build a profitable side business.

Setting Your Prices

A key part of running a successful side business is pricing yourself correctly. You need to factor in how much it costs for everything like supplies or time spent and then pair that up with the value of your product (or service) and how big the market demand is. Research your competitors' prices and try to find something that's both tempting for customers but fair towards yourself as well.

Marketing

To actually make an income out of what you're doing, marketing is key. Make sure that when creating your marketing plan, it includes things such as promotion on social media platforms, content marketing through blogging or email newsletters as well as partnering with other influencers or businesses in your niche. Focus on showing people what makes your product special and building up the brand identity which will attract customers.

Managing Time Correctly

Trying to balance all of this with everything else happening throughout your day can be quite tough sometimes. But don't worry! We got solutions for that too. If you create a schedule dedicated only to working on your side business, then it will help keep things organized for starters. Once that's set up remember these two things:

1.Prioritize tasks by order of importance.

2.Make sure workflows are efficient so productivity stays at its highest level.

Don't forget to take care of yourself though. Set aside time for relaxation and self-care so you don't end up burning yourself out.

By following these simple steps, you'll be able to build a side business that matches your passion. The next section will cover the importance of having an online presence as well as how you can create one depending on what your hobby is.

Establishing an Online Presence

To have a successful hobby based business, having an online presence is key. In 2021, the internet is everything and learning how to use it properly will definitely help when trying to showcase your work, reach potential customers or just get your name out there in general. This section will go through all the steps required when trying to create an engaging online presence which then unlocks multiple income sources.

The first thing on the list is creating a website. Think of it like this: websites are basically a central hub that holds all information about your passion projects and where people can purchase them too if they feel like it. Make sure the design aligns with your brand identity while being user-friendly at the same time.

Another important step to take is utilizing social media platforms since they benefit any type of business really. Popular platforms nowadays (and always) include Facebook, Instagram or Pinterest. Use those accounts to promote your work, engage with comments or messages from people interested in what you're doing and keep everyone updated about things like new projects. They give you a great chance at connecting with potential customers and expanding your reach.

When optimizing your online presence make sure that it's easily discoverable by using relevant keywords related to whatever niche you have chosen in this industry. If done right, this could improve visibility on search engines quite well! And finally, don't forget about networking either since the connections made there could lead into future collaborations or long-term friendships which are always nice!

Engagement

In addition to having a website and social media presence, actively engaging with your audience and networking with other professionals in your field can help boost your credibility and attract potential income sources. Respond to comments and messages promptly, participate in relevant online communities or forums, and collaborate with others to expand your reach.

Remember, creating an online presence is an ongoing process. Stay consistent with your updates and maintain a professional online image. Continuously evaluate and refine your online strategies to adapt to changing trends and maximize your potential income sources.

Nurturing Your Passion Projects

Managing and prioritizing your passion projects can be a rewarding endeavor, but it's important to find the right balance amidst your daily life commitments. Here are some strategies to help you navigate this balancing act:

Finding Time

One of the key challenges in balancing passion projects is finding the time to dedicate to them. Evaluate your daily schedule, identify pockets of free time, and allocate specific time slots for your projects. By treating your passion projects as important commitments, you can ensure that they receive the attention they deserve.

Setting Realistic Goals

When pursuing your passion projects, it's essential to set realistic goals that align with your overall vision. Break down your projects into smaller, achievable milestones, and track your progress along the way. This will help you stay focused, motivated, and prevent overwhelm.

Staying Motivated

Passion projects require dedication and perseverance. To stay motivated, remind yourself of the reasons why you began these projects in the first place. Surround yourself with supportive individuals who share your interests, and seek inspiration from like-minded communities online or offline.

Remember, nurturing your passion projects is a continuous journey. Be patient with yourself, celebrate your accomplishments, and embrace the learning experiences along the way.

Time Management Techniques

When it comes to achieving a balance between your passion projects and daily responsibilities, effective time management is key. By implementing practical techniques, you can ensure that you make progress on your passion projects without neglecting other important aspects of your life.

1. Prioritizing Tasks

Start by identifying the tasks that are most important and require immediate attention. Create a to-do list and prioritize tasks based on their urgency and significance. This way, you can focus on completing the critical tasks first and allocate time accordingly.

2. Creating Schedules

Setting a schedule helps you allocate specific time slots for your passion projects, ensuring that you dedicate regular time to work on them. Use a physical or digital planner to create a weekly schedule that balances your work, personal commitments, and passion project activities.

3. Avoiding Burnout

While it's important to be dedicated to your passion projects, it's equally important to avoid burnout. Make sure to incorporate breaks and relaxation time into your schedule. Taking care of your physical and mental well-being will help you stay energized and focused on your projects.

By utilizing these time management techniques, you can strike a balance between your passion projects and other responsibilities. Remember, finding harmony in your pursuits is essential for long-term success and personal fulfillment.

Collaborations And Networking

When it comes to balancing passion projects, collaborations and networking can play a pivotal role in supporting your endeavors. By working with others and building a supportive community around your hobbies, you can find valuable opportunities for growth and inspiration.

One of the key benefits of collaborations is the ability to tap into the expertise and experiences of like-minded individuals. By connecting with others who share your passion, you can gain new insights, learn from their successes and challenges, and expand your own knowledge base.

Finding Like-Minded Individuals

When seeking collaboration opportunities, it's important to find individuals who align with your values, goals, and vision. Look for communities, groups, or online platforms that cater to your specific hobby or industry. Engage in conversations, share your work, and be open to connecting with others who resonate with your creative pursuits.

Building a supportive community around your hobbies can also provide encouragement and motivation during times of doubt or uncertainty. Surrounding yourself with individuals who understand your passion can help you stay focused, inspired, and committed to your projects.

Benefits Of Working With Others

Collaborations offer numerous benefits that can enhance the success of your passion projects. By pooling resources, skills, and networks, you can tackle larger projects, reach a wider audience, and generate more meaningful results.

Working with others can also spark creativity and innovation. The exchange of ideas and perspectives can lead to fresh insights and unique approaches. Additionally, collaborations can provide opportunities to learn new techniques, experiment with different styles, and push the boundaries of your creative abilities.

Leveraging Networking Opportunities

In addition to collaborations, networking plays a vital role in supporting your passion projects. Attending industry events, joining professional organizations ,and engaging in online communities can help you build valuable connections expand your network.

When networking ,focus on building genuine relationships offering support to others in your field .Look for opportunities contribute expertise share insights resources showcase work .By nurturing these relationships, you can tap into a network of collaborators, mentors, and potential clients or customers. Remember, collaborations and networking are not only about what you can gain but also about what you can contribute. By actively participating in your creative community, you can create a supportive environment that benefits everyone involved.

Financial Planning for Your Passion Projects

When pursuing your passion projects, effective financial planning is crucial to ensure their sustainability and success .Balancing the financial aspects of your hobby-based business can help you overcome obstacles and achieve your goals. In this section, we will explore various strategies to help you maintain a healthy balance between your passion projects and your finances.

Budgeting for Success

One of the fundamental aspects of financial planning is creating a budget for your passion projects. A well-thought-out budget allows you to allocate resources wisely ensuring that you have enough funds to invest in business while covering personal expenses .Take time track income and expenses identify areas where adjustments align with financial goals .

The Power of Saving

Financial planning is the backbone to all your passion projects. When you put a little bit of your income away regularly, you create a cushion so that you can reinvest in your business or still make money when you come across challenges and unexpected expenses. If you feel like it's too hard to do on your own, don't worry! A lot of banks will now let you set up automatic transfers from your income to a separate savings account.

Investing in Your Hobby-Based Business

Once things get going, your hobby based business might be worth investing some more money into. You can buy better equipment, upgrade the space you work out of, or even expand your reach with some marketing efforts. Do research and take advice from professionals before making any major decisions.

Seeking Professional Guidance

As things grow, managing the financial aspects of anything quickly becomes difficult if it wasn't already. So look for someone who has worked with other creative entrepreneurs and isn't just regurgitating Google search results for advice.

By prioritizing effective financial planning, passon projects thrive without compromising their financial stability. Take control of the finances and create a solid foundation for businesses that are run by love rather than pure profit.

Diversifying Income Sources

Building a hobby-based business is already risky as it is with one revenue stream so expanding will minimize the vulnerability that comes with depending on one particular source.

There are many ways to diversify:

- Different products or services
- Different sales channels
- Collaborating and partnering up with other like-minded people
- Creating digital products
- Affiliate Marketing

When done right these different channels will compliment each other rather than distract from each other.

When it comes to your hobby-based business, effectively promoting and generating potential income sources are crucial. By building a strong brand identity, knowing who you want to sell to, and creating effective marketing campaigns will set a solid foundation for growth.

Begin by focusing on the brand identity that can appeal to your target audience. A good brand story, unique visual identity, and consistent messaging will help differentiate your business from others in the field.

Identifying your ideal customers is another vital step in the process. Find what they need and what their pain points are through market research. This knowledge will guide all of your marketing efforts as you can tailor everything including how you reach them.

Implementing Successful Marketing Campaigns

Once you've defined yourself and know who makes up your target audience, it's time to implement a successful marketing campaign. Here's some strategies to consider:

Build a comprehensive digital marketing strategy by using social media marketing (SMM), search engine optimization (SEO), content marketing, and email marketing.

Engage with your audience through regular content creation that's meaningful such as blog posts or videos.

Utilize influencer marketing where they can talk about your product or service which provides credibility for you within their following base if they align with your own brand values.

Conduct targeted online advertising campaigns on platforms where you know that's where the people who'll buy from you hangs out.

Implement SEO techniques so that you can be found easier when someone looks something up in a browser search bar.

Track how well these campaigns do using analytics tools so that if anything isn't optimal then it's changed immediately.

If all of these strategies are implemented correctly then there should be no problem in promoting your hobby-based business. The next step would be attracting potential customers then eventually generating potential income sources.

Overcoming Challenges And Obtaining Support

- Friends and Family: Sharing your projects with loved ones can help you stay connected to your passion. They can provide valuable feedback, lend a helping hand, or simply be a listening ear when you face challenges.
- Mentors: A mentor who has experience in your field can offer guidance and advice, as well as a fresh perspective on your work. Seek out mentors through networking events or online communities related to your hobby. Their wisdom and expertise will make it easier for you to navigate obstacles.

By addressing the challenges that come with pursuing passions and seeking support from friends, family, and mentors, you'll find it easier to balance your project time. Remember that you're never alone in what you do-you've got the strength to succeed if you remain determined.

Maintaining Long-Term Success

Long-term success means turning passion projects into potential income sources. The key here is balancing between nurturing creative pursuits and managing business aspects for hobbies.

To keep money rolling in, continually explore new ideas that have potential income streams. This helps enhance revenue but also offers flexibility in managing passion projects by diversifying offerings such as additional products or collaborations.

Another way long-term success stays alive is through adaptability: Trends come and go quickly so remaining open to changes is necessary along with feedback from customers. By continuously expanding knowledge and skill sets there's room for competition which benefits business longevity.

Most importantly though is finding fulfillment within it all since this isn't just about money but also happiness. Always remember why these passion projects were taken on in the first place then use that joy as motivation towards achieving financial success while making sure personal fulfillment isn't lost-open up to family and peers for support, don't hold back!

Chapter 34

Staying Relevant
in a Digital Age

In this chapter, we will be exploring the wild and ever-changing world of digital trends as well as the importance of staying literate in today's fast-paced, technological age. As technology continues to evolve at an exponential pace, it becomes more important than ever for individuals and businesses alike to keep up with trends and develop the skills necessary.

How do you go about staying ahead in such a rapidly evolving environment? Simple: by quite literally turning your brain into a sponge. Suck up all that knowledge about what's new, what's old but still relevant, and keep tabs on changes so sudden they could leave you behind in a matter of hours.

In future sections we will dive deep into these trends. We'll talk about how they shape industries and even change daily life. Digital literacy will also get plenty of time on center stage as we explore its role in personal development. We'll give strategies on how to navigate the changing digital world while keeping ourselves safe too.

But buckle up because there is much more fun in store for you! Emerging technologies like artificial intelligence (or AI) are revolutionizing everything from data analytics to food shopping experiences. Learning how AI became the monster it is today could take weeks by itself so don't worry, I'll only give you a taste here.

On top of that we'll discuss some specific skills that all professionals should have if they want any chance at career growth at all. Education isn't ignored either! It's where most people start developing digital literacy anyways so why not focus some attention there?

And if it doesn't sound like enough already, I assure you there's more! Especially when it comes to pushing innovation forward in society and industry sectors alike.

So strap yourselves in boys and girls, because we're blasting off into the unknown!

Understanding Digital Trends

In today's fast-paced digital age, staying ahead of the curb is crucial. Whether you're an individual or a business owner, not understanding trends could mean the end of you. So we're here to help.

When it comes to understanding digital trends, all you need to do is look around and find something that makes absolutely no sense and seems as random as pro-wrestling in a cooking show. That's when you know it's trending at least for this week.

But jokes aside, market trends are based on consumer behavior. By keeping up with them, businesses are able to change their offerings and keep up with customers who are going through an identity crisis every week. We'll take a look at those and see how they changed throughout history in the next section. Lastly we'll talk about emerging technologies too. They go hand in hand with these trends since they make them possible after all.

The Importance of Digital Literacy

Digital literacy is vital in today's society. Technology is part of every aspect of our lives, so having digital literacy skills has become crucial for personal and professional development. In this section, we will discuss the importance of digital literacy and how it impacts the digital age.

Understanding Digital Literacy

When you have digital literacy, you can use, understand, and evaluate digital tools and technologies effectively. This includes skills such as searching up things on the internet, using productivity software, evaluating online information and protecting your identity online.

Having these skills provides a lot of benefits. For one, it allows individuals to fully participate in a digital society. Opening up opportunities for education, employment and social interaction. It also equips individuals with the necessary skills to keep up with technology advancements which are always evolving.

Impact on Personal and Professional Development

In today's world that revolves around technology there's no longer an option about whether or not someone wants to have digital literacy but rather that its become necessary to survive. Having this skill plays a significant role in personal and professional development. When they have them individuals can enhance their knowledge skills overall competitiveness.

Professionally speaking employers love people who know their way around tech. Knowing how to leverage different tools makes it easier for them to execute tasks quickly and efficiently which leads to increased productivity better job performance and more career advancement opportunities.. It also encourages them to keep learning which helps them stay updated with industry trends.

On a personal level it only gets better because then communication critical thinking problem solving all gets enhanced too! On top of that when you know how to use your tools properly you start making responsible decisions online which keeps your personal info safe from hackers.

Tips for Improving Digital Literacy

Improving your skill is something that should be done continuously since new advancements are made regularly Here are some useful tips:

Take advantage of online resources: Access online courses webinars tutorials etc..

Explore platforms: Familiarize yourself with popular digital tools and platforms to stay connected, collaborate, and enhance productivity.

Engage in social media responsibly: Understand the impact and implications of social media, and use it responsibly to build networks, share information, and engage in meaningful conversations.

Cultivate critical thinking: Develop the ability to assess the credibility and reliability of online information, distinguishing between factual and misleading content.

Protect your digital identity: Safeguard your personal information by practicing secure online habits, such as using strong passwords, enabling two-factor authentication, and being mindful of the information you share online.

By continuously improving your digital literacy you can confidently navigate the digital world. This will also make sure that you can capitalize on its opportunities while still being able to contribute effectively to our current age.

Navigating the Evolving Technological Landscape

Keeping up with technological advancements is pretty hard. In this section though we have something that'll help. Strategies and resources that are valuable for staying updated on things happening so that you can remain competitive in your field.

Another way to keep up is to go to conferences, webinars, and workshops. That's a way for you to learn from industry experts and connect with other professionals. You can also join professional communities online or forums where you can collaborate with others who have similar interests.

With technology always growing it's important for you to upgrade your skillset. A way you can do that is by taking relevant courses online or attending webinars. These resources are valuable because they provide knowledge that'll help you adapt in the future.

You should also try your best to be curious and adaptable. Be open to new technologies and tools that come into play, because at the end of the day in our world what really matters is constant learning.

Embracing Artificial Intelligence

Artificial Intelligence (AI) has become one of the most powerful technologies in today's digital landscape. And knowing how much industries have changed across the globe thanks to it, it's important we take some time out of our days to learn about AI and other trends impacting our lives.

We all know those robots that operate in hospitals, stores, airports - yet don't even realize their powered by AI algorithms! It doesn't stop there either as it helps doctors in diagnosing diseases predicting patient outcomes. Even major trading companies use them when analyzing market trends before making an investment decision.

The list goes on as they've helped retail companies improve customer experiences and optimized route planning for logistic businesses too!

These are just some examples of how AI has been changing traditional ways that industries operate but now let's see how individuals themselves can benefit from AI education:

In this case we're fighting against each other since competition will increase when only one opening remains while 100 people apply. If we want a chance at getting these limited job opportunities than we must first understand what employers want from us: skills teachers don't teach us!

And unfortunately having proficiency in Microsoft Office isn't enough anymore as employers want workers who can automate repetitive tasks through coding. They want those who can optimize processes using data analysis, and they want someone who's able to assist in the development of intelligent systems.

Other than professionals we too can use AI in our everyday lives: virtual assistants like Siri and Alexa are powered by AI algorithms. Platforms like Spotify use it to recommend us new music, Netflix uses it to give us personalized recommendations based on our watching habits.

Lastly in a time where everyone is learning new skills to hop into the job market employers will be looking for people with digital trends such as AI experience.

Enhancing Digital Skills for Career Growth

It's all about staying relevant! The moment you let technology leave you behind your opportunities do as well. And I could only imagine how much harder it'll become when being replaced by robots is already in motion. So stay ahead of your competition by always being curious and adaptable!

In today's digital age strong digital skills will take you far. It's important that you constantly learn how to enhance them so no matter what change comes tomorrow, you're ready!

Digital literacy is a multi-faceted skill. It's the ability to find your way around digital tools and platforms, critically evaluate information online, and communicate effectively on digital channels. But it's so much more than that. Improving your digital literacy can open new doors and help you stay relevant in an ever-changing professional world.

Why Is Digital Literacy Important?

This isn't just another skill you can put on a resume - it's a necessity. Remote work, virtual collaboration, online communication: these have all become the norm. Having good digital literacy skills are crucial now more than ever before. Employers are actively looking for candidates who possess strong digital abilities because it shows adaptability, resourcefulness, and an understanding of how to use technology to meet business goals.

To take your career growth up a notch by enhancing your digital skills, start by breaking down the specific skills that match what employers want from you in your industry. You may discover it requires expertise in data analysis or coding - figure out what it is you need to learn first (if you don't know already). After that's done, go search for online courses or workshops that'll help develop those key skills.

Never Stop Learning

Keeping up with the trends of today isn't enough; professionals need to be adaptable as times change too. As more technologies emerge and current ones evolve, you've got to make sure you're always informed about them all if you want any hope of staying ahead of competitors.

Below are a few things that might keep you in the loop:

Engage in communities

Attend industry events

Follow thought leaders in your field

Something else that could help is subscribing to newsletters or podcasts relevant to the kind of work you do. By continuously taking time out of your day-to-day life to educate yourself about what's happening in the world, positioning yourself as someone who knows their stuff will become natural.

Getting better at something is always a good idea - especially when it's your digital literacy. By continuously keeping up with changing trends and technologies, you won't just have a unique selling point in the eyes of your employer, but also set yourself up for success throughout your career.

Protect Your Digital Self In Today's Digital World

In today's modern world, it is more important than ever to protect your digital self. With the increase of cyber crime and constant new and evolving threats to our digital space, it is crucial that we know how to handle and defend our personal information. By knowing what is going on in the digital world and keeping up with the latest security techniques you can avoid any risk or damage.

Best Practices for Online Security

To protect your digital identity, you must follow a few basic rules:

Use strong passwords for every account of yours online. A password manager might be a great addition as well as it can help securely store them all.

Whenever you see something related to two-factor authentication, make sure to turn it on! This adds an extra layer of security to anything.

Make sure everything is always updated. Operating systems, web browsers, antivirus programs. You name it!

Don't share too much personal info on social media platforms. Also limit whatever personal data you do share - adjust privacy settings as well.

Always be careful when clicking links in emails or downloading attachments. They could easily be phishing attempts so always verify before giving away any personal info!

Back up all of your important files regularly - either through an external storage device or cloud service in order to have them safe somewhere.

Stay Ahead of The Game

Keeling up with the latest trends and security techniques will keep you ahead of everyone else when it comes to safety against hackers:

When following cybersecurity news sources and blogs, pay attention not only to trends but also current threats.

Educate yourself about different types of attacks like phishing, malware, ransomware.

Keep all devices and software up-to-date with the newest security patches/updates.

Consider getting some antivirus software that works best for you - stay protected at all costs!

Review statements often and monitor credit reports for anything suspicious whenever possible

Keep a close eye on your accounts online just in case someone might be getting a little bit too curious.

In following these best practices you can ensure that your digital identity remains safe and secure while also staying ahead of any potential cybercrime victims!

Welcome to A New Digital Era

The future is now - or at least it's coming soon. With the rapid process of our digital era, we're lucky enough to see new technologies sprout out of nowhere on the daily. Things like virtual reality (VR) and blockchain are just two examples of what the future holds for us.. And I'm sure that doesn't make sense to you right now, but trust me; by the end of this section your mind will be blown.

Virtual Reality: Boundaries of Immersion

Imagine being able to step into a whole new world without even leaving your seat? That was only possible in movies up until recent years. Virtual reality (VR) isn't just limited to gaming or other entertainment purposes anymore. It has started revolutionizing other industries as well - healthcare, education, and architecture are only a few examples!

Healthcare professionals can use VR to train themselves in realistic scenarios, enhance surgical procedures, and treat patients who may not live close by. Education benefits from VR by providing immersive learning experiences which allows students to explore historical events, visit places they've never been before, and learn complex concepts in an engaging way. Architects can also visualize designs using VR - giving them room for better collaboration and decision making.

Blockchain: Trust and Transparency in The Modern World

Blockchain technology is normally used to have secure transactions in cryptocurrencies. However, it has far greater uses beyond finances. It's a decentralized and immutable ledger that records all transactions, this ensures security, trust and transparency. This can lead to many positive affects in other industries like supply chain management and healthcare.

Blockchain's traceability enables organizations to track every stage of a product's journey – making things easier for both the company and consumer. It also reduces fraud and promotes ethical business practices. Healthcare is another industry that stands to benefit from blockchain because it'll allow you to securely store patient records. Improving interoperability and streamlining access to critical medical information.

Through these two technologies we're going through a digital revolution. Staying informed on them is vital in this landscape we're in now.

Building Digital Literacy

Fostering digital literacy should be one of the focal points when preparing students for the future. It's the ability to confidently use digital technology effectively. Not just finding, evaluating or creating information but communicating too.

It goes much deeper than knowing how to operate a computer or browse the internet though. Critical thinking, problem-solving and creativity are all necessary so they can adapt as new technologies evolve around them.

When we instill digital literacy into education we equip students with tools that will allow them to navigate through this era we're in right now.

The Importance of Digital Literacy

Digital literacy prepares students for their careers where digital skills are increasingly important in today's workforce. By giving them these skills you enable them to adapt with new techonologies as they come out so they can be confident while engaging with digital platforms (which are everywhere). In an era of fake news spreading like wildfire, its crucial for students to develop the ability of evaluating credibility online facts as well as make informed decisions about what they consume or share on social media platforms.

Lastly, it enhances communication and collaboration which are some of the most sought after skills in the world. These skills allow students to effectively communicate with each other, collaborate and network in online environments.

Successful Programs

Educational institutions have already implemented digital literacy programs into their curriculum. One example is the "Digital Citizenship" program from Los Angeles Unified School District. The main goal of this is to educate students on responsible and ethical technology use.

Code.org has also launched "Hour of Code" which introduces basic coding concepts and computational thinking. Thousands of students have gone through it so far and they all leave with a problem-solving mentality.

Fostering digital literacy in education is a multi-faceted effort. Pairing digital literacy with established subjects like language arts, science, and social studies can give students an understanding of how these skills apply to real-life situations. Having an increased awareness of applications can make all the difference when learning something new.

But even that's not enough.

It's also helpful for teachers to be trained in digital literacy so they're able to incorporate digital tools and resources into their teaching methods. Training and collaboration are ongoing, so educators should always stay updated on the latest trends and best practices regarding different aspects of the world wide web.

Partnerships between educational institutions and technology companies bring a number of benefits as well. The most obvious being access to more tools, programs, resources that encourage growth in areas that need it.

The future is digital

In order to keep up with the rapidly changing digital landscape, people have no choice but to adapt or face obsolescence. It doesn't matter who you are or what your career is - being digitally literate is crucial for both personal growth and professional success.

Fortunately, there are several ways anyone can learn crucial skills to navigate the internet confidently. Online courses from platforms like Coursera, Udemy, and LinkedIn Learning offer insight into everything from data analysis to cybersecurity.

If you don't want to go through an entire course curriculum then try attending some webinars or virtual conferences instead. Not only do these events allow you hear from leading experts in various industries but they also let you do it wherever you choose without any travel fees.

Staying updated on the latest news in technology will also aid in keeping your knowledge relevant. There are plenty of places online where tech lovers share insights about updates they become aware of. Just know that not every source is reliable so fact-checking may be necessary before acting on information received online.

Chapter 35

A Balanced Approach
to Risk-Taking

In this chapter, we're going to dive into the world of risk-taking and explore the importance of balance. Balancing risks is a critical skill that helps us make calculated decisions that lead to growth and success. We'll also talk about the different types of risks, how to evaluate them, and ways to develop a strong risk mitigation strategy.

Let's get started!

Understanding Different Types of Risks

To navigate the complex world of risk, it pays to understand all the different types of risks individuals and businesses may encounter. Once you know what they are, you'll be able to assess potential challenges and opportunities better.

So let's take a look at some key categories:

1. Financial Risks

This type relates to potential losses that may arise from changes in market conditions, investment decisions or economic factors. Examples include fluctuations in currency exchange rates, interest rate changes and market volatility.

2. Operational Risks

Operational risks refer to potential threats that can impact an organization's day-to-day operations. These risks may arise from internal factors such as inadequate processes, system failures or human error.

3. Strategic Risks

Long-term goals can lead to strategic risks - which are potential challenges arising when organizations start making decisions with their long-term objectives in mind. Some examples include entering new markets, adopting new technologies or launching new products or services.

4. Compliance Risks

Compliance-related risks occur when companies fail to follow industry standards or adhere to government regulations. Doing so could result in legal penalties alongside reputational damage and financial consequences.

Of course, these are just a few examples; there are many more out there! The goal is simply for you recognize what they are so you can identify areas of vulnerability before it's too late.

Evaluating Risks and Rewards

When making important decisions like whether or not you should buy those cool shoes at the store last week - evaluating its associated risk is crucial (we're joking, it's probably a great purchase!). All jokes aside though, risk evaluation is the process of thoroughly assessing the potential risks associated with a particular course of action. This analysis allows individuals and businesses to make informed choices that align with their goals and objectives.

Risk-reward analysis is also a vital part of this evaluation process. It involves weighing how good or bad the potential benefits could be along with its corresponding risks. By doing so, individuals can gauge the probability of success and make more calculated moves.

To evaluate risk, you need to look at the potential outcomes of a situation. Multiple factors like market trends and industry competition need to be thought about when making a decision. This also applies to external factors that influence the outcome. By conducting a thorough analysis on each part of the risks and rewards, you can make decisions that have more guarantee.

The cost-benefit analysis is a helpful tool when trying to figure out how much risk and reward are in a situation. By calculating possible costs, both financial and non-financial, it gives an idea of all the benefits that could come with the decision. Risk evaluation and risk-reward analyzing will help people realize what could go wrong before it happens so they can make better choices during their time in charge.

Risk mitigation is important for any business in today's landscape because lots can happen. To ensure no negative impacts occur, organizations need to protect themselves from them by managing their risks.

Steps like identifying them, breaking them down into parts and prioritizing each one helps with being prepared for any outcome.

Developing ways to reduce their likelihood all together is another way companies risk mitigate. For example diversifying operations or products removes the possibility of one thing tanking your whole system because there are multiple backups already working as we speak.

As times change lots of new potential risks can spring but this doesn't mean businesses have to rework everything from scratch again just to identify these new threats. A simple review will do by monitoring possible ones regularly there isn't much room for mistakes.

Uncertainty may be scary but calculated risk-taking is always something we should embrace. Making progress without taking chances would limit us from reaching greater heights which would result in us staying within our comfort zones forever.

Calculated risks are taken by calculating a decision's potential benefits and subtracting the potential drawbacks, when there's uncertainty. Your choices reflect how you weighed the outcomes and your analysis of all available information. So, with this in mind, individuals and businesses can make their own decisions. Allowing them to make informed choices that have the potential for significant rewards. Strategic decision-making on the other hand is a process that prioritizes actions that align with long-term goals. In order to make these decisions, someone needs to understand today's market conditions and internal capabilities. And by embracing calculated risk-taking as part of the decision-making process, individuals and businesses can gain a competitive edge while putting themselves into growth positions.

However, embracing calculated risk-taking can be difficult. You need to keep caution in balance with courage. There will always be missed opportunities if you're too cautious but lose big if you're reckless. That's why successful risk-takers evaluate any possible mitigations and maintain a resilient mindset.

Below we'll discuss strategies for effectively embracing calculated risk-taking in more detail. The next section has practical tips and techniques for assessing risks, making informed decisions, and maximizing your chances of success.

Building Resilience in the Face of Risks

When it comes to navigating through uncertainties even though risks may bring challenges as well resilience is crucial. It's defined as being able to bounce back and adapt even in adversity.

Believe it or not but resilience is built by developing a growth mindset which allows us to view setbacks as opportunities for learning experiences so that we can build up our confidence through failures (yes that's right). We can then develop the courage necessary for taking risks later down the road.

Another thing that helps build resilience is having people around us who want nothing but success for ourselves as they motivate us to take risks head-on which leads to success.

The Importance of Self-Care

Keeping ourselves healthy physically, mentally, emotionally is also crucial as it lets us better handle stress and setbacks. If we're engaging in activities that bring us joy, practicing mindfulness, and prioritizing self-care routines then we're able to build our resilience.

Developing Coping Strategies

Lastly, developing coping strategies is one of the most essential elements of building resilience. It's what let's you thrive even in the face of problems so that by having effective coping mechanisms in place, we can navigate risks and challenges with greater ease.

In conclusion, building resilience is crucial for managing risks and adapting to uncertain circumstances. By cultivating a growth mindset, fostering a support system, prioritizing self-care, and developing coping strategies, we can enhance our resilience and effectively manage our risk tolerance.

Leveraging Opportunities for Growth

This section explores the inherent connection between risks and growth opportunities. In today's rapidly evolving world, embracing risks becomes crucial for unlocking personal and professional growth.

However, many individuals face challenges due to risk aversion. The fear of failure or loss often hinders their ability to seize potential avenues for growth.

By understanding that growth opportunities are born from calculated risks, individuals can overcome their risk aversion and embrace the possibilities that lie ahead.

It's important to assess the potential benefits and evaluate the risks associated with any opportunity. This helps individuals make informed decisions and strike a balance between growth and risk aversion.

Real growth requires pushing past comfort zones and embracing uncertainty. By stepping out of familiar territory, individuals can gain new insights, talents, opportunities for personal and professional development.

Seizing growth opportunities might mean pursuing new ventures or looking for innovative ideas or collaborations. These endeavors come with their fair share of risk but hold remarkable success within them.

By addressing risk aversion head-on, people can unlock a world of growth opportunities that will help them reach unimaginable heights. It's time to embrace risks, step out of comfort zones, and seize incredible potential for personal and professional growth.

The Role of Innovation in Risk-Taking

This section will explore how important innovation is in risk-taking and how it opens up new possibilities. When an individual or business embraces innovation they approach risks differently which leads to unique solutions.

Innovation gives the courage needed to take calculated risks by challenging the status quo. With this mindset people can find new ways to grow by seeking better ways to improve themselves professionally. A culture like this allows organizations to build an appetite for risk that drives them ahead of competitors.

Innovation isn't only about technological breakthroughs; it's about new ideas too. It empowers people to think outside the box while allowing them to experiment with novel approaches.

When you merge innovative thinking into taking risks people find hidden opportunities while also mitigating pitfalls before they happen. Being able to see beyond the surface helps break through fear as well as uncertainty transforming setbacks into steps forward.

Embracing innovation when taking risks requires blending continuous learning with experimentation while adapting at all times. Collaboration will be key as well as diversity when gathering thoughts from others who share different perspectives on things - which ultimately challenge assumptions towards societal norms.

Building a Mindset That Believes in Growth

Everyone must learn from failure in order to fully embrace risk-taking. Instead of feeling discouraged by setbacks, everyone must see it as an opportunity to learn and grow.

Learning from failure is key because it provides valuable insights and lessons needed to make better decisions in the future. The more you analyze what went wrong the more you'll find areas for improvement.

Failure teaches individuals resilience while also building confidence. Once we face defeat and are able to get back up their drive will push them forward knowing that they took risks just like this time before and succeeded.

Roadblocks should not be taken as a dead end, but rather a stepping stone towards growth and success. Every time you fail, take it as an opportunity to learn, adapt, and improve.

When people with the right mindset get knocked back down they don't stay down saying "why me?!" or "I can't do this!". Instead they ask themselves questions like "What can I learn from this?" and "How can I grow from this?". Failing isn't what sets successful people apart from others; everybody fails. What does set them apart is that they use their failures to their advantage, they transform setbacks into tools that will help them prosper in personal life and professional career.

It's always important to keep taking risks, no matter how many times you've failed before. You'll never reach your full potential if you're always too scared to try something new.

Striking the Perfect Balance

Proper decision making is vital when trying to find the perfect balance between risk and reward. By finding this delicate equilibrium you can maximize your gains while simultaneously minimizing your losses. Although it sounds difficult (which it is), there are a couple strategies that can make it easier for you.

One strategy that is very effective at achieving balance is evaluating each possible risk involved. This consists of thinking about every outcome and weighing its rewards against its downfalls. Once you've done this for everything on your list of decisions, you'll be able to confidently make choices that minimize risks while maximizing opportunities for growth.

Evaluating Risks: A Key Component of Decision-Making

Evaluating risks is a critical step in the decision-making process. It involves assessing the probability of each possible outcome occurring with the impact it could have if carried out successfully. By conducting a comprehensive risk assessment individuals are given more than enough time to think about potential pitfalls and develop contingency plans to lessen their effects.

But we're not done yet! You also have to think about the potential rewards when evaluating risks. Although this may sound tedious, it's a step that can't be missed. Assessing potential gains allows you to make informed decisions that will help you reach your goals and aspirations.

Strategies for Balanced Decision-Making

When we talk about achieving balance, we're not saying that you should invest in everything at once; just like how you wouldn't drain your bank account by purchasing every video game on the shelves of a store. We simply mean that you should mix things up a little.

Here are some strategies you can follow:

Diversify your portfolio: Invest in a variety of assets or projects to spread the risk and increase the likelihood of positive outcomes.

Set clear goals and objectives: Clearly defining your objectives helps prioritize risks and rewards based on their alignment with your desired outcomes.

Stay informed: Continuously monitor and assess the market, industry trends, and relevant factors that may impact the risk-reward balance.

Leverage data and analytics: Utilize data-driven insights and analytical tools to evaluate risks and predict potential outcomes.

By incorporating these strategies into the decision-making process, individuals can strike a risk-reward balance that aligns with their growth objectives. Just know it won't be easy! But taking calculated risks is essential for progress and success, but maintaining a well-balanced approach ensures long-term sustainability and resilience.

Navigating Uncertainty and External Factors

As soon as you get into risk-taking more seriously, there is one thing I must warn you about - uncertainty. It's something everybody has come across at least once in their life time; whether it's through personal experiences or work related circumstances. But no matter what it is we've all got used to adapting which isn't too bad!

External factors such as market conditions, industry trends, technological advancements, and regulatory changes can create a level of unpredictability and complexity. These factors can introduce new risks or present opportunities that we need to carefully evaluate.

Embracing Uncertainty:

In times of uncertainty, it becomes vital to proactively and flexibly approach challenges. Adapting to change and taking calculated risks can help minimize potential threats and increase our likelihood of success.

Adaptability in Uncertain Times:

Facing ambiguity necessitates staying informed and constantly considering factors that affect our decision-making. With a proactive approach, we can monitor industry news, market trends, and emerging technology.

Analyzing External Factors:

A thorough examination of external factors allows us to better understand how they can impact our choices. This involves identifying the opportunities certain factors bring about as well as the complications. Only then can we create strategies to overcome these drawbacks while capitalizing on the benefits.

Strategic Planning and Scenario Analysis

Both strategic planning and scenario analysis offer valuable ways to move forward when we have limited information. By creating different outcomes based on assumptions, we are able to predict possible scenarios before they even happen. This allows us to make decisions that are based on informed approaches rather than blind guesses.

Continual Evaluation:

Only by evaluating ourselves regularly will we be able to adapt to new situations effectively. Pausing at intervals will allow us look back at what we've done so far and determine where changes should be made or continued.

When uncertainty strikes, it is crucial that we do not freeze up or retreat into comfort zones immediately. Instead, with an agile mindset and adaptability, we must use what's given against itself for growth. It will not be easy but through this methodical process, progress can be made in any situation.

Continuous Growth and Risk-Taking

Continuous growth is a vital aspect of personal and professional development. It involves pushing beyond our comfort zones, embracing new challenges, and taking calculated risks. By adopting a risk mindset, individuals can unlock their full potential and seize opportunities for growth.

Risk-taking is not about blindly making impulsive decisions; it is about making informed choices after careful evaluation. It requires assessing potential risks and rewards, considering different scenarios, and developing a strategic approach. By recognizing and accepting that risks are inherent in any endeavor, individuals can overcome fear and uncertainty, paving the way for continuous growth.

When we embrace risk-taking, we open ourselves up to valuable learning experiences. Failure becomes an opportunity for growth, enabling us to learn from our mistakes and refine our strategies. By cultivating a growth mindset, we shift our perspective and view challenges as stepping stones towards success.

Remember, continuous growth is not about achieving perfection or avoiding all risks. It is about being willing to step outside our comfort zones, embrace uncertainty, and adapt to changing circumstances. By adopting a risk mindset and actively seeking opportunities for growth, individuals can pave the way for a fulfilling and successful journey.

Chapter **36**

Creativity and
Innovation at Forty

In this chapter, we will explore the exciting realm of unlocking your creativity and infusing innovation into your daily life in your forties.

At this age, you have gained valuable wisdom and experience. Now is the perfect time to unlock the creative potential that lies within. Whether you're an artist, a professional, or someone who wants to add a little more spice into their daily routine-this chapter will give you new perspectives on how to embrace your creativity.

These pages will also take you on a journey of self-discovery. It will help you tap into the vast reservoir of creative potential that exists within you. We want to ignite your imagination by exploring techniques, insights, and practical strategies. By doing this, it allows for new ideas to flourish.

However, don't think creativity can only be used in specific scenarios-it's quite the opposite. Creativity permeates every aspect of our lives. That's why we'll dive into how innovation can change your work and personal experiences as well.

From problem-solving complex issues in everyday tasks to improving relationships and finding joy in normal life-we'll show you how it's done.

So strap yourself in now! Together we're about to explore what possibilities lie behind embracing creativity and innovation.

The Power of Creative Potential

Unleash the untapped power within yourself and witness how it can affect all aspects of life for the better.

You might think that being creative is limited to artists and designers-but know that's not true at all. Not everyone knows they are capable of it because they haven't tapped into that side yet. Everyone has their unique abilities-which with some effort can be transformed into valuable ideas.

Embracing these abilities brings forth opportunities which leads to enhanced problem-solving skills followed by unleashed imagination powers-allowing for innovative solutions never thought possible before.

But it doesn't just stop there! Your surroundings outside work also benefit from embracing creativity. Things like bringing joy through expression and making a difference in others will be your new norm.

Now, how do you go about tapping into it? Well, it starts with being curious. Letting yourself take risks and embracing new experiences can help bring to light ideas you never thought possible. By doing this, the way things are seen outside your comfort zone can unlock hidden talents.

Remember that creativity is not something only a few people have-everyone has it. You just have to embrace that talent and let it shine.

Embracing Innovation in Everyday Life

Experience how innovation brings about more benefits than what meets the eye. Incorporating innovative thinking throughout everyday tasks will open up a world of opportunities for you.

When we think of innovation, we tend to think of groundbreaking inventions or revolutionary ideas-and while those are correct-it can be as simple as finding new ways to approach basic tasks or even embracing change in our daily routine. By having an innovative mindset, out-of-the-box solutions suddenly become unlocked and staying ahead of the curve becomes effortless.

Embrace Innovation in Everyday Life

One way to embrace innovation in your life is by always seeking out new ideas and perspectives. Diverse influences can be found through reading books, attending workshops, or engaging in thought-provoking conversations with colleagues or friends. By expanding your horizons and thinking outside the box, you'll be able to truly embrace innovation.

Another key aspect of embracing innovation is being open to experimentation and taking calculated risks. Don't be afraid of trying new things and taking a step out of your comfort zone. Innovation often involves taking chances and learning from both successes and failures along the way.

Furthermore, combining innovation with everyday tasks can help you uncover hidden potential. Look for opportunities to streamline processes and improve efficiency in your work or personal life. Utilize technology and digital tools to automate repetitive tasks freeing up time for more creative endeavors.

Remember, innovation is a mindset that can be developed over time. By embracing it every day you stay adaptable in an ever-changing world.

Nurturing Creativity Through Mindfulness

Uncover the profound connection between mindfulness and creativity while unlocking your full creative potential.

Mindfulness is the practice of intentional present moment awareness that clears a path for enhanced creative thinking – opening up a world of new possibilities.

By cultivating mindfulness, you can quiet the noise of daily life and tap into the deeper recesses of your mind where creativity resides. Embracing mindfulness allows you to fully immerse yourself in the present moment which comes free from distractions and external pressures.

Mindfulness brings an attitude of non-judgment making it easier for creative ideas to flow freely without self-criticism or fear of failure getting in the way. It helps break conventional thinking patterns enabling fresh perspectives on innovative approaches.

Techniques for Cultivating Mindfulness & Enhancing Creativity

There are numerous techniques that make incorporating mindfulness into your daily life easy:

Meditation & Breathing Exercises: Dedicate a few minutes every day to meditate or practice deep breathing exercises. Calming the mind and strengthening your creative flow.

Sensory Awareness: Engage all your senses fully in the present moment. The heightened sensory awareness can ignite your imagination and inspire new ideas.

Single-Tasking: Instead of multitasking, focus on one task at a time. Giving your full attention to each activity taps into the depth of creativity to produce higher quality work.

Nature Immersion: Spend time in nature and allow its beauty to cultivate a sense of calm and inspiration. Nature's tranquility quiets the mind stimulating innovative thinking.

By integrating mindfulness practices into your routine, you can foster creativity and uncover endless possibilities within a creative mind. Embrace it as a tool for unlocking potential then watch as creativity flourishes in all aspects of life.

Overcoming Creative Blocks

Feeling stuck because you have creative blocks that dampen expression? Don't worry, many individuals face obstacles which stop their creative flow. But don't let this stop you, with effective strategies you can overcome these barriers and unlock full potential.

Creative blocks are annoying. You're stuck, you know it, but can't do anything about it. But before you go and beat yourself up over it, realize that...you can't fix what you don't know is broken! The first step to figuring out why your creative flow is being held hostage is knowing the barriers. Things like self-doubt, fear of failure, fear of rejection and so on.

Now… no one likes breaking stuff down by tackling those fears straight on...they're scary! That's why we have to break them down into tiny pieces and toss them in the trash bin.

One way we could do this is by challenging the negative thoughts we get when trying something new or when a project fails. If we're always gonna think negatively about our work then of course the next project will be as bad as the last one. Instead let's try thinking more positively! With this growth mindset experimentation won't sound so terrifying and it'll become easier for us to learn from mistakes rather than avoiding them all together.

Another thing we could look into is mindfulness techniques such as meditation and deep breathing exercises. Just doing these things alone would provide a world full of benefits but in terms of creativity it'll help us control our minds, keep our focus sharp and give us that extra push we need to use our talents effectively!

Lastly just get some inspiration from other sources outside of your field. Sometimes seeing something outside of what you usually see gives you just enough shock value for a fresh perspective on things again. Go outdoors more often (if possible) talk with people who are passionate about their work and engage in fun activities that awaken the inner child inside you! All these things will bring back all those nostalgic emotions that made everything easy at one point.

Remember creative blocks ain't nothing but lil bugs… 1 shoe squashes em fast

Creating Space for Creativity

Sometimes you have to play around with your environment to get that spark back but here's a few practical tips!

1. Clean up your workspace: We've all been there...you sit at your desk ready to get stuff done and then that massive stack of papers you put off for weeks just stares back at you. Or maybe it's just all the junk you have on your desk. Regardless, it's hard to think clearly in a messy space. So keep things clean and organized!

2. Inspiration is key: If you're not inspired then don't expect anything amazing to come out of your head! So surround yourself with things, people or places that can make that happen. Keep books, magazines or art around you that excites you and helps keep the cogs turning.

3. Build a network: You'll need people who are like minded in terms of creativity too! Who else will understand what you're going through? Go out and find others who live this kind of lifestyle as well! Whether it be through online communities or workshops. Collaborate on projects with them because two brains are better than one.

By making the right moves in terms of your environment, everything else starts to fall into place from there.

There's no other way around it - technology is a vital part of our everyday lives now. It'd be really silly if we didn't use it to its fullest potential...especially when it comes to innovation.

With how advanced everything has become, there isn't much we can't do anymore. And if we're not taking advantage of all the new tools and platforms available then we're missing out big time!

Businesses, individuals and even children turn heads when they create something amazing using technology. But how can they use tools such as apps, graphic design software or analytics systems if they don't know about them?

So long story short...yes we should be using these tools because without them there won't be any growth or success.

One aspect of our digital age that's worth noting is the democratization of creativity. Digital tools are now widely available to everyone, so anyone can explore their creative side and contribute their thoughts. The addition of these new creative minds has made for a very diverse community where innovation knows no bounds.

Powerful Collaboration

Collaboration has also reached new heights in the digital era. Thanks to virtual teamwork platforms and tools, creatives from all over the world can work together on projects with ease, sharing their expertise along the way. This global connectivity also helps breed cross-pollination between ideas, which ultimately fuels more innovation.

Moreover, professionals have been able to flaunt and promote their work through various online platforms since the inception of the digital era. These creatives can now reach audiences from all corners of the earth using social media platforms, portfolio websites, and digital market places alike.

However, it's important to be mindful when navigating this landscape because there are plenty of options available which makes it easy to get lost among them all. Having a strategic mindset will help you figure out what works best for your creative goals while still showcasing authenticity and uniqueness throughout your process.

Innovation in this era requires adaptability, curiosity, and a willingness to embrace change. You must stay current with emerging technologies if you want to unlock endless possibilities and unleash your full potential as a creator.

Creative Collaborations & Networking

Collaboration and networking are crucial in propelling innovation forward as well as unlocking creativity's true power. By connecting with like-minded individuals who possess collective intelligence you'll be able to ignite fresh ideas you never knew were possible before.

When it comes down to collaboration in particular - meeting different perspectives provides an opportunity for breakthroughs that couldn't be accomplished individually. Pooling talents together alongside unique expertise offers access to unimaginable levels of creative potential

Establishing connections serves as one component when networking in such a field but building meaningful relationships is also just as important. Industry events, online communities, and social media acquaintances are all avenues you can take to meet new people. Doing so helps open doors for new opportunities as well as expanding your personal creative circle.

Networking allows you to discover other individuals who share the same passion for innovation while also being able to joint venture in a way that leads strictly towards growth and experimentation. When like-minded creatives combine their skills they're not only capable of pushing boundaries but inspiring each other to step outside their comfort zones.

With the use of creative collaboration and careful nurturing of an inspiring network, two things will happen: You'll begin to create a vibrant ecosystem that accelerates innovation and your own creative journey will continuously move forward at high speeds. So why wait? Reach out now and embark on this incredible adventure where ideas are shared and accomplishments are achieved collectively

Sustaining Creativity

As you turn forty it's important for you to find strategies that allow your creativity levels to sustain themselves in the long run. It's normal for burnout or lack of motivation to occur even when creativity flows naturally. In this section we'll dive into some effective techniques that help overcome these challenges which will allow you to continue exploring new avenues in the arts.

One of the key strategies for maintaining creativity is to find balance and avoid burnout. It's important to prioritize self-care and establish boundaries to prevent overexertion. Take the time to rest and recharge, allowing your mind to relax and rejuvenate. By embracing a holistic approach to health you can significantly improve your creative output.

A good way to maintain creativity is by staying motivated. Set goals that inspire you and celebrate each accomplishment along the way. Surround yourself with positive influences, whether it's engaging in supportive communities or finding mentors who offer guidance and encouragement. By keeping an open mind about learning you can fuel your motivation levels immensely, unlocking new forces of creativity.

Finally, a crucial piece of the puzzle involves adopting an attitude of exploration and curiosity. Don't hesitate to step out of your comfort zone when trying new things creatively. Engage in experiences that are diverse, expose yourself to various forms of art, culture, perspectives etc.. The more you do this the more inspiration will be injected into your work.

Chapter 37

The Benefit of
Coaches and Mentors

In this chapter, we look at the transformative power of coaches and mentors, and how they can make all the difference to our development.

Guidance has a huge role to play in our pursuit of success. It helps us with direction, clarity, and motivation. In any situation, whether it's making critical decisions or setting ambitious goals, the right guidance will always have a positive impact.

When it comes to growth, mentorship is an invaluable asset. A mentor offers guidance that goes beyond just advice; they also give us wisdom, experience and form supportive partnerships with us along our journey. Trusted advisors who give valuable insights that help us find our way through challenges.

Coaches on the other hand have a unique set of skills that can change lives. They specialize in providing targeted guidance and support which allows us to hone specific skills, overcome obstacles and unleash hidden potential.

This chapter will dive into the different qualities of effective mentors and coaches. We'll compare their approaches and benefits too. Deciding who to reach out for when you need help isn't always easy but we'll make sure you know where to go when faced with these choices.

Finally we take a look at how these relationships foster growth in others around them too. Guidance, mentorship and coaching have a ripple effect on culture of learning where everyone inspires each other to pay it forward.

We hope you're excited about uncovering the transformative impact of coaches and mentors as much as we are!

The Importance of Guidance

When it comes down to it, guidance is key for direction, clarity, motivation even inspiration sometimes. Making decisions gets easier when there's someone helping you figure things out especially if they've had similar experiences before.

Having someone share their wisdom gives you knowledge that would otherwise take years to gain yourself which only propels your journey towards success faster.

Understanding Mentorship

Mentorship is a guide to better you. It has a range of benefits that can have a lasting impact on your personal development. Today we'll talk about what those benefits are and how they can help you.

To start, mentors offer valuable insights and perspective that help individuals get clear about their goals and aspirations. They also give advice and guidance tailor-made for the mentee's specific needs, this promotes personal growth and professional advancement.

Mentorship offers a supportive environment where growing at your own pace is encouraged. They're there to provide encouragement and motivation when you need it most. Mentors will help you overcome obstacles while simultaneously building your self-confidence. If they see potential in you they'll even throw opportunities for networking and skill-building your way.

What Sets Mentorship Apart

Mentoring differs from other forms of guidance such as coaching or counseling in several ways. For now let's just focus on two things, its holistic approach and the fact that mentors use their life experiences as well as wisdom gained throughout their careers to teach.

While coaching focuses on skill development mentorship takes into account everything else along the journey of personal growth. They pull from various aspects of one's life to create an understanding rooted in reality.

Coaches also do something similar but with an emphasis on their unique skills rather than life experience. With listening being one of the many great traits coaches have, they too create safe environments for clients by putting empathy first before anything else.

The goal after all is to make sure each individual feels supported through these journeys while coaching them towards success by asking powerful questions.

Which One Should You Choose

When trying to figure out which direction is best for you it's important to remember that each path should be taken based on need- not preference.

Mentors are pretty hands-on when it comes to teaching because they look at professional development and overall growth differently than the other two platforms mentioned prior.

Coaches take a different approach by placing the individual at the center of everything. They really focus on personal development and providing guidance within specific domains like relationships, leadership skills, and even work-life balance.

Both have their own strengths that can help you depending on where your weaknesses lie. By combining that with each individual's unique set of skills it's a guarantee that you'll receive the best training possible.

When it comes to finding guidance, mentorship and support, it's important to understand the distinct approaches and benefits mentors and coaches bring to the table. Both play a key role in helping individuals achieve their goals and reach their full potential. But how do you know whether a mentor or coach is right for your specific needs?

Mentors, typically individuals with industry expertise and experience, provide valuable insights, advice and wisdom gained from their own journey. They offer support and guidance based on first-hand knowledge, bringing a fresh perspective and sharing lessons they've learned throughout their careers.

Coaches, on the other hand, use their specific coaching skills and techniques to empower individuals to develop skills, overcome obstacles and reach objectives. Focused on improving performance, coaches facilitate growth by helping individuals identify strengths, weaknesses and areas of development.

So how do you choose? It comes down to your unique goals, needs and preferences. If you need help with industry-specific guidance, connections or insights - a mentor with experience in your field could be ideal. But if you're trying to strengthen certain skills or accelerate growth/performance - A coach can give you structured support along with accountability.

Advantages of Having Both Mentors and Coaches

The choice between a mentor or coach isn't mutually exclusive - there's significant value in having both on your team. By combining the wisdom of a mentor (experience) with targeted guidance from the coach (accountability), people can benefit from a well-rounded system that addresses personal/professional development needs.

A mentor brings invaluable insights/advice derived from real-world experiences. In addition: they can show you how to navigate challenges & make informed decisions as well as help build relationships/networks along with finding growth opportunities.

On the other hand: A coach provides structure/focus during your journey. Helping set clear goals / evaluating strategies for improvement while providing feedback/support along the way so progress can be tracked in real-time.

The client relationship is built on trust: a coach serves as a motivator/accountability partner ensuring you stay focused towards success.

Ultimately, the choice between mentor / coach comes down to goals, preferences and the level of support you need. But the potential advantages of having both aren't something to just overlook. They provide unique perspectives / expertise to maximize personal/professional growth.

Unlocking Potential Through Mentorship

Mentorship holds an immense power in unlocking one's full potential. By leveraging guidance/support/valuable advice provided by mentors - individuals can overcome challenges, develop new skills and achieve goals.

The Transformative Impact of Coaching

Coaching has the ability to drastically change lives and lead to transformative outcomes. As individuals embark on their coaching journey: they'll be empowered to understand themselves deeper, overcome hurdles that stand in their way and reach their FULL potential.

Coaching provides a safe and supportive environment for individuals to explore their goals, aspirations, and challenges. A coach is there to guide them through self-discovery, helping them identify strengths and areas they need to grow in. By building this kind of awareness, individuals are able to achieve more success.

People learn invaluable strategies and tools from coaching that they can use for problem-solving. No matter what area of life the problem exists in (career, relationships, overall health), coaching will help them develop resilience. With guidance along with being held accountable by their coach, individuals will be able to see progress in all aspects of their life.

Coaching also helps challenge beliefs and mindsets-each person has different ones that either help or limit personal growth. When someone is able to change their perspective on things, possibilities become endless. People unlock potential they never even knew was there.

To sum it up: Coaching gives people the ability to overcome obstacles while embracing strengths. This leads individuals down a path of personal development which enhances how successful they can be in both work and life.

How Important is Guidance? Very

The impact of guidance goes beyond just one person's life-it ripples out into the lives of others too! It creates such an effect that affects personal growth, professional development, and overall success.

Once someone receives guidance through mentorship or coaching-they gain knowledge that transforms everything around them as well as themselves. Others start noticing differences within those who received it-since they're applying what was learned-and begin asking how they did it!

The ripple effect makes people want to seek out guidance for themselves so they can pursue dreams and reach unimaginable limits too! Having a culture like this one where support comes first allows an environment where everyone feels empowered enough to go after anything.

A workplace example-we wouldn't need fancy office spaces if everyone came together to create a company-wide culture like this one! Job satisfaction would skyrocket since productivity would increase, and the entire team would be motivated.

But let's not forget about our personal lives too. In relationships, happiness, and overall well-being-guidance makes a world of difference. We learn how to communicate effectively while building connections with people who matter most to us-we wouldn't want it any other way!

So let's embrace what guidance can bring to our lives! It starts with us, the people around us will begin following suit once they see success stories. Let's create a world where support, learning, and success are boundless because the ripple effect is forever flowing.

Nurturing Mentor-Protégé Relationships

Building and nurturing mentor-protégé relationships is vital for a rewarding and successful mentoring experience. A strong bond between mentor and protégé is built on trust, effective communication, and shared goals.

The Key Factors for a Fruitful Mentor-Protégé Relationship

To foster a productive mentor-protégé relationship, several factors play a crucial role. Firstly, both parties must establish clear expectations and goals. Open and honest communication is essential to ensure that the mentor's guidance aligns with the protégé's needs and ambitions. Secondly, trust is the foundation of any mentoring relationship. The protégé should feel comfortable opening up about challenges, seeking advice, and receiving constructive feedback. Lastly, maintaining confidentiality is paramount to create a safe and supportive environment where personal and professional matters can be discussed openly.

Trust and Communication: The Building Blocks

Trust is the cornerstone of mentor-protégé relationships. A mentor must demonstrate reliability, confidentiality, and consistent support. Trust encourages the protégé to take risks, explore new opportunities, and embrace personal growth. Communication is equally crucial. Active listening, empathy, and effective feedback enable mentors to understand their protégé's needs and tailor guidance accordingly. Regular check-ins and open dialogue help establish and maintain a strong connection, fostering a nurturing environment for mentorship to thrive.

The Responsibilities of Mentor and Protégé

Mentors and protégés both have essential responsibilities within the mentor-protégé relationship. Mentors should provide guidance, share relevant knowledge and experiences, challenge and inspire their protégés, champion their development - essentially doing whatever it takes to empower them as they grow in their career or personal life path.

For their part, protégés should be receptive to feedback (and actively seek it out), apply learnings from each interaction with their mentors toward bettering themselves professionally or personally.

By embracing these responsibilities, both parties contribute to the overall success of the mentor-protégé relationship.

By nurturing mentor-protégé relationships through trust, communication, and shared responsibility, individuals can unlock their full potential, accelerate growth, and achieve their goals.

The Role of Accountability in Coaching

When it comes to coaching, accountability plays a crucial role in driving progress and achieving goals. It acts as a guiding force that keeps individuals focused, motivated, and committed to their desired outcomes. Accountability ensures that clients stay on track and take responsibility for their actions, ultimately leading to personal growth and transformation.

Coaches establish accountability measures through various strategies tailored to their clients' specific needs. These may include regular check-ins, progress assessments, goal setting, action planning.

We help our clients develop plans with actionable steps which we hold them accountable for as they go along this journey. Some people find this pressure helpful while others might struggle with it. This helps us identify what best works for each client when it comes to keeping them on track.

By holding clients accountable for their commitments and actions coaches create a supportive and structured environment conducive to growth and development.

The Benefits of Being Held Accountable

Being held accountable throughout the coaching process offers numerous benefits. Firstly it fosters a sense of discipline and consistency encouraging clients to follow through with their commitments taking proactive steps towards achieving their goals - maintaining momentum during tough times.

Accountability also enhances self-awareness and self-reflection allowing clients to identify obstacles limiting beliefs or patterns that may be holding them back-this way they accept responsibility for changing those aspects even if it's uncomfortable. Furthermore accountability provides clients with valuable feedback from someone who has no bias or is subjective about your life decisions - you get raw truth here.

In simpler terms, accountability is a fundamental pillar of coaching. It helps clients stay committed to their goals, take responsibility for their actions, and overcome obstacles. Coaches help facilitate growth and development through this system.

Repeated Growth

Development and mentorship isn't just temporary; it has a lasting effect on people's lives. This section will go over the continuous benefits of coaching and mentorship.

Personal Change

Self improvement never stops with coaching and mentorship. Individuals are given the tools to continuously grow themselves by raising self-awareness providing guidance, and encouragement. With that support individuals will be able to get past anything in their way and transform themselves.

Becoming a Leader

Leadership develops drastically from coaching and mentoring practices. Just being guided all the time by experienced mentors or coaches can make someone's skills skyrocket. Long term investments like these make leaders influential empowering figures.

Cultivating a Lifelong Learning Mindset

Effective coaches and mentors instill a lifelong learning mindset in their mentees. By encouraging curiosity, intellectual development, and continuous improvement, they foster a hunger for knowledge and a commitment to personal and professional growth. This mindset enables individuals to adapt to changing circumstances, embrace new challenges, and continuously expand their horizons.

In the next section, we will explore the importance of embracing the potential of supportive relationships for fully benefiting from guidance and mentorship.

Embracing the Potential of Supportive Relationships

To fully benefit from the guidance and mentorship available, individuals must embrace the potential of supportive relationships. Supportive relationships provide a nurturing environment where personal and professional growth can flourish. They offer a safe space to share ideas, seek advice, and gain valuable insights from others who have walked a similar path.

Seeking out and cultivating meaningful connections is vital. Start by surrounding yourself with individuals who inspire and motivate you. These can be mentors, colleagues, or friends who share your aspirations and values. Engage in open and honest conversations, exchanging thoughts and experiences to foster mutual growth.

Peer support is equally important. Engaging with a community of like-minded individuals allows for ongoing learning, collaboration, and shared experiences. Actively participate in networking events, industry conferences, and online communities to build a support system that will encourage you to reach new heights.

Remember, as you receive guidance and support from others, it is essential to give back by mentoring others. By sharing your knowledge and experiences, you not only contribute to the growth of others but also reinforce your understanding. Embrace the potential of supportive relationships, and together, we can create a community that thrives on continuous learning and personal development.

Chapter 38

Mindfulness and Presence

In this chapter, we dive into the transformative practice of mindfulness and how it can positively impact our everyday lives. Mindfulness allows us to embrace the present moment, cultivating a "be here now" attitude and connection to the world around us.

In our fast-paced lives, it's easy to get caught up in the whirlwind of responsibilities and distractions. Living in the moment can become a distant concept, felt only in fleeting moments. However, by incorporating mindfulness practices into our daily routines, we can re-introduce presence and bring more joy, calm, and fulfillment into our everyday experiences.

In the following sections you will learn about the various aspects of mindfulness and its practical applications. From understanding the core concepts of mindfulness to exploring its benefits in different areas of life (such as work, relationships, and self-care), we aim to provide you with all tools necessary for incorporating mindfulness into your daily life.

Whether you are a beginner or have some experience with mindfulness, this chapter offers a range of techniques and tips to help you start or deepen your mindfulness journey. Together let's explore the power of living in the moment and discover all ways in which mindfulness enhances our overall well-being.

What is Mindfulness?

In today's fast-paced world finding moments of peace and clarity may seem like an impossible task. That's where mindfulness comes in. Mindfulness is simply defined as bringing your attention to the present moment without judgment or attachment. It involves being fully aware of your thoughts, emotions, bodily sensations as they arise in everyday life.

Mindfulness isn't about emptying your mind or trying to achieve a particular state of being. It's about acknowledging whatever is happening at that moment with acceptance without getting caught up in worries about future or regrets from past.

By practicing mindfulness you can cultivate heightened sense awareness allowing full engagement with each moment/experience. It's an extremely powerful tool that only requires simple integration into everyday life helping navigate ups & downs with greater clarity and resilience.

In the following sections we will explore the benefits of mindfulness in everyday life and provide practical techniques to help you integrate mindfulness practices into your routine.

Benefits of Mindfulness in Everyday Life

Living in the moment & incorporating mindfulness practices into your every day life can yield a plethora of benefits. By cultivating presence and prioritizing mindfulness, you can enhance overall well-being while improving various aspects of daily experiences.

One key advantage is stress reduction. Through mindful awareness it becomes easier recognizing/ managing stress triggers which allows for greater sense calm/balance during day-to-day interactions.

Another positive impact is on focus/concentration. Training mind to stay present enhances ability to stay focused on task at hand ultimately boosting productivity in both personal/professional settings.

Improved Well-being

Mindfulness practices contribute to overall sense well-being. Being fully present in moment fosters deeper connection within yourself, emotions, surroundings which leads to increased self-acceptance/compassion & improved relationships with others.

Furthermore, mindfulness can enhance sleep quality and overall physical health. By decreasing stress levels and encouraging relaxation, practices like these can help alleviate sleeping disturbances and enhance overall sleep patterns. Also, research reveals that mindfulness is able to have beneficial effects on blood pressure, heart rate, as well as other physiological markers of health.

Incorporating mindfulness into your daily life leads to a more meaningful existence. By living in the present moment and practicing mindfulness, you can fully embrace the richness of everyday experiences. Discovering joy and gratitude in even the simplest of moments.

Mindfulness Techniques for Beginners

You may find incorporating it into your everyday routine daunting if you're new to mindfulness. However rest assured, starting small with simple techniques can help you cultivate presence and embrace living in the moment. Here are some practical tips to get you started:

1. Mindful Breathing

Begin by focusing on your breath. Close your eyes for a moment, then inhale deeply through your nose, exhale slowly through your mouth. Pay attention to how it feels when it enters and leaves your body.

2. Body Scan Meditation

Find a comfortable position laying down or sitting up straight then bring all of your attention to different parts of our body from head down to toes while doing so notice any sensations that come either tension or relaxation without judgement.

3. Mindful Walking

Take a short walk but this time pay FULL attention to each step you take notice how it hits the ground notice how it makes your body move notice what sounds or sights are around you doing this will allow calmness on your journey.

4.Eating mindfully

During meals slow down taste each bite really savor them think about texture at least once smell aromas think about nutrition eat until satisfied not full! Even though we should do nothing but practice gratefulness practicing mindful eating helps develop healthier relationships with food as well as fully enjoy nourishing yourself!

Remember its not about reaching perfection nor trying to get rid of our thoughts. Its about being fully aware and accepting the present moment. Regular practice allows it to become normal in daily life helping us cultivate mindfulness in every aspect of your days.

Mindful Eating

When was the last time you truly savored the taste, texture, and aroma of a meal? Mindful eating is a practice that encourages us to slow down, pay attention, and fully engage with our food. By bringing mindfulness to our eating habits, we can transform our relationship with food and nourishment.

Mindful eating is all about cultivating awareness and presence during meals. It involves being present in the moment, savoring each bite, and listening to our bodies' cues of hunger and fullness. By fully immersing ourselves in the eating experience, we can develop a healthier approach to nourishment and foster a greater sense of satisfaction.

The Benefits of Mindful Eating

Mindful eating has numerous benefits for our emotional and physical well-being. Slow down, pay attention, and you'll get to:

Develop a healthier relationship with food

Improve digestion

Love food more

Control portion sizes and make good choices

Cut down on mindless snacking or emotional eating.

Boost your body's signals of hunger and fullness.

By practicing mindful eating, we also foster gratitude towards the nourishment our food provides. And develop a stronger connection to the earth that gives life to our table.

Techniques for Mindful Eating

Below are several techniques and practices you can incorporate into your daily life to improve mindful eating:

Savor each bite: Take your sweet time tasting every single flavor and texture in your meal. Chew slowly, savor each bite, allow yourself to fully feel all the nourishment.

Listen to your body: Tune in when hungry. Stop when satisfied. Pay attention to what's happening internally at both stages.

Engage senses: Use everything on top of your neck during meals. Observe colors, smells, textures. Embrace all sensations offered by the present moment.

Avoid distractions: During meals try not using things like cell phones or TV's. Instead silence them so you can create an environment that allows complete focus on your meal.

Cultivate gratitude: Before and after each meal take a moment to be grateful for what's about to enter you stomach or what just provided nourishment. This act alone will shift perspective and help promote a more mindful eating experience.

By incorporating these techniques into everyday life one is embracing mindful eating which comes with many benefits. Start being aware during the next meal you have because it may transform how you feel inside.

Another important part of bringing mindfulness to work is growing mindful communication and active listening. This means being completely present in conversations, truly hearing others without judging them, and giving a response that's full of compassion and empathy. With this practice, we can make our relationships with coworkers stronger. We can also build better teamwork which makes the workspace more positive and pleasant.

Finally, integrating mindfulness into the workplace isn't just about speech. The physical environment plays a big role too. That's why it's suggested to set aside a quiet area for meditation or other mindfulness practices. Through this people are given an area where they can solely focus on their thoughts while feeling safe from any distractions.

By adding these small changes into your daily life at work you'll see a major change in how you look at your job. Stress will be reduced, you'll be able to focus way better, and of course wellbeing will improve as well.

Mindfulness in Relationships

When it comes to building strong connections it's important to always have mindfulness in mind (no pun intended). By living in the moment and practicing what was mentioned earlier we're able to fully connect with others which makes socializing very rewarding.

One big technique is active listening. In order to do this you must be fully present and engaged so that you're able to understand someone else's feelings accurately rather than making assumptions.

Just like before, empathy plays another huge role here too. We need to build the ability of understanding when someone is barely holding up so that we can show them compassion when needed.

And last but not least, having a nurturing presence helps build strong relationships as well.

Incorporating these techniques into our everyday lives will give us much more meaningful connections than ever before if we stick with them consistently.

Mindfulness and Technology

Unfortunately we live in a world where technology is thriving by making everything easier for us but at the same time worse for our mental health. There's a constant battle between being mindful and indulging ourselves with the endless possibilities of smartphones, social media, etc.

While yes, it does help us stay connected to others and makes things much more convenient for us. It also distracts us from what's going on around us and causes disconnection with the present moment.

The constant notifications, endless scrolling, and the pressure to constantly stay connected can prevent us from truly being present and fully engaged in our experiences.

Every now and then take breaks from tech by doing a digital detox. Dedicate an entire day, or even the whole weekend to abstain from devices. Instead, engage in activities that'll let you live in the moment. Whether it's going outside and spending time with nature, reading a book near a window, or meditating - taking breaks will help you recharge.

3 Use Mindful Technology Apps

In an ironic twist of fate; technology can actually help us when it comes to practicing mindfulness. There are plenty of different apps available that'll help you accomplish this. From giving short guided meditation exercises to just having you breathe normally, these apps are here to remind you to just stop and calm down.

4 Practice Mindful Consumption

When using any form of technology always keep mindful consumption in mind. Be intentional about what kind of content your eyes come across and how much time you spend on digital platforms in general. Unfollow accounts that aren't healthy for your mental well-being anymore, and start engaging with things that uplift and inspire you.

By such aware about our relationship with technology we can make conscious choices when it comes to it. The goal is to find a balance between living in the present moment without disconnecting ourselves completely from everything else around us. Keep reminding yourself that technology is just another tool we use daily, so it's up to us how we utilize it to benefit our mental health as well as our connection with the present moment.

Mindfulness and Self-Care

Self-care is important for anyone who wants to maintain a balanced lifestyle overall. So when talking about self-care practices mindfulness takes front stage because they pair perfectly together. When incorporated into your routine properly mindfulness can help support your own overall well-being while also fostering a sense of self-compassion.

This kind of thinking pushes individuals like yourself towards being fully present at all times of the day - as well as acknowledging their thoughts, emotions, physical pain, and everything else happening within their body. And then of course taking intentional actions when it's necessary. The main goal here is to support mental, emotional as well as physical health.

A simple practice of mindfulness that anyone can do at any time is mindful breathing. All you have to do is gently focus your attention on your own breath, and let everything else go quiet in the background. This way you'll be able to calm your mind so much easier after a long day at work or school.

Another great way to practice self-care with mindfulness is through movement. Engaging in activities like yoga and tai chi are perfect because they force individuals to connect with their bodies first. By doing this we're able to release tension faster than before, while also bringing joy into our lives - which plenty of us need more of.

Additionally, treating yourself with kindness and understanding is another important aspect of practicing self-compassion. In order for anyone to really succeed in life they have to be "on their own side" if you will. It's all about acknowledging your needs and setting healthy boundaries that won't break down as soon as someone crosses them.

All Mindfulness practices serve as a foundation for self-care by helping you stay present, listen to your needs, and make choices that actually benefit yourself instead of others around you. Once you start incorporating it into your daily routine slowly but surely a deeper sense of self-awareness will grow within yourself - thus nurturing both physical health as well mental well-being along the way.

As we get ready to bring this chapter to a close, let's go over some practical tips and techniques you can implement into your everyday life. By doing this, we can ensure you're always living in the moment, and fully embracing the power of mindfulness. One of the most fundamental practices is meditation.

Carve out just a couple minutes each day to sit quietly and focus on your breath as well as observing your thoughts without judgment. This simple act can help anchor you in the present moment while enhancing your awareness. Breathwork is another powerful tool that anyone can use at any time of day. Take a few moments throughout your day to consciously connect with your breath and practice deep breathing. Through this, you'll calm your mind while inviting relaxation and presence as well. Next up on our list is mindful movement which can be done through many different activities such as yoga or even simply walking outside for fresh air.

While doing these activities, pay attention to how it feels within your body, what movements you make in what rhythm, and also the environment around you. Making note of all these things will help you fully engage with the current moment which results in a deeper sense of appreciation for everyday experiences.

Finally incorporating these mindfulness practices may take time and patience but there are proven benefits on why it's worth trying them out such as reduced stress levels! So start small by being consistent so that eventually mindfulness transforms every experience of yours!

Chapter 39

Raising a Family
While Flourishing

It can be hard to balance family life while trying to reach your own goals, but the good news is it's possible. You can create an environment that helps both aspects of your life blossom together. In this chapter, we'll go over some practical tips and strategies for finding and keeping that delicate balance.

The Importance of Balance in Parenting

Balancing parenthood is important for your own well-being as well as the health and happiness of your family. It requires you to carefully navigate through various roles and responsibilities, where sometimes you have to be there for your children, while other times you have to be there for yourself. It might feel like a chore getting everything right, but it's essential for the betterment of everyone involved.

When achieving balance in parenting, you can effectively nurture your personal aspirations while also being a present and supportive parent. You become more than just someone who looks after them all day long. Striking this delicate balance allows you to prioritize not only their needs but also yours as well. By doing so, you create a positive environment that promotes growth and happiness.

The Advantages of Balanced Parenting

Achieving balance in parenting comes with its fair share of benefits too! For one thing, it reduces stress in parents which makes them more patient with their kids. It's easier to find joy when things are going smoothly at home, so naturally they'll be happier too (and we can't forget about how much we love seeing our loved ones happy). Balancing parenting with personal aspirations also promotes self-growth and fulfillment because parents continue striving towards their dreams even when they have a family.

Lastly, a balanced approach sets up a good example for children too. When they see someone valuing their own goals and dreams while raising a child it teaches them the importance of self-care. They learn what resilience is by experiencing it first hand from watching their parents pursue their passions as well. This way when they have their own family, even if they don't understand it right away, they'll know how to find the perfect equilibrium.

Finding Balance

Being a parent is never really easy but we can make an attempt at it. The first thing you should do is prioritize your time and energy. You mustn't forget about yourself or else nothing will be done! Everything that you do for them every day is out of love, so isn't treating yourself the same way also out of love? The fact of the matter is, no one deserves self-care more than parents do! Establishing clear boundaries and communicating openly with your family about aspirations and balance are also important.

It's not all set in stone though because sometimes life just hits us with the unexpected. This means sometimes we won't be able to follow our plans as we expected. Being okay with that is key because when you're adaptable to change it makes things so much easier on your end. Following this path has led me to meet some amazing people who've helped me along my parenting journey as well. I hope you too can build a strong support group filled with like-minded parents who can provide guidance, empathy, and encouragement.

Remember that achieving balance in parenting takes time and looks different for everyone since no two people are alike. But by setting goals for yourself and showing your children how important it is to follow through on them even after having a child, not only does it improve your life but makes theirs better too!

Identify and prioritize your personal aspirations. Which ones are most important to you? Determine which of those dreams need immediate attention, and which ones can be saved for later. By doing this you will be able to allocate your time and energy effectively.

Build a Supportive Environment

Surround yourself with people who understand the value of nurturing your own dreams while raising a family. It can be friends, mentors or other parents just like yourself. Their support and guidance can make all the difference in your journey.

Make Goals You Can Reach

Break down bigger aspirations into smaller goals that you can actually reach without overwhelming yourself. Doing this will give you a sense of accomplishment without neglecting your responsibilities as a parent.

Get The Most Out Of Your Time

Search for little pockets of time throughout the day where you can work on your personal aspirations. Maybe it's waking up earlier by an hour everyday or using nap times for something productive.

Expect The Unexpected

Parenthood is unpredictable, sometimes things don't go to plan so we have to adapt to situations quickly. Embracing unexpected changes when they come helps us keep balance between our goals and being parents.

And remember: Focusing on our own happiness isn't selfish, it's needed for us to grow as individuals and provide better care for our families.

When it comes to setting priorities, it's important to be realistic and flexible. Understand that there will be times when one area of your life requires more attention than the other. Balance, adaptability and constant reassessment are key to overcoming difficult situations while maintaining your personal aspirations and honoring your parenting responsibilities.

Always remember, setting boundaries and realigning priorities allow you to better integrate your parenting role with personal goals. By finding this harmonious balance, you can nurture your own growth and wellbeing while being an attentive and loving parent to your children.

Communication and Collaboration with Your Partner

Effective communication and collaboration between partners is crucial when it comes to parenting while striving for personal aspirations. Honesty has the power to lay a solid foundation on understanding each other's needs as well as finding common ground. A collaborative approach allows for shared responsibilities which both partners can use as support in raising a family along with fulfilling individual ambitions.

To effectively communicate with one another, learn how to actively listen. Create a safe space where both of you feel comfortable expressing concerns or aspirations without judgment. Effective communication isn't just about talking but also empathizing as well as understanding one another's points of view.

Collaboration involves working together as a team in order to divide parenting responsibilities that'll later translate into time allocating for pursuing personal goals. By striking a balance that accommodates both partner's aspirations, you can create an environment that fosters their own personal growth while providing a nurturing environment for their children.

Supporting Each Other's Dreams

This type of support is an integral part of collaboration. Encourage your partner by actively engaging in their goals which they have set out for themselves. The ways by which this can be done may vary depending on what is needed such as taking turns caring for the children or simply lending moral support or practical help. When genuine interest and enthusiasm are shown towards supporting one another's dreams, bonds between partners strengthen while creating a supportive environment for each other's personal aspirations.

Remember, balancing parenting and personal growth is a shared responsibility. Keep in mind that both partners have unique needs and ambitions to which, they must actively work together in order to find a compromise that benefits the family as a whole. By leveraging effective communication and collaboration, both will be able to navigate through the joys and challenges of raising a family while flourishing personally.

Balancing Work and Family Life

For many parents, finding the right balance between work and family life is one of the biggest challenges they face. The balancing act of managing a career while being present for your children along with achieving personal aspirations requires careful planning and effective strategies.

One crucial strategy is setting clear boundaries between work time and family time. No matter what you may be doing at the moment, prioritize your priorities as it goes hand in hand with allocating dedicated time for both work and family activities. This strategy will help you maintain balance overall instead of overwhelming one aspect more than another.

Effective time management is another key factor that'll contribute towards this goal. You should learn how to prioritize tasks properly as well as delegate when possible freeing up more free time to allocate for family or personal endeavors. Take into consideration technology tools or resources that could streamline your work processes by maximizing efficiency as well.

Communication is key to finding balance. Keep in constant contact with your employer and let them know about the needs of your child. Try to find flexible work arrangements, like working from home or sticking to a simple schedule. This open dialogue will help create a work environment that acknowledges family life as important.

Don't forget to take care of yourself as well. Self-care is crucial for maintaining both physical and mental health. Prioritize activities that recharge you, whether it's exercise, relaxation techniques, or just indulging in hobbies.

Lastly, adopt a kind of work-life integration rather than making strict lines between the two worlds. Find ways for work and family life to blend and compliment each other. It might mean having your child do some of your tasks or having coworkers participate in family events.

By following these tips and keeping an adaptable mindset, you can maintain the thin line between work and family life. No one finds perfect balance right away so be patient with yourself as you adjust along the way.

Self-Care for Parents

Parents often put their own aspirations aside when raising children but self-care should always have priority. If you don't take care of yourself then burnout becomes inevitable, which makes becoming a good parent much harder too. By making self-care a high priority, you're investing into your own health while also setting an example for your children.

Physical health usually takes center stage when talking about self-care since without it everything else falls apart fast. Take time out of every day to exercise, even if it's just stepping outside for five minutes while on break from work. Physical activity isn't only good for the body but also boosts mood and reduces stress levels significantly. Lastly, make sure you're eating well-balanced meals throughout the day so that your body gets all its necessary nutrients.

Just like physical self-care should be practiced daily, mental/ emotional self-care should be given attention too. Find things that bring joy into your life, whether it's reading a book or just doing whatever hobby you enjoy. Taking time out of the day to do something you like recharges your energy and lets you be the best version of yourself in front of your children.

Creating a Supportive Environment

Sometimes you'll need help and that's okay. It's important to vocalize these moments though so friends, family, or other parents can come assist you. Besides lightening the load on yourself, building a support network also creates a feeling of community which is extremely important for mental health.

Setting boundaries with your partner and children is necessary too. Be open with them when discussing how much alone time you might need on certain days. The clearer everyone is about their needs, the easier it'll be for each person to respect those needs.

Making Self-Care a Priority

Always remember that self-care isn't selfish. It's essential for overall well-being and will make navigating parenting much smoother. By taking care of yourself, there will be more energy, patience, and resilience in order to manage personal aspirations alongside raising children.

Cultivating a Supportive Network

Parenting and pursuing personal goals can feel like you're juggling. You need a network of friends, family, and other parents to make it work. They can lend support and guidance when you navigate the ups and downs of parenting while chasing your aspirations.

To balance being a parent and focusing on your goals, you have to lean on a strong foundation. Surrounding yourself with people who understand the hardships you face will be priceless for advice, empathy, and encouragement.

You should actively seek connections with parents who share similar values as well. Join groups or communities for parents online or in person where you can find those like-minded individuals. Engage in conversations, they've probably been through what you're going through already so seek their advice. As much as we talk about finding new friends it's also important to remember about the ones that are already there though. Friends & Family might not be parents themselves but they'll still offer support regardless if they don't know how to help or what words to say. Reach out to them no matter what stage of life you're in.

Remember that creating a supportive network isn't just about receiving support either. Being there for others is just as important as getting someone when you need it. Lend an ear when someone needs an extra one from time to time or even lend physical help around the house sometimes too!

As rewarding as it may be trying to reach your own goals while caring for another life can get exhausting but extremely fulfilling at times ... yet doesn't mean that road has to be walked alone! By cultivating a supportive network, families will find the strength, guidance, and encouragement needed to navigate challenges faced along the way without losing touch with each other.

Embracing Flexibility and Adaptability

When it comes to balancing parenthood with personal aspirations flexibility is key! Life doesn't go according to plan many times! When those moments arise being adaptable is crucial since plans adapt too over time. Always be ready for change so you can maintain a healthy family life while overcoming challenges.

Adjusting to Change

Being a parent means being prepared for the unexpected. Whether it's shifts in your work schedule, sudden family obligations, or unforeseen circumstances adapting will help fight through tough times and even grow from them. Change should be seen as an opportunity to become better! Find creative solutions to adjust plans without negatively impacting the well-being of your loved ones.

Communication and Collaboration

A flexible mindset goes hand in hand with communication that gets things done effectively. Keep the lines open so if something is needed or bothering you it can be shared no matter how small it might seem at the time. Work together when problems arise, parenting is a team sport after all! Strong relationships and supportive environments are bred from collaborative decision-making.

Putting Priorities into Perspective

When faced with sudden changes everyone must reassess their priorities. Balance doesn't mean sacrificing personal aspirations nor failing as a parent either... it's about understanding what's important then making decisions based on those values every day!

For instance, if a professional opportunity arises that requires more of your time and effort, consider how it may affect your family life. Think about whether the potential benefits align with your long-term goals and if it can be handled without throwing off balance too much.

The Power of Adaptability

You are setting a powerful example for your children by embracing flexibility and adaptability as core values in your parenting journey. They'll get to see first-hand how problems can be fixed, plans can be adjusted, and balance is always possible even when life is chaotic. These skills will come in handy as they navigate their own lives.

Modeling a Balanced Life for Your Children

We play a big role in shaping our children's values, beliefs, and behaviors. One of the most powerful ways we can guide them is by modeling a balanced life. We show them how important it is to balance personal aspirations while still nurturing strong family relationships.

Kids are often mirroring our attitudes and actions because they're perceptive and observant. When they see us prioritizing our own goals and maintaining a healthy work-life balance, they learn that we don't have to sacrifice being great parents just to follow our dreams.

By establishing routines that allow us to give quality time both our personal growth and our families, we show them that harmony really does exist. Letting them into some of the things you're doing builds trust between parent and child but also inspires them to find what they love doing one day.

Open conversations about the meaning of balance are important because they let kids know why we choose certain activities over others. This teaches them how to make conscious choices early on in their lives which will lead to better use of their time later on down the line.

As parents we must also put ourselves first sometimes. Our physical health has an effect on more than just us emotionally so letting them know why you take care of yourself shows its importance to loved ones too.

All in all, modeling a balanced life for our children is more than just an individual endeavor. It's a collaborative journey that involves everyone in the family. By encouraging open conversations about balance and continuously reflecting on our own progress, we create a supportive atmosphere. One that instills the importance of personal growth and forging deep connections with others.

While we strive to find our own balance between parenting and pursuing personal aspirations, let us remember that actions speak louder than words. By modeling a balanced life we inspire our children to become well-rounded individuals who understand the value of both ambition and nurturing relationships.

Celebrating milestones and progress

Parenthood is littered with milestones, and it's always great to feel rewarded for your hard work. Be it your child's first steps or reaching a career goal - stopping and acknowledging these achievements gives us the motivation to keep going.

As parents, we tend to get caught up in the everyday aspects of raising a child. We almost never acknowledge the victories no matter how insignificant they might seem. By doing so, we validate our efforts all while showing our kids that hard work pays off.

Balancing parenthood and personal aspirations are tough. That's why achieving milestones is so satisfying. They remind us where we were, reigniting our drive to push even further. Make sure you celebrate these steps along the way or else you'll burn out before you reach your desired destination.

Celebrating Parenthood Milestones

In parenting there's one thing that's constant: growth (not just your child). As they grow so do our skills as parents. A single day can teach you so many new things about being a mom or dad that it'd make your head spin! As cliche as it may sound - each milestone comes with lessons waiting to be learned from them.

Take some time out of your day whenever these pop up and relish in them however you see fit! It could be anything from writing notes, having special meals, or simply hugging whomever's closest when they come around again. Celebrate those days, as long as they're important to you then everything will be fine.

Recognizing Progress in Personal Aspirations

Becoming a parent does not mean giving up who you are. And there's no better way to prove that than by accomplishing goals alongside raising children! Don't fall into the trap of thinking small steps forward don't matter - because they do!

When pursuing personal aspirations track every single accomplishment happenning along the way - big or small! It doesn't matter how you do it, just as long as you visually see progress happening in front of your eyes. Celebrate those moments that every milestone represents and always reward yourself. You've earned it after all!

Remember, celebrating milestones isn't about trying to one-up others or searching for validation from those around you. It's all about appreciating what you've accomplished so far - fostering a sense of fulfillment - and enjoying the beautiful journey that is parenting.

Moreover, it encourages us to consider what we've been doing right - and wrong. By acknowledging what has been effective, we can continue to improve our parenting style while also trying to find ways to better balance family time with personal goals.

Along this journey, it's important for us to seek continuous improvement. Meaning we need to explore new techniques and resources that could help us become even better parents than we already are. Whether that means finding support from other experienced parents or even professionals when needed. Through this commitment of growth and self-improvement, a fulfilling parent life is possible.

Chapter 40

The Art of Letting Go

The Power of Embracing Change

Life is a never-ending rollercoaster. We experience ups, downs, twists and turns along the way. Change is something we can't avoid, but it's something we need to learn how to adapt to if we want to succeed in life.

Adapting to change can be a bit difficult at times. It requires us to step out of our comfort zones and let go of everything we thought we knew so well. But when you truly embrace change, you're opening yourself up to an entire world of opportunities that you wouldn't have seen before.

Your previous lifestyle may slow you down and hold you back from making any real progress in your life. And while it's nice staying where things are familiar, sometimes it takes change for us to reach our full potential.

Change isn't bad either - as long as you're willing enough to do something about it then chances are things will work out well for you. Take the leap first then ask questions later is typically what works best here.

And if that doesn't convince you - think about all of the personal developments and professional achievements that would come your way if you just welcomed the change with open arms? Who knows? You might even discover hidden strengths or talents that were just waiting for you!

Once we fully accept it into our lives… well there's really nothing else left that could hold us back from anything.

Releasing Your Past For A Brighter Future

We've all made mistakes and wish things went differently in life at some point or another, but one thing's for sure: There's no use crying over spilled milk. And there's definitely no use holding onto them either.

The past does nothing more than weigh us down heavier than an anchor on a small boat trying to sail far away from shore for freedom and clarity. It keeps us locked away from all the new experiences waiting for us, which might even be better than the ones we've lived.

More importantly though, it stops us from doing anything else to progress our lives. And when you look back at things, why would you intentionally want that for yourself?

If you're ready to create a new life with a fresh start and no burdens holding you back then follow along as we go through some strategies to help you let go of your past:

Acceptance - Understand that you can't change the past and let it go. Acceptance isn't about approval; it's about understanding what happened and deciding to move on from it.

Forgiveness - Forgiving yourself and others is a powerful tool for closure. Holding grudges or resenting only causes negative emotions to linger. Choose to forgive, not for them, but for your own healing and personal growth.

Reflect - Take time to think about the lessons you've learned from your experiences. By examining what went wrong and what you could have done differently, you gain wisdom that helps prevent similar mistakes in the future.

Seek support - Letting go can be hard, so don't be afraid to ask for help. Reach out to friends, family members or a therapist who can offer guidance and listen with an open ear.

Stay in the present - Use your energy on now instead of before. Do activities that bring joy, work on yourself or just make new experiences that align with what you want.

By embracing this practice of moving forward, you allow new beginnings, growth and inner peace into your life. Get rid of things that hold you back and make room for endless possibilities.

Finding Clarity in Chaos

In today's world we're all living fast-paced lives surrounded by distractions making it hard to stay focused on goals and make good choices - especially when there are so many uncertainties around us. Luckily clarity is the magic key to unlock our true potential so we can live fulfilling lives regardless of how chaotic things get.

So how do we find clarity when everything else is chaos? Here are some tricks:

Mindfulness - Stay present while ignoring noise around you by focusing on breathing. Journaling - Writing your thoughts down clears up space in your mind and lets you understand what actually matters most to yourself giving insights on decisions aligned with values/aspirations.

Prioritizing - Make clear goals/priorities which leads to easier decision-making and removes distractions.

Remember: Clarity doesn't mean no chaos - it means being able to make informed choices through it. Practice these tips daily to create a future that aligns with your wants and needs.

Discovering Your Purpose

Our purpose is what gives us meaning and direction in life. It's about aligning our actions with passions/values to live the best version of ourselves.

Discovering our purpose takes a lot of inward thinking and reflecting. It has us ask ourselves deep questions to figure out what we care most about, what makes us happy, and the things we hold to high value. This might take a while and require some trial and error, but the process will change you.

One way to start is to think back on experiences where we felt like we were in tune with yourself. These moments often hold clues about our passions and what brings meaning in our lives. Also try looking at your strengths, values, and interests because they can give more insight into your unique gifts.

When our actions align with why we exist, it feels so much easier to be authentic and find fulfillment in life. We're driven by something deeper than what gives us external rewards or societal praise. Instead, it's an internal motivation that pushes us forward towards who we truly are.

This is not something that happens overnight though. As time goes on so will you and your purpose may evolve as well. Keep an open mind while exploring new things because life can throw curve balls at you that lead to something amazing.

Change for Personal Growth

We know change is good for us in terms of personal growth, but it's even more than just adapting to whatever situation you find yourself in. It's a transformation within ourselves that appreciates opportunities for self-improvement. Change puts us out of comfort zones which challenges beliefs and desires for betterment. You'll have no choice but to let go of old patterns, embrace uncertainty, and step into unknown territories just because life demands it from time to time.

Here's the great part though: through all this discomfort you become stronger mentally every single day that passes by. Resilience starts growing along with flexibility and adaptability which makes difficult situations look laughable compared to others who haven't embraced change yet.

When embracing change you have no option other than discovering yourself inside out. Strengths, weaknesses, and limits all become clear which helps identify areas for improvement that you probably would've never realized on your own. It's like having a compass that tells you where to go every time because the path will always resonate with who you really are.

This also expands horizons by exposing us to different perspectives. Cross culture experiences should be consumed as much as possible because it broadens our understanding of the world and enhances empathy and compassion. And once all this information is absorbed, we'll continue learning more intellectually and emotionally.

Embrace all this change because it paves the way for personal growth which then gives us a strong enough mindset to embrace change without hesitation. By doing so we're able to experience a fulfilling life full of meaning.

Letting Go

We all have hurtful memories or past grievances that linger in our heads. They prevent us from living fully in the present by weighing us down. The only way to truly find peace is by letting them go though. Doing so allows us to move forward, heal ourselves, and forgive whatever needs forgiving.

Releasing the past is not an easy process. It requires acknowledging our pain, accepting our emotions, and choosing to move on. However, it's in this journey of letting go that we free ourselves from the chains that hold us back. And as we do so, we open new possibilities for ourselves and welcome positive change into our lives.

Strategies for Finding Healing and Forgiveness

Healing and forgiveness are personal journeys that look different for everyone. However, there are strategies and practices you can use to guide yourself towards this transformative process:

Self-Reflection: Take time to introspect about how past wounds have affected your life. Understand how holding onto these wounds has impacted your well-being and connections with others. By being self-aware, you're already taking the first step towards releasing the past.

Seek Support: Find people who you trust enough to share your experiences with. This can be friends, family members, or even professional counselors who can provide guidance when needed. Sharing your emotions with others will give you insight and support as you work on healing.

Embrace Self-Care: Be sure to prioritize your well-being throughout this process by taking care of yourself physically, mentally, and emotionally. Engage in activities that bring joy into your life while also prioritizing mindfulness and self-compassion.

Focus on the Present: Now is what matters most right now! When practicing self-discovery it's important to direct energy into the present moment rather than focusing on the past or future moments. Doing this will create space for emotional growth while bringing new opportunities for fulfillment.

Letting go of past hurts isn't something that can be done overnight. Remembering this will help build up patience within yourself as you continue working through any internal conflict that arises during the process.

Uncovering Your True Self

Have you ever asked yourself if you're living someone else's life? Are societal expectations too much to handle? Do they overshadow who you really are?

Self-discovery is a transformative experience. Sure, it's not something you can do in one sitting, but it does involve letting go of everything you think you know about yourself and embracing your true self. This process requires introspection, reflection, and a willingness to understand your emotions, values, and passions. It's the only way to find out who we truly are at our core.

When we stop caring about what others think of us and focus on ourselves instead, we break free from the chains that hold us back. It gives us the ability to express ourselves freely, chase after our dreams with full force, and make choices based on our own values.

Embracing Self-Discovery

The journey of self-discovery isn't always easy. There will be moments when you'll have to confront fears that make your stomach drop or take mental blows from insecurities that seem impossible to shake off. However, it's through these moments that growth happens and evolution as an individual takes place.

Self-discovery lets us strip back the layers of conditioning and tap into our inner wisdom. We become aware of our strengths, weaknesses, and the patterns that shape us. It empowers us to make conscious decisions and live life on our terms.

Moreover, self-discovery allows us to build a deeper connection with ourselves and others. When we are in alignment with who we truly are, we attract like-minded individuals and form more meaningful relationships.

So, take some time to embark on your own journey of self-discovery. Reflect on your passions, values, dreams, etc. Embrace the process of letting go and uncover your true self. Your uniqueness is a beautiful thing! Live a life that feels right for you.

Embracing Change in Relationships

Relationships are constantly changing. By embracing this change we open ourselves up to growth and deep connections. If resistant, relationships can stagnate but if not they will grow healthy dynamics that allow for personal and collective development.

Embracing change within relationships requires adaptability, communication (being able to chat openly), and being receptive to the needs of partners.. People change over time so it's important supporting each other's growth because it leads to stronger connections.

One way of embracing this change is by going through self discovery together as partners. When both people commit it creates excitement which leads to challenges that come with personal transformation. This creates understanding empathy and encouragement.

Another important element is Navigating through challenges or conflict together because It's inevitable in any relationship . By doing this we approach disagreements with openness which lets us find solutions . Combining this mindset with understanding gives compromise/resilience.

A third factor is not expecting much from your partner instead be flexible about roles or responsibilities as those things evolve within the partnership . As circumstances/people change our roles may need adjusting so we can keep balanced . Allowing each partner comfort when expressing themselves makes decisions easier too .

In conclusion embracing change within relationships is an ongoing process . You need adaptability, open communication, and a commitment to personal and collective growth. By embracing change, we navigate challenges with resilience and create a nurturing and fulfilling dynamic within our relationships.

The Importance of Clarity in Decision-Making

Living in this fast-paced world makes decision making harder . Lacking clarity can lead to doubt or confusion which usually results in indecisiveness or impulsive choices that don't align with goals/values. On the other hand it lets us make well-informed decisions that bring us closer.

So how do we do it?

1. Define your goals

Before any decision, you need a clear vision of what you want to do. Define your goals and understand the result you're looking for. You don't want to start doing something only to realize that the whole time, it was not what you wanted.

2. Research everything

Educate yourself before making a big decision. Research as much information as possible and consult experts in that field. Get different viewpoints from other people (even if they are negative). This will give you a better understanding of whatever you are doing and reduce uncertainties.

3. Look into future

Realistically evaluate what each path could lead to. Think about both immediate and future implications of all your options. Use this knowledge to weigh the pros and cons so that your decisions align with your values.

4.Learn when to trust intuition

While gathering information is important, sometimes our gut feelings can offer insights logic alone may miss. Tune into your inner voice by using self-awareness and learn when it's best to follow it.

Having clarity in decision-making will make life easier to navigate through choices because we have an end goal in sight.

Living on Purpose

Our main goal on earth is living a meaningful life with purpose towards something greater than ourselves which drives us every morning we wake up. It lets us live life focused but in today's world, there are so many distractions fighting for our attention which makes it harder than ever before.

Everyone goes through different things at various times in their lives so each individual has a unique journey. You have to know who you are inside and out then go deeper by asking questions like "What am I good at?", "What do I value?", "What do I love?" etc… this can help uncover what truly makes us happy because we lose ourselves trying please others when we should be focusing on bringing joy personally.

After finding the reason why you get up every day life starts moving faster but not always in a perfect smooth line. People will make fun of you because it's something they don't understand, your family might not agree with what you're doing but that shouldn't matter - success is the best revenge.

The last thing to remember through all this is that no two people can have the same purpose so stop comparing yourself to others because if you do you'll never be happy and always find a reason why you need more.

Chapter 41
Finding Harmony in Health, Wealth, and Relationships

In this chapter, we will explore how health, wealth, and relationships connect in different parts of our lives. Achieving a balance between these three things is key to leading a fulfilling life. We're going to discuss what exactly having a balanced lifestyle means, how you can achieve it and why it's important. When people talk about living a balanced lifestyle, they mean having the perfect balance between different aspects of their lives. It's all about finding the right balance that nurtures your physical and mental well-being. Ensuring financial stability, cultivating meaningful relationships, managing work-life harmony and integrating leisure and recreation are also part of this equation.

Just understanding how important it is to have balance is already a big step towards achieving it. When we recognize the interconnectivity between different areas of our lives we can make conscious choices to create harmony and promote overall well-being.

We're going to go into detail throughout this chapter on the different dimensions of what makes up a balanced lifestyle. By doing so you'll be able to see how each area influences others. Our goal here is to provide you with insights, strategies and practical tips that will help keep balance in your health, wealth and relationships.

Understanding Just How Important Balance Is

Having balance in your life is essential for overall happiness as well as good health. Balance means you're keeping everything steady between all aspects of your life instead of letting one thing dominate while neglecting others. This way no single area is compromised making sure every part gets its fair share.

Being able to maintain an equilibrium is crucial when trying to find balance since everything needs just enough but not too much attention or care. However when we choose one aspect over another it throws off our whole equilibrium causing stress dissatisfaction or even leaves us with no fulfillment at all.

A fulfilling life comes from striving for a balanced lifestyle which allows us to manage time energy and resources effectively across multiple areas like health wealth relationships work-life personal growth etc. When we maintain a balance we can feel greater joy satisfaction and personal growth in all of these areas.

Taking Care of Mental and Physical Health

There's nothing more important than making sure you're physically and mentally healthy when trying to achieve a balanced lifestyle. This should be our main focus because well-being is connected with the interplay between other aspects of life.

Physical health acts as the foundation for a balanced lifestyle. Being in good shape allows us to go full force into various activities that could potentially make us better people. We need to make sure we get enough sleep eat nutritious meals and exercise regularly in order to keep optimal physical well-being.

Mental health on the other hand is what keeps us stable happy and helps us think clearly. By taking care of our mental well-being it gives us strength to battle stress make smart decisions and cultivate real relationships with real people. Practicing mindfulness engaging in hobbies or even just setting aside some "me" time are just some things that contribute to living a balanced life.

The Interplay Between Health And Other Areas Of Life

The state our minds and bodies are in significantly impacts other areas of life. When we take care ourselves properly energy levels rise allowing us to perform better at work etc. Resilience is also built through taking care of ourselves leading to an easier road when dealing with setbacks or challenges

Prioritizing our health is important in relationships. It lets us show up fully and be there for people we love. We can provide support, empathy and companionship if we are physically and mentally well. Strong relationships depend on this because it makes harmony between both parties.

Having balance in life depends on how well you take care of yourself. Once your mental and physical being is great, then that's when the magic happens. You'll have a strong base to work with when it comes to financial stability, meaningful relationships, personal growth etc.. Stress will be easier to manage too because of the stability you have built.

The next section goes into detail about how financial stability helps create a balanced lifestyle.

Financial Stability

A lot of aspects in life depend on how stable you are financially. It has an impact on your wellbeing overall.

Stress levels go down once your money is right

You don't need to worry about living check to check anymore either

You can start investing more time into your passion because you're not heavily worried about finances anymore

Helps build a better environment for family or friends, which brings peace

Gives space to give back to communities or causes that mean something to you

Our relationships influence more than just our emotional well-being. They impact all aspects of our lives, including our physical health, professional success, and personal growth. By filling our lives with positive people who support us, we create a culture that helps us maintain balance in life and strive for our goals.

It's not about the number of friends you have, but rather the quality of your friendships. Building deep relationships with those who matter most to us is what helps us find fulfillment and overcome any obstacle thrown at us.

Building these relationships starts with effective communication skills, active listening, empathy, and respect. We should be willing to invest time into nurturing them because they are an investment in ourselves and happiness.

If you understand that a happy life is built on strong relationships then your job is to do one thing. Build meaningful ones..

Whether it's chasing interests, exploring the outdoors, or spending quality time with friends and family, leisure activities bring a sense of balance. This lets people focus on the present and enjoy life. Engaging in hobbies that bring pleasure can boost creativity. It can also strengthen relationships and even make people more productive.

The benefits are plentiful when prioritizing leisure activities. A well-rounded routine with activities for fitness and well-being will make individuals happier. They will then be able to create a fruitful life.

For example, sports can help keep people physically fit while making friends along the way. Painting can unlock someone's creative side while giving them an enjoyable activity to look forward to doing.

Leisure activities aren't always physical either. Listening to music is a great way to relax and unwind after a long day at work.

By focusing on things that make us happy we can live more fulfilling lives.

Putting Time into What Matters

In order to achieve balance, our environment needs to support it as well. Where we spend most of our time plays a huge role in how much harmony we're experiencing in life.

If everything around us is cluttered it'll likely have an effect on our minds as well, so getting rid of clutter is important. Additionally, surrounding ourselves with positive influences will put us in better mental states overall.

A simple walk outside during break periods at work can go a long way too. By removing ourselves from whatever environment we're used to being in every day it gives us room to breathe and think clearly.

When it comes to personal growth, many factors interact with one another. Your physical and mental health can act as a solid foundation for self improvement. Adding regular exercise, maintaining a proper diet, and practicing mindfulness or meditation can all help you thrive in other aspects of life.

Building financial stability is a must when it comes to personal growth. Managing your wealth in the best way possible gets rid of financial stress, and creates more opportunities for you to grow as an individual. Investing in education, attending seminars or workshops, and just overall expanding your knowledge will take you very far on your journey for self-improvement.

Without meaningful relationships it's hard to grow personally and develop. To be able to do so you have to build healthy connections with loved ones, friends, and colleagues. When engaging in open conversations, you get lots of opportunities for growth. Supporting others while also asking them for support when needed helps make us better people. A sense of belonging goes a long way too.

Being able to manage both work and personal life is also very important. If not done well you may experience burnouts which isn't good if you're trying to grow. Giving yourself time off is essential.

Doing things that bring joy into your life has immeasurable value.By doing these things we create environments that are supportive which then promotes growth within ourselves.

When we want to grow as individuals we shouldn't just stop at the moment where we feel like we've achieved something big.Reflecting on ourselves at all times is something we should get used too.Rest assured knowing that personal growth never stops.Taking up new challenges here and there will allow us to continue growing.One simple change leads us down paths that eventually lead us towards the perfect person we want to become

When we allow ourselves to grow and develop, it leads to fulfillment. If you embrace learning new skills, gaining knowledge, and just exploring life's many aspects you will evolve. This gives us the ability to keep progressing in any area of our life and work towards reaching our full potential.

Putting practical tips into play is how we balance our health, wealth, and relationships. The more we can implement what's discussed here the more harmonious our lives will be.

Chapter 42

Advanced Organization
for the Midlife Mind

As we journey through the ups and downs of midlife, it becomes more important than ever to declutter our minds, optimize our productivity, and leverage the tools around us. In this chapter, we'll explore advanced organization techniques that are designed specifically for people like us. By using them, you can supercharge your efficiency, unlock a sense of calm, and pave the way for a better future.

Getting More Done

Increasing productivity is a surefire way to get more done in less time. Below are several tips and tricks that will help you unlock your maximum potential:

1. **Manage Your Time:** The first step to boosting productivity is making sure you're spending your time wisely. Identify your most valuable tasks and focus on them first.
2. **Avoid Procrastination:** Procrastination can be deadly if not handled correctly. We'll take a stab at teaching you how to overcome this nasty habit so that you can stay motivated throughout the day.
3. **Optimize Your Workspace:** If your workspace is cluttered or uncomfortable, then it's probably not helping with productivity. Follow our advice below on how to improve your setup.
4. **Fix Your Daily Routine:** Did you know small tweaks to your daily routine can have big effects on productivity? Learn how to establish effective routines that take advantage of your body's natural rhythms.

Following these strategies will lead to an immediate increase in overall productivity levels as well as help you build habits that last a lifetime.

Tools You Can Use

There are plenty of digital tools out there designed specifically for people who want to speed up their workflow and boost their efficiency:

1. **Digital Productivity Apps:** These apps double as personal assistants (just without all the annoying questions). They're capable of managing tasks, tracking time spent on projects, prioritizing objectives - basically anything under the sun!
2. **Project Management Software:** If you work on bigger projects or with teams then having project management software can be a game changer. Its features allow you to assign tasks, track progress, and communicate without ever having to leave the app.
3. **Workflow Streamlining Tools:** There's a tool out there that can do everything for you - whether it's automating repetitive tasks or transferring data between different platforms.

In today's world where technology plays such a huge role in our lives, we would be crazy not to use it to our advantage.

Optimizing Workspaces

In a world that's moving at high speed, keeping an organized and clutter-free workspace is crucial for productivity and peace of mind. When your desk is filled with junk, it becomes harder to concentrate on your work. However, having an organized workspace boosts concentration and efficiency. In this chapter, we'll run through some practical tips on how to declutter and organize your workspace to create an ergonomic environment that will inspire more hours of productivity.

Boosting Concentration And Creativity

Begin the process by removing items that aren't needed and only keeping the essentials. Clutter can be distracting or even overwhelming, making it tough to complete tasks efficiently. But if you remove unnecessary items from your workspace, you'll have a clean workspace that inspires focus and creativity when needed. Upgrading to ergonomic furniture is also recommended because they promote proper posture while reducing physical strain. This includes getting yourself an ergonomic chair, adjustable desk, as well as good lighting - these all make significant differences in comfort.

Efficient Storage Solutions

The importance of storage solutions cannot be stressed enough when it comes to maintaining orderliness in a workspace. Invest in shelves, containers or desk organizers that'll allow you to keep supplies neatly arranged while still being able to reach them when needed. Store documents, materials and supplies like this too if possible. Categorize every item so they're easier to locate later on. Minimize the time spent looking for things by simply labelling containers after categorizing what's inside them.

Keeping The Workspace Orderly

After tidying up your space by removing junk and organizing everything else left behind, it's important to establish a system. By doing so, you'll spend less than 5 minutes each night cleaning up instead of 30 minutes doing so once the mess piles up. Starting off each day with a clean space makes you feel better about getting work done for the rest of the day. Similarly,it would also be a good idea to set time aside every week or month to declutter and remove items you no longer need. Doing this will prevent clutter from piling up over time.

Digital Strategies

Are you tired of going through an inbox full of emails or spending hours trying to look for a file on your computer? If that sounds like you,it's time to take control of your digital world and start organizing it. With these strategies,you can effectively manage emails,documents,and other files - resulting in a clutter-free digital environment that enhances productivity.

An important first step is managing your email.Use folders to organize them by priority and relevance. Putting things in folders will make things easier to find months down the line when searching for something. But also remember that not all emails are important,so try to unsubscribe from any newsletters,promotions or anything else that clogs up your inbox.

Make a more complex folder structure for documents and files.Creating main folders for different categories or projects is suggested because it makes navigating easier from the outset.If needed,create subfolders so they're further categorized as well.A descriptive name should be given to each document too so people who don't regularly work with the files know what it is all about.Purging unnecessary files should be done on a regular basis too because this actually helps free up storage space on a computer.

Use digital tools and techniques to maintain a clutter-free digital workspace. You can even look into productivity apps and software that are designed to help you stay organized and focused. There's tons of applications like Trello, Evernote or Google Keep that all assist in managing tasks, notes and reminders so you can be on top of your digital responsibilities.

Another way to declutter your space is through cloud storage solutions such as Google Drive or Dropbox. It's an easy way to collaborate with others while also giving you access to your files from any device. The best part? These services come with an automatic backup system for the ultimate security.

By implementing these organization strategies, not only can you save time when searching for a file but it'll unlock the full potential of your digital workspace.

Filtering and Prioritizing Information

In today's day in age, information overload has become a common challenge. With so many emails, notifications and online content coming at us it's no wonder we sometimes feel overwhelmed. However, there are ways you can manage this problem and keep a focused mindset.

First thing is first - filter out what information is worth consuming. Instead of trying to do it all, focus on what's important and will benefit your goals/tasks. Not only will this make you more efficient with your time but it ensures that what you're focusing on matters.

Then comes note taking systems… yes they matter too! Depending on what works for you (whether its online note-taking apps or good old pen plus paper) find something that sticks. All you have to do is take concise plus organized notes during meetings/presentations/consuming content in order to process info better later on when needed.

Last but not least - avoid distractions! Turn off notifications if unnecessary and create blocks of dedicated work time where nothing will harm your concentration. For some people using methods like the Pomodoro Technique work wonders (short bursts of intense focus followed by short breaks). It improves concentration and reduces the feeling of overwhelm.

Lastly, be mindful when consuming information. No one likes to hear they're being a picky reader but in this case it's a good thing! You want to make sure you're reading from trusted sources to avoid misinformed info. Wasting time is not okay here so set goals for yourself whenever you engage with content!

As a facilitator, it's your job to make sure people are comfortable and willing to share. Encourage everyone to speak up with their ideas. Use effective listening techniques. Summarize what you've heard from others.

Collaborate!

Use tech in meetings! There's project management software, digital whiteboards, and shared document platforms that can help you brainstorm better. Plus it makes it easy to track action items or collaborate on tasks. These tools will help engage everyone in the virtual room.

Don't Fall Into The Pit

Always look out for common meeting problems and avoid them at all costs. For example going off on tangents or being unfocused is a big one. You'll also want to be careful around participants who dominate the conversation. Set rules for your meetings and make sure everyone feels supported enough to speak. If needed, steer people back on topic.

By using these strategies you'll have better meetings that lead to more collaboration and progress overall.

Getting Help From Others

You can achieve so much more when delegating and outsourcing tasks to others. Using other people's skills allows you to focus on what you do best while still making ground elsewhere,

Finding areas where this can be done is step 1. Find things that don't require your unique skills or expertise but are still important enough that they need doing by someone else other than yourself.

Communication plays a big part here so start there first when delegating. Make sure expectations are clear as day and leave detailed instructions to anyone taking over for you - even if it's a team of people rather than just one person. Regular check-ins will allow for any necessary adjustments too.

Using agencies

When outsourcing anything finding reliable places or people is pivotal in preventing headaches later down the line.. Upwork, Fiverr, Freelancer are platforms full of professionals who dedicate themselves solely towards specific projects or ongoing tasks

Review ratings and reviews carefully before finalizing an outsourcing agreement. This will give you insight on their reliability and capabilities. If you want, feel free to hold interviews or ask for work samples so that you're confident in your decision.

Remember that just because you outsourced doesn't mean it's out of your hands now. Keep clear communication channels open and set expectations from the start of the project to ensure a successful working relationship. Regularly evaluate how well things are being done and adjust if necessary.

If used right delegating and outsourcing can save time freeing up energy to focus on other important tasks. It's an effective tool to use when trying to reach goals and stay productive overall.

Productive Lifestyles

After you've already gotten into habits that have helped you with productivity don't stop there! You'll want these things to stick around for a long time since they are what make up good habits in the first place.

One thing you can do is identify the things that give you energy and work towards them. Put these activities at the front of your day. Get enough prioritized throughout. Whether it's starting your day with exercise, knocking out important tasks first or taking breaks whenever you need to recharge. That way you'll keep a high level of energy and focus.

Doing what it takes to not burnout is super important if you want to stay productive at all times. Don't get me wrong, hard work is great but so are regular breaks, practicing self-care and knowing when to cut yourself off from work altogether. By giving yourself time to relax and taking breaks for your own good every now and then you'll be able to avoid burning out completely, while also maintaining a healthy balance between life and work.

Fulfillment is hands down the most important part of always being productive. You'll never be able to go hard 24/7 if whatever you're doing isn't fulfilling enough for you in both personal and professional ways. Set goals that inspire both areas of your life equally as much as each other. Celebrate the goals once they're met but don't ween off from there, stay happy about them till completion or even beyond that if possible! Taking this route will make staying motivated super easy because all the fulfillment will just drive itself into your system!

Chapter 43

Midlife Dating and
New Relationships

Here's the deal: Dating in midlife is tricky. But if you know how to stay true to yourself, you'll be golden. In this chapter, we talk about finding balance between personal independence and meeting new people.

Whether you're fresh from a breakup or haven't dated in forever, there's something everyone can relate to: it's different when you're older. Join us as we dive into the challenges and opportunities that come with seeking new relationships later in life.

A healthy relationship needs each person to have their own thing going on. We give tips on how to keep doing things your way while also growing closer with your partner.

And what about those fears? The insecurities? The baggage? Don't worry - we've got you covered. We discuss how to overcome these roadblocks so you can experience love at its fullest potential.

Trust is important af no matter how old you are; yet, it hits a little harder as we get older. Check out our ways on building trust and creating an unbreakable bond with your S.O.

Communication is another important part of any relationship that often gets overlooked. But not here! We show you how to tell bae what's up without steppin' on toes (or breaking hearts).

But remember: Self-care is key! Yes, make time for date nights and trips together - but also make time for yourself too. It's all about finding balance and knowing when enough is enough.

Everyone plays different roles in different relationships - that's just life. However, it's still important to find a solid foundation within yours by rewriting what being supportive means and setting clear expectations from the get-go.

This one goes without saying: You need closeness! We spill some tea on maintaining emotional intimacy with your partner while keeping things spicy throughout the years.

We all have our fair share of emotional baggage… but nobody wants it thrown onto them like some lost luggage at the airport. Learn how to keep your baggage at bay and be there for one another in ways no other person can.

Opening up is a lot harder than it seems… especially as we get older. We'll show you how to let someone in without losing yourself, so you can feel all the love while keeping your independence.

Lastly, we take a peek into what's on the horizon when it comes to finding love later in life. It's a fun section that reminds you that there really are possibilities around every corner.

So join us as we dive headfirst into the world of midlife dating and new relationships. There's no better time to find balance in love and embrace endless beginnings!

One of the amazing things about dating in midlife is that priorities shift. People have a clearer sense of what they need and want. This makes their connections intentional and fulfilling. The pool grows, so there's more opportunities to meet someone who has the same values and perspectives as you.

However, this landscape also comes with its own set of challenges. Past experiences can shape new relationships. Baggage can make it difficult to move on, which is needed for a healthy relationship start. Life responsibilities don't help either because that takes time away from going out and actually meeting people.

Still, even with these issues there's growth and opportunity. Midlife dating allows for self-discovery, an exploration of new interests, and building a stable foundation with someone who appreciates all your wisdom.

In the following sections we will go over strategies for maintaining independence in a relationship, overcoming fears, building trust, communicating effectively, and embracing vulnerability.

Maintaining Independence

Independence is important when starting any new relationship. Especially in midlife when both partners have their own lives established already.

It's very normal to want what's best for us while still trying to explore new romantic connections. To do this you should communicate your needs clearly to your partner. It shows them that you aren't trying to be selfish but rather just maintain personal space along with time dedicated to your own hobbies.

Another way to maintain independence is simply continuing doing what you love most outside of work or being withe friends - alone or not.

By setting healthy boundaries like respecting each other's personal space as well as autonomy lets both individuals know that their decisions are respected by one another equally.

Don't forget: independence doesn't mean isolating yourself or avoiding vulnerability!

Overcoming Dating Fears

Reentering the dating scene during midlife is scary! But don't worry… things have changed in many ways than one since the last time you've dated!

Rejection is a common fear. The idea of putting yourself out there just to be turned down can be tough. You have to remind yourself that being rejected is something everyone goes through. It's not a reflection of your worth or desirability. With the right mindset and seeing rejection as a learning experience you'll start developing meaningful connections in no time.

Another frequent fear is vulnerability. Opening up to someone about all your experiences and emotions can be scary. It's probably one of the most intimidating things you'll have to do when building deep connections. The best way to get comfortable with it is by sharing your thoughts with people you trust first because as you build trust these relationships will make it easier for you to open up more and more.

The fear of being judged also comes up often in midlife dating. After being out of the game for so long, what will others think? Well, keep in mind that everyone has their own insecurities and stories too, so don't sweat it too much! Just focus on being authentic and true to yourself while embracing your uniqueness. You've lived this long so someone who appreciates and values you for who you are will come along.

Steps for overcoming fears

Overcoming fears isn't easy but here are some strategies that should help:

Challenge negative thoughts: Replace self-doubt and negative beliefs with positive affirmations. Remind yourself of your strengths, achievements, and the qualities that make you a desirable partner.

Take small steps: Start by dipping your toes into the dating scene through online platforms or social activities. This allows you to get comfortable with the idea of dating again at your own pace.

Seek support: Share your feelings and fears with trusted friends or join support groups for individuals navigating midlife dating. Hearing others' stories and receiving support can provide reassurance and guidance.

Educate yourself: Learn about modern dating practices, etiquette, and relationship dynamics. This knowledge can help alleviate anxiety and give you a better understanding of the dating scene in today's digital age.

Practice self-care: Prioritize self-care activities that boost your confidence and well-being. Engage in physical exercise, indulge in hobbies you enjoy, and practice self-compassion. Taking care of yourself will help you approach dating with a positive mindset.

Remember, dating in midlife is an opportunity for personal growth, companionship, and fulfilling connections. By acknowledging and overcoming your fears, you can embrace the possibilities and create meaningful relationships that bring joy and fulfillment to your life.

Building Trust in Midlife Relationships

Trust is a cornerstone of any successful relationship, and it becomes even more crucial in midlife when embarking on new relationships. Building trust with a new partner requires time, effort, and open communication. Here are some effective ways to foster trust and cultivate a strong and lasting connection:

1. Be Open and Honest

Open up about everything! Your feelings, thoughts, expectations all of it! And encourage your partner to do the same as well so that there's no miscommunication or confusion. Transparency builds trust which helps create a solid foundation for your relationship.

2. Keep Promises When Making Them

Consistency is the key to any good relationship. When you make a promise, no matter how small, it's crucial that you follow through with it. Show your partner that they can trust you and that you value their trust. Not only will this strengthen your bond but it also shows that you are dedicated to the relationship.

3. Respecting Boundaries

No matter what kind of relationship it is, respecting boundaries is vital for maintaining healthy connections with others. Talk to your partner about what they are comfortable with and never cross those lines. A strong sense of safety and security will be built from this foundation, which will help strengthen trust.

4. Show Empathy and Understanding

Trust grows from understanding one another and being able to connect on a deep emotional level. Putting in the effort to listen, validate your partners feelings, and understand where they are coming from is essential in all relationships. By doing so, we create an environment where open and honest communication can flow freely.

5. Be Reliable

In order for someone to fully trust you, they must first know that they can count on you at all times; not just when it benefits them in some way or another. The key here is consistency - if someone knows you'll be there when everything seems hopeless then they'll definitely have faith knowing that even when things go well, you'll still be there for them.

6. Always Stay True To Yourself

It goes without saying but being yourself is always the best thing anyone can do in any given situation (as long as who we are doesn't involve causing harm to others). If we constantly pretend or hide our true selves then the person on the receiving end won't ever know who we actually are - thus making it impossible for them to ever trust us fully since trust cannot exist without honesty.

No matter how many steps there may be - if both people put in their full effort into these guidelines then building a solid foundation of trust will be smooth sailing. Remember, trust takes time to build and when you don't have it you'll need a lot of patience.

Taking care of yourself is one of the most important parts of staying independent in a relationship. It's easy to lose sight of your own well-being when you're focused on nurturing a new partnership. But by balancing how much you care for yourself and how much you commit to the other person, you can create a bond that feels good.

Self-care means tending to all aspects of your life: physical, emotional, and mental. You have to focus on activities that make you happy, reflections on who you are and what's going on inside your head right now, setting boundaries, and keeping yourself healthy.

When starting a new relationship in middle age, it's natural to dive deep into getting to know each other, building intimacy, and doing everything together. But don't forget about these two things:

Your personal needs

Things that make you happy

Communicating those two things with your partner is key because it'll help them understand what makes you feel good while letting them know how to support you as well. A balanced approach will also promote individual growth within the partnership.

Here are three things that'll help develop strong love in later years:

Laying out roles and expectations

Creating an intimate connection

And finding new ways to experience pleasure side-by-side

Remember that everyone has different comfort levels and boundaries. Having open conversations and getting consent is key. As long as there's ongoing communication, you should be able to create a safe space for touch.

There's no other way to put it: creating intimacy and connection in midlife love is all about having emotional openness, shared experiences, and physical touch. Prioritize these three things if you want your relationship to last.

Don't let past baggage ruin your new relationship

Old baggage just has a way of making itself known when you're trying to start something new. You should always be aware of your own emotions because it can impact your dating journey. And although we don't have an answer as to why, everyone seems to develop some sort of dealing strategy with any unresolved issues that come up along the way. Remember that everyone has their own baggage

We all come with our own share of baggage into relationships - whether or not we're aware of it at first. It could be from past relationships or even personal challenges we've overcome over time. Either way, this stuff impacts how we enter new connections.

Working through it

First things first, you need to understand your past before being able to move on from it. Doing so will help you see how previous experiences have impacted the way you act in new connections.

If the unresolved feelings make themselves known once again and impact the healthiness of said connections, seeing a therapist is always an option. They'll guide you through the feelings and work towards finding resolution on them.

Stop holding onto the past

It's pretty much impossible for us humans to embrace what's in front of us if we keep holding on tight to what no longer exists behind us. Remembering this during times where old wounds creep back up will be key in building a solid foundation for a healthy relationship.

How do you talk about it?

When old baggage resurfaces and starts affecting your current partner negatively, it's time to sit-down and have a good old heart-to-heart. Let them know what you're feeling and fearing. Through this, they'll be able to support you in growing and healing together as a couple.

Forgiveness and self-compassion

One important part of getting over our past is by learning how to forgive ourselves, as well as others. This lets us get past negative emotions, which in turn opens up space for new experiences and connections. Another crucial thing to do is practice self-compassion in this process too. It helps you acknowledge and validate your own feelings and experiences.

It's good to remember that everyone has a past. How we navigate and move on from it is what shapes our futures. Creating new relationships when dating at middle-age might be hard to trust at first, but if you learn how to handle your baggage in a healthy way, while being proactive about it too, then you can create relationships built on trust, understanding, personal growth.

Embracing Vulnerability and Emotion

Becoming vulnerable with someone new while dating at middle-age can be daunting too. After all, life tends to hurt pretty bad sometimes and once you've gone through it all it feels like the safe play would just be avoiding feelings altogether. But true connection needs real vulnerability and emotion. Here are some ways you can walk that thin line of remaining independent while embracing these things:

Reflect And Release Past Fears

In order to embrace vulnerability fully, reflect on past experiences so that you may release any fears or insecurities left over from them. Remember every relationship is unique so don't expect the future based off of the past! By dropping fear we make room for better possibilities.

Communicate Your Needs

Communication is everything when it comes to relationships - old or new! When being vulnerable express your wants/needs with your partner openly.. There will always need to be balance so that your independence doesn't have too much negative effect on emotional connection!

Practice Self-Compassion

You'll never truly be able to build an emotional connection with another person unless you're willing to be compassionate towards yourself first! Being vulnerable is not being weak. Let love happen.

Take Small Steps

You don't have to pour your heart out day one.. Building trust and opening up can take time. Share little by little, slowly getting them used to you as well as you getting used to them!

Celebrate Emotional Intelligence

This one's super important too! Emotional intelligence often gets overlooked but it's an amazing tool that will allow for independence while embracing vulnerability. You need to recognize how you feel about things, how they do, and manage those emotions as well as possible.

Looking Ahead: Future Possibilities in Midlife Love

As you embark on your midlife dating journey and embrace new relationships, it's important to keep your independence intact. The dating scene can be both exciting and daunting, but by maintaining a sense of self and embracing the future, you can make the most of your romantic endeavors.

Midlife love offers a wealth of possibilities and potential. It's a chance to explore new connections, experiences, and emotions. While it's natural to have reservations and concerns, remember that this is your time to shine and create a fulfilling romantic life.

When it comes to starting a new romantic relationship, the key is not losing yourself in the process. To put yourself first and still continue to pursue your dreams and hobbies while nurturing the initial connection with your partner. Once you set your limits and express yourself openly, you'll be able to strike the perfect balance of intimacy and "alone" time.

Chapter 44

Reinforcing Your
Reservoir of Patience

In this chapter, we explore the concept of patience and its profound impact on achieving success during your second act. Patience is not just a virtue but a vital ingredient for personal growth and resilience. Modern society has conditioned us to prioritize instant gratification, making it easy to forget the importance of patience. However, embracing patience will strengthen your ability to overcome midlife challenges while setting the stage for greater achievements.

Throughout this chapter, we discuss how patience is a reliable tool for navigating life's curveballs. We'll dive into why it's crucial in midlife and how you can cultivate it across different aspects of your daily routine.

So if you're ready to learn how to reinforce your reservoir of patience, unlock its potential for personal growth and experience midlife success, let's get started!

Understanding the Power of Patience

When most people think about patience, they often picture waiting. Waiting for traffic lights to change or maybe waiting on a slow service clerk.

But in reality, there's much more complexity that lies beneath the surface. It includes acceptance, trust and perseverance which are all necessary traits for growth.

Once you truly understand what makes up patience you'll be able to navigate life's challenges with grit and resilience. It allows you to keep calm even when going through adversity so that better decisions can be made and purposeful actions taken.

Patience is not passive! It doesn't simply involve accepting where we are in life but actively working towards our goals while understanding certain things take time.

Growth is an ongoing process with no destination at sight which means infinite learning. So instead of getting frustrated when things don't go as planned use this time as reflection - maybe there's something else that could be done?

Above all else though… Trust The Timing Of Your Life!

Instead of trying to control every aspect have faith that everything will unfold as it should. When doing so unnecessary stress drops off from your shoulders inevitably leading towards a more fulfilling life.

In summary, patience is a powerful tool that helps us reach our goals. It keeps us composed and enables us to make better decisions during adversity. By understanding this we'll be able to experience the transformative potential of personal growth and midlife success.

The Role of Patience in Midlife Success

Midlife success comes from navigating challenges and uncertainties with resilience. And in this stage, patience plays a significant role towards achieving greater fulfillment.

Slow progress or setbacks are common obstacles whenever reaching for success but it's usually these times where people quit. But through patience you'll understand that things take time… And every step forward matters!

During midlife, you will experience various changes internally and externally when it comes to developing yourself. This is why patience becomes so important because it guides you through the process of change!

When used as a guiding force individuals are able to open themselves up for new opportunities and possibilities since they're given space to reflect learn and adapt.

As is often the case in personal growth, being patient will get you further. Patience will be your tool for diving into the unknown and embracing what comes with it. It'll help keep your spirits up and motivate you to overcome any setbacks or challenges that arise.

Boost your patience through mindfulness

Patience is a virtue, one that's easily developed through mindfulness practices. By incorporating these into your daily routine, you can make staying calm and focused in adversity all the more easier.

The Power of Mindfulness

Without judgment, being fully present in the moment is what we call mindfulness. It gives us the ability to observe our thoughts, emotions, and physical sensations with kindness and curiosity. And by doing so we can see where impatience stems from and how to respond more patiently.

Another trait of mindfulness is training your attention skills to improve presence. This helps prevent getting caught up in negative thought processes or anxieties about the future. With a focus on right now, any challenges that come can be faced head on without worry.

Mindfulness Exercises for Cultivating Patience

1. Breathing Exercises: Take time out of each day to think about nothing other than breathing. Observe how it feels as it enters and leaves your body. Once you start thinking about something else bring it back to your breath gently. To cultivate patience it's important to stay present and not let anything distract you.

2. Body Scan: Start at your toes and imagine moving a spotlight slowly up until it reaches your head while focusing on different parts of your body along the way.. Notice any changes but don't judge them or react in any way just take notes.The goal here is building an unreactive observer mindset.

Strategies for Enhancing Patience

1. **Acceptance:** Understand that some things are simply out of control when facing given situations. Learn to accept what life throws at you whether instant gratification comes with it or not.. There's a special type of peace and personal growth that can only come from having patience.

2. **Changing Perspectives:** Try to look at hurdles from different angles. Think about how this obstacle could help you grow or what new opportunities it might bring along. The goal here is to foster patience and resilience in any situation.

Developing the patience needed for personal growth involves incorporating mindfulness practices and strategies into your life. Navigating challenges becomes easier with patience, stress is reduced and fulfillment ultimately becomes attainable.

Fulfillment

Patience is a key component to emotional intelligence. It's with practice that we learn to regulate our emotions as well as respond with empathy and understanding. Instead of impulsively reacting, patience allows us to take a quick pause and consider things from different perspectives. While we strengthen this skill, managing relationships, resolving conflicts, and making an impact on those around us will become easier.

Patience also helps foster resilience. When faced with challenges or setbacks, having this trait present keeps our mindset positive and determined. Giving into frustration or impatience will never get you far. But when we approach obstacles with a calm attitude, bouncing back from adversity becomes possible leading to personal growth and success.

Opening ourselves up to the world of personal growth and transformation starts by embracing patience.. This single trait lets us cultivate self-awareness, develop emotional intelligence, and foster resilience. And in our journey towards continuous self-improvement, it serves as a guiding light illuminating the path towards personal growth and fulfillment.

The End of Impatience and Frustration

It's common for impatient feelings along with frustration to begin manifesting when navigating through midlife.. These negative emotions can hinder your drive for personal growth which will directly prevent you from achieving goals.

The first step is recognizing what exactly is triggering these impulsive thoughts. They can be anything ranging from career problems all the way down to unfulfilled aspirations.. Figuring out the root cause will provide some insight into how you can better manage those emotions more effectively.

Focusing on the present moment could also do wonders.. Practicing mindfulness techniques such as deep breathing exercises or meditation help ground us while reducing stress levels at the same time which can lead into less frustrating moments.

We want progress now but in reality it doesn't come overnight which is why setting realistic goals are so important... Little victories should be celebrated throughout your journey so that motivation remains high.. Remind yourself that personal growth never stops and so patience will always be needed.

There are many tips out there but by implementing these two, managing impatience and frustration should become easier over time.. Fueling personal growth and leading a more fulfilling life is all the result of overcoming these negative emotions.

The Catalyst for Goal Achievement

As we journey through midlife, patience becomes the driving force behind achieving long term goals. It's through this skill that allows us to set realistic expectations along with breaking down tasks in order to stay committed to success.

The ability to navigate the ups and downs of endeavors while understanding progress takes time and dedication makes anything possible. And although it seems hard now, with patience we can weather setbacks and obstacles with ease which will ultimately lead us towards our desired outcomes faster.

Setting realistic expectations is the key to mastering patience. It's important to understand that great things don't come overnight. Your goals will take some time to achieve and you'll most likely encounter setbacks along the way, but by maintaining a patient mindset, you can ensure you won't get discouraged. You can also break down tasks into smaller steps with patience. By taking small victories and celebrating them, you keep yourself motivated while slowly making progress towards your goal. This leads to more momentum over time, which then takes you further and faster towards your end goal.

In addition to this, patience helps us stay on track long term. The road gets rough every now and then and we might even want to give up sometimes. But with a patient approach, we remind ourselves that all of this is part of the journey; it's our job to persist no matter what obstacles come our way if we truly want success.

When used correctly in our pursuit of success during midlife, patience allows us to revel in the incremental progress made towards our goals. Allowing us to feel genuinely accomplished when desired outcomes are achieved.

Building Patience in Relationships

Patience isn't just important for personal growth but also for building strong relationships overall. We must understand how impactful it can be on our interactions with others.

Cultivating patience allows us to fully hear others out instead of jumping ahead half way through their sentence or assuming what they'll say next before they can finish speaking.

Effective communication techniques are a huge factor in practicing patience with people around us. Being present when talking to someone else makes it harder for misunderstandings and validating their feelings becomes easier on our end too.

Coping Mechanisms That Help Embrace Patience

No matter how well we get along with those close to us there will always be some bumps in the road; disagreements or challenges of sorts, but with practiced patience these obstacles become much easier to navigate through without causing any harm.

Taking a step back and doing something that calms you down when faced with a difficult situation will help you come to the problem more rationally. This way it's easier to focus on resolving it instead of reacting off of impulse, which could potentially make things worse.

Respecting One Another's Differences And Personal Growth

Another aspect of patience is accepting people's differences and understanding that we all grow at different rates throughout life. You're not always going to be moving at the same pace as your friend or family member, and you must allow them time and space for development.

When patients is embraced within relationships, it creates an environment that allows both individuals involved in it to grow. Celebrating progress whenever made, encouraging one another when they feel like giving up and even providing some space for reflection can strengthen connections and make them more meaningful.

Remember, patience isn't always the easiest thing to have, but it can bring a lot of rewards to our relationships. If we use effective communication, come up with ways of coping, and respect personal growth then we can develop patience and create long-lasting bonds with those we care about most.

The Impact of Patience on Well-being in Midlife

As we reach midlife, it's important for us to cultivate patience for our overall wellbeing. Patience isn't just about waiting - it's a powerful tool that can reduce stress, improve mental health and elevate our life satisfaction.

During this part of our lives, where we grow as people and discover ourselves more so than ever before, there are going to be plenty of challenges and uncertainties. And that's why patience is important -

because it allows us to navigate through these obstacles gracefully and resiliently. This helps us find clarity and make informed decisions that will support success during midlife.

When we practice being patient with ourselves, we allow space to explore new possibilities and embrace the journey of growing as a person. This leads to better understanding ourselves and others which builds stronger relationships since we're able to empathize more.

This is also the time where you'll reflect on who you are and whether or not you've been living your life correctly up until now. And guess what? Being patient is key here as well. It prevents us from forcing outcomes or rushing anything while embracing the process of self-discovery. Through cultivating patience you learn how to trust the timing of your life which gives contentment in the present moment - ultimately leading to better overall wellbeing.

Lower stress levels essentially means better mental health; And practicing patience does exactly that by helping manage frustration, anxiety ,and impatience when unexpected challenges occur. Instead of losing control over yourself you'll be able to approach these situations calmly which dramatically reduces negative impacts on your wellbeing.

Patience even increases gratitude along with appreciation for the midlife journey. It encourages us to celebrate small victories and milestones that we reach, which boosts motivation and speeds up our growth as a person.

In conclusion, embracing patience at this stage of life isn't just good for our overall wellbeing but also our success. By practicing it you reduce stress, enhance your mental health, and find contentment in the present moment - leading to a more fulfilling second half of life.

Integrating Patience into Your Second Act

When trying to become successful during this part of your life, becoming patient during it will be transformative. So as you begin, make sure to integrate patience into everything you do so that it can push you towards new achievements.

Cultivating patience means knowing that progress takes time. Instead of focusing on when something is going to end or happen, focus on embracing the process since things take time. Use grace and resilience when trying to overcome obstacles which will lead to better results in the end.

One helpful way to remain patient is by setting realistic expectations for yourself. Divide goals into smaller steps so that they're manageable. And when these milestones are reached, don't forget to celebrate them! This provides a sense of accomplishment while cultivating an essential patient mindset that's needed for sustainable growth and success.

Nurturing self-awareness and self-compassion also plays a big role in harnessing the power of patience. Understand that personal growth is something continuous - it's not going anywhere anytime soon! So give yourself some grace and understand that things take time. If you ever find yourself being impatient or frustrated with how slow something is going practice mindfulness techniques; This'll allow you to respond with clarity and composure rather than anger or aggression.

Chapter 45

Celebrating Your Forties

Your forties are a prime time for personal growth and self-reflection. You can learn to set goals for your future, as well as looking at the past and seeing what you've learned. You can develop yourself while nurturing meaningful relationships.

We will help you understand how to navigate this stage in life, which comes with both challenges and triumphs. With every new challenge there is an opportunity for personal growth, of course not everything is going to go your way but it's never too late to try again.

We also believe that building strong relationships and connections are very important during this time in life. We'll provide insights on the best ways to grow those connections, from old friends or new ones too. We'll also discuss having a healthy work-life balance, self-care tips, and even career satisfaction.

As we reach the second half of our lives it becomes crucial to have financial plans locked down. This will allow peace of mind while we embrace all the possibilities that lie ahead.

Now the most important thing about life is taking care of yourself physically and mentally. It's crucial that we find ways to make sure we're thriving in all aspects of life because there's nothing more important than feeling fulfilled.

Come join us through this journey that will lead us through self-discovery and personal growth as we navigate through our forties.

Our forties are a time for personal growth. Not only do we learn to adapt to the many changes happening around us, but we also grow internally. By looking inward, we can find our strengths and weaknesses, as well as what areas need improvement.

A career change

This is the perfect time to change careers if you're thinking about it. We'll help you with strategies and tips to make that leap of faith easier. Whether you want to take your passions seriously or move up in an already established field, we have the advice you need. So many people find success through this stage in life.

Family matters

As we get older, our family relationships change too. Empty nest syndrome can be hard on most people, but there's many ways to ease into it better. The dynamics of our family isn't the only thing that changes though-our relationships with others do too.

It's scary when it feels like everything is changing so fast. But know that by moving forward with a positive attitude and strong mindset, you can handle anything that comes your way. It's going to be exciting knowing how much potential you truly have once you tap into it.

Celebrating accomplishments

This section will help guide you through reflecting on your past accomplishments. We ask for some self-appreciation here! Looking at how far you've come should make any nervousness disappear-seriously! Growth doesn't happen over night (unless it's bamboo). Look back at all the skills and knowledge gained over the years too.

Focusing on areas for improvement

Don't be afraid to acknowledge where there's room for growth though! It's natural and always will be. Reflecting on those major growing pains is important to ensure future success. Some people might not even realize they're lacking in certain fields until they decide to self-reflect.

Most likely everyone has a goal or two they wish they achieved by now as well... It's not too late though! Use this time to figure out exactly what you want and how you're going to do it. By thinking about your future goals, it becomes much clearer on how your present actions should be.

Your forties are a time of change and opportunity. Whether you're looking to grow personally, professionally or both, effective goal setting is key to mapping out the next stage of your life.

When setting your goals, it's important to consider what truly matters most to you. Reflecting on the things that bring you joy and fulfillment will help ensure your goals are realistic and meaningful.

One method for doing this is breaking larger aspirations into smaller tasks. This way you can progress step-by-step while staying motivated along the way. Additionally, by setting specific and measurable objectives, you'll have a clearer understanding of how far you've come as well as how much further there is to go.

Creating a timeline for these tasks can be helpful too - adding pressure while also making sure you're continuing to move forward. That being said, adapting them as needed is important because let's face it: life throws curveballs.

Next, think about sharing your goals with others. By discussing them with family members or friends, they'll be able to provide encouragement or advice if necessary. And if altruistic goals like volunteering or mentoring interest you, not only will they benefit others but also give yourself an opportunity for growth too.

Your forties are filled with possibilities and brand new beginnings where anything can happen. So today is a great day to take the steps towards living a happy and successful life full of purpose.

Building Relationships

Relationships are everything; it's what makes up our lives after all! And when we reach our forties they become more important than ever before. This crucial stage provides us with a chance to build both personal and professional bonds that will last a lifetime. From keeping old friendships alive, down to building ones from scratch - this section offers some tips on nurturing meaningful relationships.

When it comes down to friends there isn't a better time than now to reassess and grow existing connections. It's time to reflect on all the amazing people who have stuck by you since day 1. And from there, it's about cherishing them and the experiences you've had together. Then going forward, all one can do is stay dedicated to being a good friend and have meaningful interactions that promote growth.

From this point on, your forties are filled with an ideal opportunity to expand your social circle. There is no need to fear going outside of your comfort zone in order to meet new people at this age - everyone's looking for new friends! By joining clubs or organizations you're interested in, attending networking events, or participating in community activities; finding like-minded people will be easier than ever before.

Building Professional Relationships

When it comes down to the professional side of things - as we all know - there will be ups and downs throughout our careers. Fortunately for us though, our forties are filled with chances where we'll need our network in order to make it through some tough times. So make sure that no bridge has been burned up until this point.

Keep in contact with individuals you've met along the way whether they were former colleagues or industry experts. Consistently let them know that you're here for them just as they have been for you throughout these years.

In addition, take advantage of trade shows and conferences in your industry. They give you a chance to meet new people and learn from them. When going to these events, don't just focus on yourself. Show genuine interest in others, ask questions that make sense, and listen actively. These small gestures can lead to powerful connections that may influence your career path later on.

To summarize everything, your forties are a time when you should nurture already existing relationships while creating new ones. Try to build meaningful relationships with people who share the same mindset as you. By doing this, you'll have multiple supportive pillars that will help you move forward.

Balancing work with personal life

When reaching your forties it's paramount that you learn how to balance your work and private life. At this point of our lives we have become very busy people both at work and home which is all the more reason why we need to figure out ways of being able to master both without having any issues.

The first strategy would be prioritizing self-care. Being able to take care of ourselves mentally and physically allows us to be productive no matter where we are or what we're doing. Make sure you have time for activities that recharge and rejuvenate you like hobbies or spending time with family.

On the subject of careers find satisfaction in what it is that you do every day. It won't always be perfect but it's important for your own mental health if there are times where the days tend to fly by because they were so much fun! And remember growth is crucial so continue learning and challenge yourself!

Lastly manage your time effectively while setting very clear boundaries between work-related tasks and personal ones - if possible completely block out one afternoon or morning per week strictly dedicated towards things not related to work.

At the end finding balance is never easy but make sure you prioritize self-reflection above all else.

Planning ahead

The final piece here has nothing to do with work or personal life but your future. Entering our forties should be a wake up call to take our finances seriously before it's too late. We need to start taking steps towards building a solid foundation for what's about to come next.

Investing wisely: The biggest part of this is making smart investment choices. Consider consulting with a financial advisor who can make sure your investments are aligned with your end goals and risk tolerance - diversify where you can and keep track of market trends.

Preparing for retirement: Although it might seem like it, retirement isn't that far away and by now we should have already started planning. Assess what your current savings look like and determine if they're enough, chances are they won't be so consider increasing them if needed. Then take full advantage of different saving options such as IRAs and 401(k)s because trust us when we say by starting early you'll benefit from the power of compounding and build a substantial nest egg for when you do retire!

Building an emergency fund: Life is full of surprises, and it's important to have a financial cushion in place. Create an emergency fund that can cover at least three to six months' worth of living expenses. This will help protect you against job loss, medical emergencies, or unexpected costs. Regularly set aside a portion of your income so that if anything happens, you're ready for any financial setback.

Managing debt: Debt holds us back from our future goals and hampers our financial security. Start by getting a detailed overview of your debts before creating a strategic plan to pay them off. Remember to prioritize which ones should be paid off first while still making the necessary payments on others. The key here is to create discipline when it comes to managing the debt so that over time, the stress decreases.

Regular check-ups: As life goes on, our needs change along with them. Regularly reviewing and adjusting your finances every year ensures they stay up-to-date with your aspirations and goals. That sounds like no fun at all but don't worry! Set aside just a little bit of time each year so you can evaluate everything with ease: investments, long-term goals and make any possible adjustments. Although this next part might not sound fun either... Think about speaking with someone who specializes in financial planning - their professional guidance will help reassure that you're doing things right.

Taking these steps now will build a strong foundation for the future. By doing these small things now we ensure we are setting ourselves up for long term success as well as relieving stress now.

Wellness Plus Self-Care

This stage of life brings many new responsibilities and challenges so making sure we take care of ourselves physically and mentally is crucial.

Physical Health:

In this stage of life it's easy to forget about physical health but remember... It's never too late! A healthy body equals less trips to the doctor! Taking 30 minutes out of everyday, even just to take a walk or try out that workout class you've been eyeing can make a huge difference. Don't stop there, make sure you're eating well balanced meals too!

Mental and Emotional Well-being:

Don't forget about your mind! It's equally important to take care of it as well. Managing daily stressors can be difficult but there are many techniques that help. Try some out like meditation or journaling and see if they work for you.

Self-Care Rituals:

Taking 15-30 minutes out of the day to yourself can do wonders. Do something that brings joy no matter how small it is... Even reading a book does wonders.

Importance of Sleep:

Something so simple yet often overlooked. Make sure you're getting enough sleep... Your body will thank you in many ways! Aim for 7-9 hours each night to support your physical and mental health.

Don't forget: self-care isn't selfish. By investing in your well-being, you're able to serve others and fully enjoy the experiences that come with being 40. Make sure to take care of yourself and keep wellness a priority during this stage of life. It's crucial.

Recognizing Milestones

As you enter your forties, it's important to look back at what you've accomplished so far. This is the perfect time to acknowledge personal growth, accept achievements, and celebrate the path you've taken.

Milestones like reaching career markers or starting a family remind us how far we've come from where we started.

Celebrations are a great opportunity to honor these moments and make them last forever. You can do this by throwing small gatherings with friends and family or even planning a weekend getaway - anything that suits your style. These celebrations bring happiness and joy while fostering gratitude for all the things that have shaped us.

Don't limit celebrations to external milestones either - be sure to also celebrate personal growth and self-discovery. Think about the values and passions that have defined you as a person in your forties then find ways to honor them. Share this experience with people who have supported you on this journey so far - they deserve it just as much as you do!

"At the age of forty, life is no longer just a painting. It's sculpted with wisdom that only comes from experience. The strength that only comes from resilience. And the grace that only comes from acceptance."

Epilogue

As we reach the end of our journey exploring concepts of personal growth, spirituality, relationships, and more, I would like to leave you with a few final thoughts. This book was intended as a starting point - an invitation to further reflect on these profoundly insightful topics and continue your exploration. My hope is that within these pages, you found perspectives that sparked new ideas, challenged conventional thinking, or shed light on your own experiences.

By delving into research, studies, wisdom traditions, and diverse viewpoints, we uncovered an array of insights across different subjects. However, knowledge alone does not equate to true understanding or application; it is an ongoing cycle requiring continuous practice. With further self-inquiry, conversation with others, and real-world experiences, these learnings can continue to take shape and deepen within you over time. I encourage staying open to learning through unconventional paths, whether through conversations, nature, creativity, or life's unexpected turns.

Though we explored diverse topics individually, each section is deeply interconnected - from spirituality to relationships and learning, our evolution is an elaborate tapestry of experiences, conversations, challenges, lessons, and journeys of self-realization. There is no definite endpoint or finishing line, only ongoing refinement of our abilities to think, understand others, and positively shape the world around us. My hope is you leave feeling energized and motivated to apply fresh insights into your own life's adventures.

On that note, I'll sign off by wishing you the very best moving forward. May your personal quest for knowledge, growth, and meaning continue to unfold in remarkable ways. Thank you for taking this journey with me-I hope it has offered helpful perspectives and inspiration as you continue pursuing your aspirations. The possibilities that await you and the positive impact you can make are boundless. Farewell, and here's to our shared endeavors in cultivating happiness, wisdom, and prosperity.

Case Studies

Rephrase Stacey's Leap from Employee to Travel Business Owner

Stacey, a woman in her 40's, courageously quit her job. She started a brand-new career, creating her own travel company.

Determined and supported by her cousin, Stacey created her business from scratch. She studied the market carefully, found a special niche, and designed one-of-a-kind trips to suit her clients' wishes.

Despite early challenges, Stacey's love for travel and her strong commitment to great service pushed her forward. She used her knowledge and built strong connections within the industry, earning a respected place as a travel entrepreneur.

Over time, people began to love Stacey's business. Positive reviews and word of mouth spread from happy travelers. Her talent for planning amazing trips and her custom service helped her stand out from others.

Now, Stacey's travel business is thriving. She loves helping others explore and make unforgettable memories. Her story shows us that even a major career change in your 40's can lead to fantastic success.

The Story of Faye—From London Life to a Bed and Breakfast in Cornwall

Faye and her spouse took a daring leap. They said goodbye to fast-paced London and hello to scenic Cornwall. They decided to chase a dream: starting a bed and breakfast. They found cute cottages tucked in an idyllic forest. Then they put their minds and strength to work, transforming it into a successful business.

Letting go of their old jobs, Faye and her spouse faced the hurdles of switching careers in their 40's. They gave their all to make a warm, inviting place for guests, giving them a special journey. Through careful details, friendly service, and yummy breakfasts, they earned a name for their lodging.

Making a bed and breakfast was a winning and satisfying venture for Faye. It not only awakened her business spirit but soaked her in the peaceful beauty of Cornwall. The stunning local sights kept reminding her of the good that can come from stepping out of comfort and welcoming fresh starts.

Year after year, Faye's bed and breakfast blossomed, luring travelers seeking quiet getaways. The thriving business proved it's never too late to chase a new career and inspired others wanting professional change.

Lisa's Journey: Turning Passion into Profits

Lisa adored planning events. In her 40s, she made it her business. Thanks to industry knowledge and a knack for designing memorable moments, Lisa started her event planning venture.

Her expertise made each of her events unique. Corporate functions or weddings, Lisa handled everything smoothly. Her knack for details, creativity, and turning visions into realities made her popular in the field.

By leveraging her potential and knowledge, Lisa became a trusted name in the industry. Her focus on delivering remarkable, personalized events set her apart from others.

Happy clients and word-of-mouth referrals made Lisa's business grow. Trusted by clients and vendors, her company boosted her reputation. Her excellent work led to partnerships with big-name brands.

The Beauty of Being Your Own Boss

In her 40's, Lisa began a business journey which highlights that age is no barrier when chasing dreams. Her joy and skill changed her interest in event planning into a thriving business.

This tale can inspire would-be business starters in any field. It shows, sticking to what they love and being brilliant at it, can yield amazing results. The mix of bliss, skill, and strong commitment in Lisa's journey shows success is within reach at any age.

Randi's Rapid Rise in Coaching Business

Entrepreneurship in later life has its success stories and Randi's coaching business is an inspiring illustration. Randi achieved striking success in her 40's in just two years and established a profitable 6-figure coaching business.

Andrea Sexton's PR Business: From Kitchen Table to Success

Andrea Sexton proves that success in your 40's holds great promise. Starting a PR business from her kitchen table, she saw substantial growth in just four years.

With just two clients to start, Andrea's drive and entrepreneurial streak led her to grow her client list to 14. Her PR expertise equipped her to build a successful business and earn a solid reputation in the industry.

Andrea, in response to her booming business, smartly recruited two part-time aides. This move not only bettered client management but also boosted her business growth.

Her journey embodies the might of entrepreneurship and the limitless potential for growth regardless of age. Andrea's triumph in PR illustrates what's attainable for those brave enough to chase their passions, even in their 40's.

Switching from Finance to Fashion

Let me introduce you to Paula, a brave entrepreneur, who dared to switch careers in her 40's. She ditched her finance job and followed her fashion dreams, opening her own vintage fashion shop.

The change from finance to fashion may sound intimidating, but Paula never let go of her grit and perseverance. She faced many hurdles, but her ardent passion led her to success.

Paula's vintage fashion shop rapidly rose to fame, luring in fashion enthusiasts and collectors. With her exquisite selection of unique items and extraordinary customer service, she carved out a shopping experience second to none.

By harnessing her entrepreneurial drive and chasing her fashion dreams, Paula demonstrated it's never too late to change careers. Her inspiring journey serves as a great example for those pondering about diving into a new career field.

Paula's journey from finance to fashion showcases the transformative power of entrepreneurship, demonstrating that pursuing your passion can lead to a fulfilling and successful career. So, if you've been contemplating a career change, don't let your age hold you back. Take a leap of faith, follow your dreams, and create a new path that aligns with your true passions.

This is Your Life to Live

Johannah, a woman in her 40's, used her wealth of life experience and the knowledge she gained from her previous job to embark on the journey of starting her own business. Armed with a deep understanding of her industry and a passion for entrepreneurship, Johannah turned her dreams into reality.

Her story serves as a powerful reminder that you don't have to wait until you're young or have a specific background to create a successful business. Your life experience, whether it be in a corporate job, raising a family, or pursuing personal interests, can provide the foundation for a thriving entrepreneurial venture.

Entrepreneurship in your 40's allows you to leverage the skills and expertise you have developed over time, giving you a distinct advantage. You can draw upon your industry knowledge, problem-solving abilities, and interpersonal skills to navigate the challenges of starting a business.

Building a business based on your life experience also means that you have a deeper understanding of your target market. You can identify gaps in the market and create products or services that genuinely resonate with customers. Your life journey has equipped you with insights that can lead to innovative solutions and a unique perspective.

Launching a venture when you're 40 shows the strength of change. It illustrates it's never too late to follow your dreams. Johannah's narrative encourages those thinking about business. It proves the present, with your gained wisdom, is the best time to begin.

Boosting Women's Confidence

In fashion's forefront, Michaela's mission is boosting women's confidence. Her clothing business offers a space for women to feel good about themselves. But, it's more than stylish clothes. It's a platform encouraging women to express their true selves.

Beginnings in the Clothes Trade

Sky, a hopeful business person, entered the clothing industry in her 20's. Despite early success, she faced unexpected hurdles, leading to her venture's downfall. This failure didn't dampen Sky's business spirit. She chose to begin again in her 40's.

Guided by endurance and resolve, Sky refounded her apparel business. She overcame challenges, drawing on past mistakes. She shows the inner strength entrepreneurs have. It proves that age isn't an obstacle, and it's always a good time to chase your dreams.

No More Mediocrity!

Steph Robson broke away from the norms of her age. Sandwiched between running a business and family life, she was a fearless specimen at 40. She dove into the business world, proving conventional ideas wrong, and showed that combining professional success and family joy is anything but fiction.

40s Entrepreneurs Outshine Youthful Startups

Common misconceptions are challenged by research. It finds that 42 is the average age of business starters. Shockingly, the mean age of founders in top-notch startups is 45. So, it's time to rethink the claim that entrepreneurship success is the playground of only the young.

Launch a Business in Your 40s: The Perfect Time

Studies hint at the 40s being the prime time to plunge into startup culture. This ripe age sees people equipped with both, financial stability and business insight, which boosts their entrepreneurship potential.

Rephrase During your 40s, you've probably spent significant time enhancing your career and gathering rich expertise. This substantial knowledge base is your stepping stone into business ownership. It aids in tackling startup pressures and offers an upper hand in the commercial realm.

Switching careers in your 40's is pretty normal. Lots of folks look for fresh paths or chase their dreams. Beginning a business at this phase can incorporate your current skills, while also hitting the more rewarding trail. It's an opportunity to use what you know differently and construct a business that fits your beliefs and hobbies.

No more is age thought of as a hurdle to business triumph. Nowadays, a growing number of people are setting up businesses later in their lives and they're hugely successful. The 40's can be a great time for kick-starting a business, combining the right mix of knowledge, financial security, and the zest to make a notable touch in the business world.

References and Additional Reading

References

Duckworth, A. (2016). Grit: The power of passion and perseverance. Scribner.

Seligman, M. E. P. (2011). Flourish: A visionary new understanding of happiness and well-being. Free Press.

Brown, B. (2010). The gifts of imperfection: Let go of who you think you're supposed to be and embrace who you are. Hazelden Publishing.

Burchard, B. (2003). The Buddha walks into a bar...: A guide to life for a new generation. Penguin Books.

Sanders, J. (2015). Yoga mind, body, spirit: A return to wholeness. Shambhala.

Dweck, C. S. (2006). Mindset: The new psychology of success. Random House.

Seligman, M. E. P., & Csikszentmihalyi, M. (2014). Positive psychology: An introduction. In M. Csikszentmihalyi, Flow and the foundations of positive psychology (pp. 279-298). Springer, Dordrecht. https://doi.org/10.1007/978-94-017-9088-8_17

Additional Reading

The Power of Kindness: The Unexpected Benefits of Leading a Compassionate Life by Brian Goldman

A Mind for Numbers: How to Excel at Math and Science (Even If You Flunked Algebra) by Barbara Oakley

Grit: The Power of Passion and Perseverance by Angela Duckworth

Deep Work: Rules for Focused Success in a Distracted World by Cal Newport